Biblical Knowing

Biblical Knowing

A Scriptural Epistemology of Error

DRU JOHNSON

With a foreword by Craig G. Bartholomew

CASCADE *Books* • Eugene, Oregon

BIBLICAL KNOWING
A Scriptural Epistemology of Error

Copyright © 2013 Dru Johnson. All rights reserved. Except for brief quotations in critical publications or reviews, no part of this book may be reproduced in any manner without prior written permission from the publisher. Write: Permissions, Wipf and Stock Publishers, 199 W. 8th Ave., Suite 3, Eugene, OR 97401.

Cascade Books
An Imprint of Wipf and Stock Publishers
199 W. 8th Ave., Suite 3
Eugene, OR 97401

www.wipfandstock.com

ISBN 13: 978-1-61097-726-5

Cataloging-in-Publication data:

Johnson, Dru.

    Biblical knowing : a scriptural epistemology of error / Dru Johnson ; with a foreword by Craig G. Bartholomew.

    xxii + 242 pp. ; 23 cm—Includes bibliographical references and indices.

    ISBN 13: 978-1-61097-726-5

    1. Knowledge—Theory of, in the Bible. 2. Knowledge—Theory of (Religion). 3. God—Knowableness—Biblical teaching. 4. Bible—Criticism, interpretation, etc. 5. Polanyi, Michael, 1891–1976. I. Bartholomew, Craig G., 1961–. II. Title.

BT40 J545 2013

Manufactured in the USA

This work is dedicated to

Stephanie,

Benjamin,

Claudia,

Olivia,

and Luisa

—through whom I have come to know with excellence our Creator, his creatures, and creation.

Contents

Foreword by Craig G. Bartholomew   ix
Acknowledgements   xiii
Introduction   xv

1   How Should We Conceive of Knowledge and Error?   1
2   Knowing in the Garden: Genesis 2   22
3   Error in the Garden: Genesis 3   45
4   Erroneous Knowing in Exodus and Beyond   65
5   Knowing under the Prophet-Messiah: Mark, Luke, and John   97
6   Scientific Epistemology, Wisdom, and the Epistles   122
7   Broad Reality and Contemporary Epistemology   149
8   Analytic Theology and Biblical Scholarship   181
9   Implications for Theologians and the Church   202

Bibliography   219
Scripture Index   231
Subject and Name Index   239

Foreword

IT IS A PRIVILEGE to write the foreword to Dru Johnson's creative and excellent work on *Biblical Knowing*. I had the privilege of being his external examiner for his PhD and am glad to see his work there now gathering further momentum in this impressive book.

Recent decades have witnessed a remarkable renaissance in Christian philosophy, a development unimaginable some thirty years ago. This renaissance has yielded a whole new generation of young Christian philosophers who are steadily making their mark. Dru is one of them. Amidst this renaissance a neglected element has been the relationship between Scripture and philosophy, an important gap that we are starting to see bridged. *Biblical Knowing* makes a significant contribution to a fresh opening up of the relationship between Scripture and philosophy. This is no easy task, requiring the author to navigate philosophy, biblical studies, and theology. Dru does this masterfully. Having done the hard, rigorous work on this topic in his doctorate, Dru has continued to work away at biblical knowing, and the result is a lucid, accessible text, and yet one that makes an original contribution.

With all the elements at play in an examination of the biblical view of knowing it requires real mastery to be able to present one's case with lucidity and ease. Dru demonstrates just such mastery. Readers will be struck by how accessible this book is with its warm, direct style and its clear, logical structure enhanced by illustrations, diagrams, and very helpful summaries throughout. *Biblical Knowing* not only makes its case but in the process it introduces the reader to key dialogue partners and the state of play in contemporary epistemology *and* biblical studies. For example, not only does Dru map out the contours of a biblical epistemology, but he also brings this into dialogue with the major options in epistemology today, including such well-known approaches as Virtue epistemology and Reformed Epistemology. He is well acquainted with the contemporary work in the areas he examines; readers will find introductions to the most recent biblical work

Foreword

on epistemology *and* movements such as Analytic Theology, all of which are brought into critical engagement with Dru's model of biblical knowing. The result is a book that will function well as a textbook for undergraduate students in their later years of philosophy, as well as in biblical studies and theology. It is the sort of book that I for one have been waiting for when teaching epistemology and I suspect that many professors will have the same experience.

But *Biblical Knowing* is more than a textbook that introduces readers to the debates and main thinkers. The introductions are there, to be sure, but they occur in the context of Dru's own understanding of biblical knowing, explored in detail in his doctorate and made available here in a more accessible, but no less rigorous, form. The biblical text is front and centre in his work, as it should be, and he ranges across the canon, both Old and New Testaments, with more detailed excavations at particular points. In the process he demonstrates unequivocally that Scripture has a great deal to say about knowing, that a discernible, unified approach can be detected throughout, and that Christians ought to *listen* to Scripture in this area if they are to see and thus know the world aright. In this way Dru rightly avoids the dangers of both biblicism and dualism. He neither approaches Scripture as a philosophy textbook from which we can easily extract a full-blown epistemology (biblicism), nor as a church book which has nothing to say to philosophy (dualism). Instead he finds in the grand, sweeping narrative of Scripture an orientation to epistemology, which can be brought into dialogue with philosophy and developed into a contemporary epistemology.

Philosophically, the hero of the book is Michael Polanyi, whose work Dru finds congruent with what he finds in Scripture. In this Dru follows in the footsteps of his former professor, Esther Meek, who has herself published two excellent studies on epistemology, namely *Longing to Know: The Philosophy of Knowledge for Ordinary People* (2003), and *Loving to Know: Covenant Epistemology* (2011), both of which build on Polanyi's work. Meek's and Dru's work serve as a reminder that amidst the resurgence of Christian philosophy we should not forget to attend to the major contribution of Michael Polanyi, especially in his *Personal Knowledge*.

My hope is that this book will further set ablaze the work we are starting to see being done on the Scripture-philosophy-theology relationship. Dru would be the first to acknowledge that there is far more work to be done on the Bible and epistemology, to say nothing about the Bible and ontology, anthropology, and ethics, as well as second order philosophical

Foreword

disciplines such as political philosophy, philosophy of art, of law, etc. Rich work cries out to be done in all these areas and the work is far more than one scholar can do alone. We need a community of biblical scholars, philosophers, and theologians who will work together with people like Dru in order to reap the rich harvest of the direction in which Dru points us in this work.

I conclude this foreword with two more personal comments. At The Paideia Centre for Public Theology in Ancaster, Ontario, of which I am Principal, we recently hosted a consultation on *Transdisciplinarity*. The basis for discussion was a paper that I and the psychologist Eric Johnson produced, arguing that the "integration model" in Christian higher education has failed and that we need a new model, one which we name "Transdisciplinarity." It occurs to me that Dru's work is a good example of the kind of trans-disciplinary work we urgently need if we are to overcome the fragmentation of the disciplines bequeathed to us by modernity.

Secondly, I suspect that Dru's exploration of biblical knowing could be richly explored specifically in relation to Continental philosophy. While his frame of reference is understandably mainly that of analytic philosophy my hunch is that it is in the tradition of the much neglected work of Johann Georg Hamann, of Kierkegaard—to whom Dru does attend, and of the hermeneutic philosophers, and the current theological turn in phenomenology that resources and allies might be found for the exhilarating project of *Biblical Knowing*.

I anticipate that we will hear much more from Dru in the years to come. *Biblical Knowing* is a feast and I encourage Dru to keep serving up such meals for there is a hungry world out there needing just such sustenance for the journey.

Craig G. Bartholomew
H. Evan Runner Professor of Philosophy,
Redeemer University College, Ancaster, Ontario;
Principal of The Paideia Centre for Public Theology
Easter 2013

Acknowledgments

THIS WORK HAS BEEN an endeavor that began a decade ago in an epistemology class at Covenant Theological Seminary with Drs. Michael Williams and Esther Meek. There, I first encountered both the great philosophers and attempts to reconcile the philosophical aspects of biblical texts. Under their direction we asked the question, "Does the Bible have anything substantive to say about knowing?" I owe nothing but thanks to the time and energy that Drs. Williams and Meek surrendered to me. The training that I received from professors such as Hans Bayer, Jerram Barrs, Brian Aucker, Jay Sklar, and Jack Collins allowed me to confidently approach the biblical text years later and explore what it has to say about theories of knowing.

After seminary, I immediately entered a philosophy program at the University of Missouri–St. Louis while I worked as a pastor during the day. I am grateful to the excellent training that I received there from professors Paul Roth, Jon McGinnis, Andrew Black, James Buickerood, Eric Wiland, and especially David Griesedieck who taught me Nietzsche and Asian philosophy. These skilled practitioners of analytic philosophy at UM–St. Louis were especially gracious to this philosophical neophyte who asked weird questions and wrote so imprecisely.

My gratitude extends especially to a cadre of scholars who have all directly helped me to scrutinize my thinking about the biblical texts, philosophy, and theology. My doctoral supervisor Professor Alan Torrance (University of St Andrews, Scotland) shepherded me through the entire process of doctoral research from which this book is funded. His insight and guidance were and still are indispensable to me. Professor Torrance additionally recruited Drs. Nathan MacDonald, Mark Elliott, and Kelly Iverson, who volunteered their expertise to help me avoid every tragic error as well as I would listen to them. Professor Craig Bartholomew (Redeemer University College, Canada) has been a great theological role model over the years and a personal encouragement to me as I have continued to research in the admittedly dicey interdisciplinary waters of philosophy, theology, and biblical studies.

Acknowledgments

A group of colleagues have also contributed to my thinking on this topic more broadly. The Institute for Advanced Studies (Shalem Center, Jerusalem, Israel) has committed to helping scholars explore philosophical matters in the Tanakh. Dr. Yoram Hazony has been a good friend of my work and has enlivened the sense of importance for such projects through his work at the Shalem Center. Their annual conferences titled "Philosophy of the Tanakh, Midrash, and Talmud" have been a sweeping success for allowing this scholarship to proceed. As well, Katherine Munn (Oxford University) has been a wonderful interlocutor in the world analytic philosophy and some of my dialogues with her have found their way into this book.

My colleagues and students at The King's College have also been a wonderful support in this endeavor, allowing me to teach a seminar on epistemology and Scripture. I wish to thank those students both at The King's College (NYC) and Covenant Theological Seminary who listened to me "think out loud" and helped me to sculpt the ideas in this book throughout 2012. Thanks also goes to the various people who volunteered to read and critique various stages of the book: Alessandra Haynes, Ray Davison, Nadia Barduson, Taylor Lindsay, and Laurel Recsetar. A special thanks goes to Susan Moeller's keen mind and careful editing eye, which greatly improved later drafts.

Finally, it is my family, my friends, and the catholic church—expressly my father, step-mother, and mother along with my life in the catholic church in the United States, Kenya, Brazil, and Scotland—who inspired this research. The particular communities who dedicated themselves to shaping my thought were GracePoint of Webster in St. Louis, Missouri; The Parish Church of the Holy Trinity in St Andrews, Scotland; and Christ Community Presbyterian in Newark, New Jersey. Knowing God and knowing creation well is not merely a philosophical model to be worked out, but a way of being in this world according to which we were created. My wife Stephanie, my son Benjamin, and my daughters Claudia, Olivia, and Luisa all have helped me to see why knowing well matters profoundly. All thanks goes to them for enduring the voyage patiently and loving me the whole way through. And lastly, if anything at all is fruitful in these pages, I know that the God of Abraham, Isaac, and Jacob makes it so.

Introduction

THE CHRISTIAN SCRIPTURES COULD be theologically described as beginning and ending with an epistemological outlook. The first episode of humanity's activity centers on the knowledge of good and evil. The final stage of humanity is pictured by Jeremiah as a universally prophetic and knowing society: "And no longer shall each one teach his neighbor and each his brother, saying, 'Know the Lord,' for they shall all know me, from the least of them to the greatest, declares the Lord" (Jer 31:34). What happens to knowledge in between? We intend to hash out epistemology with the tool of biblical theology: an approach to knowledge as developed in Genesis 2 and explored throughout the Tanakh (i.e., the Old Testament) and New Testament.[1]

In short, due to the resemblance of Genesis 2–3, both in the theology and narratives of Israel's canon, we will work from the beginning of the Pentateuch forward. But we are not bound to a particular school of biblical theology. In this manner, we will follow this epistemological process through the narratives rather than make theological statements about individual passages.

The goal of this book is to lay the groundwork for a biblical theology of knowledge–how knowledge is broached, described, and how error is rectified within the texts of the Protestant Christian canon. Essentially, this

---

1. Of this problematic term "biblical theology," we only mean that we will work through the story of Scripture as it is developed canonically in the Protestant Christian bible. First, we want to avoid rigid modes of biblical theology. We are not endeavoring to see epistemological process as necessarily bound to just one approach: salvation-history, promise-fulfillment, typology, or covenant theology. Methodologically, we recognize that "The possibility of biblical theology remains, even for its own practitioners, a very precarious thing . . ." Barr, *Biblical Theology*, 229. Hence, this study is guided by Watson's call to lower the "lines of demarcation" between biblical studies and systematic theology. Watson, *Text and Truth*, 1–29. This biblical-theological approach allows us to be co-readers of the biblical texts, just as first century Jews saw themselves as co-readers of the Tanakh. See also, Bartholomew, "Story and Biblical Theology."

study is meant to be a pry-bar, a tool to open the lid on the neglected idea that Christian Scripture might be developing robust descriptions of knowing that can direct us today. Proper knowing as it occurs in the Scriptures means that there are better and worse ways to know. Even more, the epistemology that we find advocated in Scripture is not relegated to religious knowing. We will argue that scientific epistemology and biblical epistemology, if we can allow such a term in an introduction, make significant points of contact—enough to suggest that they are fundamentally consistent with each other.

This project comes with inherent difficulties. The consistency of epistemic vocabulary varies, even in the early texts of the Hebrew Bible (i.e., the Old Testament).[2] For instance, if we merely consider the breadth of connotations concerning knowledge in the first four chapters of the Pentateuch (i.e., knowledge from a tree, knowledge of one's own nakedness, and knowledge qua sexual intimacy) then our methodology cannot be limited to a word study of "know."[3] This effort means to reflect a biblical-theological approach inasmuch as it attends to the Bible's manner of disclosing what a proper or improper epistemology might look like, from the beginning of the history of humanity through the earliest moments of the post-Pentecostal messianic movement (i.e., the church described in the New Testament canon). This biblically-attuned view of knowing *unfolds* in the history of Israel and we are attempting to locate the trajectory of knowledge as it unfolds within these texts.

Throughout, we will employ a three part system of checks to constrain ourselves, as much as is possible, from reading epistemological concerns *into* the texts. The three criteria for examining a text for epistemological description are that epistemological language and concepts must be 1) present, 2) relevant, and 3) persistent.

First, in looking for the presence of terms and concepts, we are asking ourselves the question: Are epistemological concerns present or are we reading them into this text? Second, the presence of vocabulary is not sufficient. Epistemological language and concepts must be relevant. For instance, Roman execution methods are present in the Passion narratives, but

---

2. By "Hebrew Bible," I am referring to the same collection of Israelite literature commonly called the Tanakh in Judaism and the Old Testament in Christianity. Specifically, I am referring to the Masoretic Text of the *Biblica Hebraica Stuttgartensia*. Unless specifically noted otherwise, I am not including the emendations of the Septuagint (LXX) or portions of the Apocrypha.

3. E.g., Hebrew: *da'at* (דעת); Greek: *gnosis* (γνοσις).

those stories are clearly not about crucifixion. We are asking: Would any attentive reader of the text be able to notice the epistemological concepts in the text? Third, even present and relevant talk of "knowing" does not make a text epistemologically interesting. The concept and terms must be persistent—developed by the text to yield a fuller description of the epistemological process beyond mere passing use of the term (e.g., Judges 13:21: "Then Manoah knew that he was the angel of the Lord."). Is knowing mentioned once and then never returned to? Or, is it a theme that the author employs and re-employs (or revisits at different times)?

As we follow the story and language of knowing and error, knowing looks more like a process than a mechanism that yields a product called knowledge. Epistemological process then must be discerned through a literary reading that will sometimes involve the common terms for knowledge, but sometimes not. In other words, focusing our attention on the various manifestation of the word "know" will not render the entire picture of epistemology and that has been the shortfall of some earlier attempts to develop a biblical epistemology.[4]

Further, focusing current epistemological models *onto* the texts of Scripture does not render the entire picture either. We will have to be cautious about affirming too much about the modern notion of propositional knowledge such as "S knows P" (i.e., "*Subject* knows *Proposition*"). At certain points, such models are not entirely alien to the narratives. For example, YHWH wants for Abraham to "know for sure" (ידע תדע) that his promises to him will come true (Gen 15:13). At first glance, it appears that "Abram *knows that* YHWH's promises are veracious" accurately reflects something about Abram's knowledge according to the narrative. However, we will find that defining this scene in terms of propositions alone cannot reflect Abram's knowledge *sufficiently*.

As we wade into these texts, we seek to explore how "the Subject" knows anything at all and we are especially concerned to figure out what happened when characters of the stories know erroneously. We want to describe both what characters came to know, but even more, how they erred in the epistemological process per the narrative.[5]

---

4. For my critique of those attempts, see "Epistemology and Ancient Texts" in Johnson, "Error and Epistemological Process."

5. In this same thinking, Robinson argues that narrative analysis can restore perspicuity to biblical theology providing some of the corrective historical, literary, and theological tension. "Narrative Theology and Biblical Theology."

Introduction

Why study error?⁶ A shortcoming with deriving epistemology from ancient texts is that the object of knowledge itself is often ambiguous or obscured to the reader. Knowing is often portrayed as seeing something that never quite equates to a proposition, although it can be expressed sometimes in a sentence. For instance, Adam comes to know that the woman is his proper mate and states his discernment as a matter of fact, "This at last is bone of my bones and flesh of my flesh . . ."⁷ But it was the man's ability to *see that this was his mate* that is constitutive of his knowledge and we are interested in how that *seeing* is honed.

Moreover, the object of knowing is often God himself and thus what is meant to be known still lies outside the perspective of the reader (e.g., Exod 29:46). What could it possibly mean, after all, that Israel could know YHWH as her God, or that the man and the woman knew that they were naked?⁸ These could mean many things, none of which would be entirely plain objects called "knowledge" to us.

Part of the difficulty is the contemporary discussion of epistemology. The epistemic objectives found in Scripture are generally ascribed to knowing-in-relationship rather than the analytical formulation in current fashion: "knowing that."⁹ For instance, someone might *know* their own child, but they also *know that* their child is a human being. For many and seemingly good reasons, relational knowledge is not the popular parlance in much of current epistemology.

Even where "knowing that" is stated in the biblical texts, it is often stated in terms that are explicitly covenantal or resemble covenantal relationship. For instance, when God states "surely *know that* (ידע תדע) your offspring will be sojourners . . ." (Gen 15:13), he speaks within what appears

---

6. This book and the methodology was birthed from my doctoral work at the University of St Andrews, Scotland. As a second-generation of work, the devilish exegetical details that I sometimes rely upon here can be found in my doctoral thesis. Where appropriate, I will refer the reader to that work. This current work, however, makes the doctoral work more accessible and extends some of those ideas out further into the Christian canon. As well, I include a more precise analysis of Michael Polanyi's scientific epistemology and its relationship to the biblical texts plus a critique of the Analytic Theology movement that has arisen since that doctoral work was completed.

7. Gen 3:23.

8. Gen 3:7.

9. Attempts in analytic philosophy at reducing "know how" to "know that" remain unpersuasive given the nature of knowledge in these texts. See Stanley and Williamson, "Knowing How," 411–44.

to be a covenantal ceremony.¹⁰ YHWH appears to bind Himself, possibly unto death, with Abram's descendants and the texts expects the reader to see the covenant ceremony as *the justification* for YHWH's declaration "know for sure."¹¹ So "knowing that" is contingent upon knowing-in-covenant-relationship. Similarly, to *know that* we are naked, in the sense that Genesis 2 juxtaposes it against Genesis 3, is to say that we are related to our body in a different way than we were before. What appears as "*knowing that* we are naked" is actually "knowing that we have a particular relation to our body." Genesis 2–3 expresses this as an ultimate epistemological concern of the narrative, not on the periphery of the story. Again, the problem is precisely this: the Scriptures tend to focus exclusively on knowing in relationship, *in contractum*, rather than knowledge as an object.

Where the nominal form is used, "knowledge" still generally reflects knowing-in-relationship. The contemporary philosopher, Thomas Nagel, made an inventive argument about consciousness that seems analogous here. Against the physical reductionists who want to reduce humanity's mental activity down to the chemical activity of the brain, Nagel argued that there is something ineffable and irreducible about the human mind that does not equal a chemical depiction of the brain.¹² In defense of this position, he argued that there is *something that it's like* to be a bat. While we might not know what that is like, because we will not ever be a bat, we can imagine that there is *something that it is like* to navigate sonographically, for instance. And if there is *something, anything at all*, that it is like to be a bat, then that *something* cannot be reduced to a chemical description.

In the same vein as Thomas Nagel's clever argument for what it is like to be a bat, the Scriptures appear most concerned that people know *what it's like to be* a knower primarily as an obeyer of YHWH and Jesus respectively. Knowing appears as a skill, figuring out to whom we should listen, where we should look, and how we should understand what is being said. Even if we figure out to whom we should listen, skilled "looking" and "understanding" has equal weight in knowing and avoiding error. Jesus

---

10. In the Hebrew, there is no equivalent to the English "that." It is supplied by the interpreter. However, the force of the statement is equivalent to the English "know that." The point is, the presence or lack of linguistic convention is not a defeater for the larger argument that many epistemologists are attempting to make: the notion of knowledge being propositionally related to us (e.g., "*knowing that* the sky is blue"). The argument that all knowledge is "knowing that P" remains despite mannerism of different languages.

11. Kline, *By Oath Consigned*, 17–21.

12. Nagel, "What Is It Like To Be A Bat?"

Introduction

hounds his peers on this point in his Sermon on the Mount (Matt 5–7). Merely knowing to whom they should listen (i.e., the Mosaic Law) does not bring them to understand what was meant to be known—the principles that undergird the Mosaic Law. Moreover, knowing is relationally bound and the epistemological process does not produce propositions (i.e., abstract facts) whose veridicality we can justify. The object of knowledge is not always clear, but error is patent at many points in Scripture. Thus, we will study the constituent factors where characters of the narratives get it wrong.

In the current philosophical discussion, many contemporary epistemological models posit abstract entities such as propositions, properties such as truth (not necessarily the biblical sense of truth found in Hebrew terms like *emunah* or the Greek *aletheia*), and necessary relationships between the two such as correspondence. By positing a world where there are such abstract entities and qualities, epistemological models have sometimes suffered from the possibility of being mere phantasms of knowledge—the way we would like knowledge to work and to be.

Some epistemological models have attempted to overcome the phantasms of knowledge, seeking instead to root their epistemology in description of the way the knowing world *actually is* rather than how *we would like it to be*. Naturalized epistemology is probably the best representative of an attempt to work descriptively, showing how humans *actually* rationalize, consider, conclude, and therefore, how they actually know. But in the search for fidelity to the actual lives of knowers, naturalized epistemology cannot defend better ways to know anything other than what is pragmatic. Indeed, the most-known standard of veracity for these naturalized views of knowing is pragmatism: it is true if it works, if there is engineering payoff.[13]

Beginning an epistemology with the *is* rather than the *ought* appears reasonable *prima facie*, especially for epistemologists who believe that the universe is only physical. For them, there *is* no *ought*. Continental philosophy has offered an even fuller description of knowing according to how reality *is*, but the Continental philosophers' impenetrable writings risk being labeled as irrelevant by many trained in the Anglo-American tradition of Analytic philosophy.[14]

---

13. I am borrowing this phrase, "engineering payoff," from Prof. Paul A. Roth (UC-Santa Cruz, formerly at the University of Missouri—St. Louis.).

14. Whether this dismissiveness by the Analytic tradition in philosophy is fair is a wholly other matter.

Introduction

It seems that we need both the descriptive and prescriptive view of knowing. The Christian Scriptures give us both: the way knowing is *supposed* to work and how it *actually* works. Further, the Scriptures describe in detail how the attempt to know goes horrifically wrong. In the Scriptures, we have a creation narrative that dominates much of the epistemological understanding of that which ensues in the Tanakh and New Testament. That creation story pictures a world in which knowing occurs apart from brokenness. Because we read of both covenantally responsive ways of knowing described in these texts *and* the egregious violation of the covenant in seeking knowledge, then we have the obligation of maintaining the dual perspective: assessing what is being prescribed by Scripture apart from what has been described. This book will struggle to see Scripture's description of knowing in order to understand what might be prescribed.

This work will begin with some ground-clearing. Chapter one tackles how we conceive of error and how that informs our reading of Scripture. Chapters two through six focus on the texts of Scripture, from Genesis to Kings, the stories internal to the Gospels, the rhetoric of the Gospel writers, and a discussion of scientific epistemology as compared to the Proverbs and Epistles. Chapter seven engages contemporary epistemology in Analytic philosophy in order to assess what fits best with what we have found in the Scriptures. Chapter eight deliberates the Analytic Theology movement and the fruits of recent biblical scholarship about epistemology. Finally, chapter nine concludes with some over-arching implications for theology, both in how theologians could think about their task (theological prolegomena) and how the actions of the church follow epistemological paths found in Scripture (practical theology). Very brief implications will be offered concerning teaching, preaching, counseling, and discipling in the church.

N.B. While I will note (in parentheses) the Hebrew and Greek terms/passages where they seem particularly appropriate, a reading knowledge of neither language is required for this book. I merely post that information for those who need a bit more persuasion about the lexicography behind the claims.

1

How Should We Conceive of Knowledge and Error?

WE WALK BY FAITH and not by sight (2 Cor 5:7). What does this mean? Certainly, picturing the Christian life as a walk fits within the collective imagination of the biblical writers. But what are we to do with Paul's juxtaposition of faith and sight? Regardless of the Apostle Paul's intended meaning, a common Christian interpretation has pictured something akin to "faith as a blind walk." Depicting the Christian life as a walk, where Believers grow in knowledge of the Creator and His creation, certainly fits the biblical picture. From ancient Israelite faith to its extension into Christianity, the metaphor of life as a walk (the *peripatetic* life) has been common, though not always the kind associated with Socrates and his followers.[1] But what kind of walk do we envision? Is it like a frustrating stumble and grumble through the wilderness with Moses, a maddening walk with Socrates, or a peaceful stroll with Jesus?

Whether it is representative for historical Christianity or not, many Modern Christians view walking by faith like the game minefield played at youth camps. A field of play is strewn with objects to find and obstacles to navigate. The players, except for one designated to be the caller, are all blindfolded. The caller verbally directs her blindfolded teammates around the obstacles to retrieve their objects and win. The players walk by faith and not by sight.[2]

---

1. E.g., Deut 29:19; 1 Kgs 3:14; Prov 2:13; Pss 26:3; 82:5; Mark 7:5; John 8:12; 12:35; Eph 2:1, 10; 4:17; 5:8, etc.

2. The analogy is then construed this way: We Christians are like the blinded players in this world of spiritual and physical obstacles. The Scripture and the Holy Spirit together (at least for Protestants) act like the "caller" who we trust through faith to navigate this

Biblical Knowing

I want to suggest in the following pages that this analogy is *wrong*. Well, if not flat out wrong, it is at least flawed in a crucial way. It does not adequately capture the view of knowing advocated in the Scriptures themselves. However, the analogy can be redeemed, but we will have to adjust our understanding of two facets. First, we need to ensure that we all mean the same thing when we use the word "faith." Second, the blindfolds have to come off! In the totality of the Scriptures, "not by sight" means something different from the ever-popular blind faith connotation. Indeed, even within the Pauline corpus it cannot mean that we are blind, for Paul clearly believes that we do indeed see, even if "in a mirror dimly" (1 Cor 13:12).

The idea of listening to a caller who can see where we need to go is still ripe for usage because the Scriptures are intent on us being good listeners in order to know reality well. Blind or not, listening is the fundamental priority when it comes to knowledge. In fact, we will argue later that to whom we listen determines what we can know. However, *we do not wear blindfolds when we listen.* Instead of the blindfolded players in the game described above, I would like to replace it with three examples: a docent at a museum, a golfing coach helping us with our swing, or a pilot teaching us to fly. Good knowing occurs when the novice listens to her guide *and also* looks at what

---

obstruction-wrought reality. The more closely we listen to the "caller" (i.e., the Scriptures and Holy Spirit), the better we come to know this world for what it really is. As we walk by blindfolded faith, our sight is useless in favor of our ability to listen to our Most Holy Caller: God.

the guide is showing her. For instance, what separates me from knowing the significant features of Egyptian hieroglyphics or the graphs of space exploration cannot be bridged by closing my eyes (see image above).[3] I must open my eyes and look at the relevant features being pointed out to me while listening to the acknowledged authority who can guide me to know.

Corresponding to this, the Scriptures insist over and again that walking by faith means: 1) recognizing the docents through whom God speaks and listening to them alone, 2) embodying the actions they prescribe, and 3) looking at what they are showing us. When the people of God do all three to the extent required, then it is considered knowing. When we transgress any of these three, it is considered error (or, erroneous knowing).

Not walking by sight then signifies that there is no such thing as *brute seeing*. There are no self-interpreting events for Israelites to know, not even the exodus plagues nor the miracles of Jesus. *Not walking by sight* does not mean being blind to the world before us, instead, our sight needs to be guided by an authority so that we can see what is already before us. This brings us back to the former issue of that peculiar word: faith.

In American English, "faith" has collected so many connotations that it is unclear if people would even recognize the biblical denotation. Most biblical instances of the Hebrew term *aman* (אמן) and its most prominent Greek peer *pistis* (πιστις) can equally mean something like trusting belief, which begs the question: Who or what is being trusted? Again, to whom we listen determines what we can know. If I could reword 1 Corinthians 5:12 in light of a broader biblical connotation of faith: "We walk by *trusting authentic authority* and not *merely* by sight." Faith and sight are not opposed to one another. Trusting the correct guides, docents, or prophets is the first step that enables our eyes to see.[4] Listening to the right voice determines, at least in part, what we can see and therefore what we can know.

---

3. Public domain image: Photographer unknown, "NASA's first major attempt to tell the story of the U.S. Space Program graphically."

4. Interestingly, Jesus' rhetorical patterns in the synoptic Gospels uses "ears to hear" and "listen" much more intensely than "eyes to see" and "look." Even though the two phrases are found in parallel in both Deut 29:4 (MT 29:3) and Isa 6:9–10. Jesus chooses listening to characterize his ministry to Israel.

CHRISTIAN VERSIONS OF ERROR

Not only must we listen and look in order to walk by our trust, we must also sort through several misconceptions of error. On the one hand, we want to be sure that we are *getting it right* when it comes to knowing in this world. On the other hand, we want to have some confidence that we are not *getting it wrong*. Aristotle tells us that to know something well, we must understand what it is (*genus*) and what it is not (*differentia*). We will discuss more fully why we have chosen to focus on error in knowing (i.e., the *differentia* of proper knowing). But for now, we should consider some of the ways in which people conceive of epistemological mistakes, i.e., errors.

Insufficient Information

There is a category of error that may or may not be a legitimate error, but one that must be dealt with nonetheless: error caused by ignorance or a lack of information. This supposes a situation where someone attempts to know something, but all that hinders them is a supposed lack of information. We must consider this view of error is because the solution ensues directly from it. If our mistakes in knowledge are due to not having the right amount or caliber of information, then the solution is to correct the quantity or quality of our information stream.[5]

Let us briefly examine what appears to be an error of the disciples after Jesus' resurrection when they initially question the apostolic authority of Saul. In this episode of Acts, the author has already revealed to the reader both the veridicality of Paul's claim to apostleship and the ignorance of the disciples (Acts 9:26–31). As a reminder, the disciples back in Jerusalem have heard about their zealous persecutor Saul who has reportedly become a Jesus follower. But, the apostles have good reasons to be skeptical and the story centers upon the change in their belief from skeptical about the reports to knowing the truth. It appears that if the brothers in Jerusalem

---

5. In theological thinking, we must go much farther than this. The chasm between error and solution must always include a theological anthropology that is sensitive to our human condition. There have been many discussions about our mistakes owing to *sinfulness* (i.e., the so-called *noetic effects of the Fall*: finitude, broken mental mechanisms, etc.) and *sin* (i.e., the acts of omission and commission). We do not need to rehearse those discussions in order to understand that the most important errors of concern in the Scriptures do not fall into the category of "just needed more information."

only had more information, then they too, along with the reader, could know that Saul the persecutor is now Paul the apostle.

Is this an error on the disciples' part or on Paul's part or is there is any error at all? We will argue that this is not an informational error because information is not what resolved the conflict internal to that story.[6] Rather, it was trust (πιστις) in Barnabas' testimony which resolved the conflict, and this testimony evinces a different epistemological framework that is not based on a modern notion of information. To show this, we must compare the meaning of "information" and "testimony." The idea that the disciples simply needed more information connotes that autonomous rational agents were, as a court, weighing the possibility that Saul is now an apostle, a datum-centric view of the scene. But the apostles did not merely need more evidence. Even though we often speak this way by convention, there is something more than brute evidence being presented here.

To resolve what was deficient, the narrative itself shows us the different phases of the apostles' epistemic assent. The apostles began in fear of Saul and did not trust (Acts 9:26; μὴ πιστεύοντες).[7] What disposed them to go from "not believing" (Acts 9:26; μή πιστεύειν) to "learning" (Acts 9:30; ἐπιγινώσκειν) that Saul had become Paul, and by implication, believing that Paul is an apostle? If we assert that the apostles needed more information, then new information ought to resolve the narrative. However, the resolution begins not with their willingness to learn information, but to hear the testimony of Barnabas. Equally, claiming that they needed more information is akin to claiming that maps direct people to where they need to go. This manner of speaking may correspond with our experience as long as we acknowledge that the cartographer actually guided us *via the map*. Testimony of the cartographer undergirds the so-called information on a map.[8]

To know whether or not Paul is an apostle, the Jerusalem apostles must accredit Barnabas as an authoritative guide. They must not only listen to Barnabas, but entertain the possibility that Jesus' *good news* may be more inclusive and transformative than they had previously expected, even including people such as Saul the persecutor. This possibility is not incongruous with the kingdom of God that they learned from Jesus, but

6. This whole scenario reveals the problem of an ahistorical, contextless, and modernist term like "information."

7. We will prefer to translate the Greek πιστεύω as "trust," which is an equally viable English translation. The reasons for this are given in more detail in chapter 5.

8. Kevin Vanhoozer makes this same point in his essay on how to interpret *theodrama*. "Lost in Interpretation?"

rather, this possibility appears incongruous with the apostles' collective understanding of the kingdom of God. In yielding to Barnabas' testimony, they must participate in the larger paradigm that we could call "knowing the kingdom of God." And the apostles must integrate these new events and possibilities into that paradigm, *despite the apostles' independent ability to gauge their veracity*. The possibility of knowing the expansive nature of the kingdom of God required the disciples' commitment to a precarious degree, considering the apostle in question (i.e., Saul the persecutor).

The point here is that these apostles were disposed to know certain things about the kingdom of God and its expansiveness (e.g., Mark 4:30–34; Acts 1:6–11). But the apostles were not disposed to discern that Saul could become Paul under that same rubric. Only in their commitment to know through the guidance of Barnabas could these indiscernible particularities of Saul's life become discernible to resonate with the grander scheme of knowing the expansiveness of the kingdom of God.

The disciples' initial skepticism towards Paul appears to be an error on their part only if we remove the story from its larger epistemological context. But if we plot this account in a more comprehensive path toward knowing, which we could title "the disciples coming to know that the kingdom of God expands to all humanity," then we see this episode as disposing the disciples to know the kingdom of God. We could also include episodes such as Peter and the Gentiles (Acts 10), the apostolic council (Acts 15), along with many similar instances in the Gospels themselves where the disciples couldn't comprehend the expansiveness of the kingdom.[9]

We will not argue that the apostles were wrong or mistaken in the sense of error, but that the process by which they came to know, because it is fundamentally social, lends itself to tentativeness in knowing. Something similar could be said of Thomas Didymus (John 20) or even the scientific enterprise in general. The author and reader are the only ones disposed to assess this situation as an error on the part of the disciples and then only from within a constrained view of this particular passage. However, this scene reveals the disciples were not meant to know this new particularity (i.e., Saul was now an apostle) apart from their submission to Barnabas' testimony.[10] Given the volatile nature of the Levant in the early first century,

---

9. See Gibson, "The Rebuke of the Disciples"; Iverson, *Gentiles in the Gospel of Mark*. As Blakely summarizes: "the harshness of Jesus' rebuke in Mark 8:14–21 is occasioned not by the disciples' lack of faith or incomprehension but by their active resistance to his Gentile mission." Blakley, "Incomprehension or Resistance?" vii.

10. We will not engage the current philosophical debate between reductive and

to invite Saul into the apostolic circle without Barnabas' testimony would have been far more than an error, it could have been a calamity.

The errors that we are interested in exploring are not like these episodes from Acts. They are not stumblings on a learning curve or being wrong when someone is faithfully following the epistemological process (i.e., the disciples weighing the testimony of Barnabas regarding Saul). Rather, the errors that we need to explore in Scripture are those where persons or communities have the guidance and evidence in place that would dispose them to know, yet they fail in some discrete way that ends in erroneous knowledge.

Being Wrong versus Getting It Wrong

What does it mean to *be* wrong? It is a funny expression to say the least: *to be* wrong. It grabs onto existential/ontological language and adds a direction: *being* wrong. Do we actually exist in error when we get it wrong? Kierkegaard would have whole-heartedly embraced the permeation of this phrase *being* wrong in modern vernacular, but I suspect that most people believe that they *are wrong* in very non-Kierkegaardian ways. In his book *Philosophical Fragments*, Kierkegaard clearly believes that humans do not merely commit error, but we *exist* in error.

Before we consider Kierkegaard's position more fully, I should explain why the phrase "getting it wrong" is superior for a biblical description of error. First, *getting it right* is not the antithesis of *getting it wrong*. Rather, knowing happens when we simply *get it*. *Getting it* (whatever *it* might be) connotes a process that ends in an intuition, insight, or even a knack for seeing something; as in, "He gets *it*."[11] To *get it* is to understand. To *get it wrong* does not merely mean that we *are existentially* wrong, but that we have done something wrong in the process that ends in our misunderstanding, miscalculation, or misconstrual of a situation. In short, we either *get it wrong* or we are on the path to *getting it*.

The matter of error becomes much more worrisome for Christians, as traditional understandings of Scripture imbue layers beyond merely

---

non-reductive accounts of testimony. For a survey of that work, see Johnson, "Error and Epistemological Process," 191, n 80. For an apt summary of testimony, see Lamont, "A Conception of Faith in the Greek Fathers."

11. See Benjamin Yagoda's apt examination of the dizzying array of meanings that "get" can fund. *When You Catch an Adjective, Kill It*, 215–20.

getting it wrong. These could best be stated under the headers: sinfulness and sin. First, sinfulness admits something about our nature as creatures in the world. The world is broken and so are we, even in the ways that we know the world. This is sometimes termed the *noetic effect of the Fall*, but it means that we malfunction in how we arrive at knowledge. But more than that, we are flat-out broken, down to the very core of our existence.[12] In the best of human circumstances, things still do not work as they should, and we see this reflected in the laws of Israel. For instance, there is a Levitical offering exclusively devoted to atoning for unintentional sins (Lev 5:14–19). Conscious of our tendency toward remiss in the area of sinfulness with others and God, Jesus also addresses the matter of our brokenness when it comes to broken relationship and their import (e.g., Matt 5:23–24; Luke 13:25–27).

Second, we do particular things that we call sins. These are actions, that according to Scripture, begin in the heart and culminate in embodied performance.[13] We will see that knowing the world, or *getting it*, not only involves listening to authorities and appraising their guidance, but also acting upon their instructions. This type of error is repeatedly seen in Scripture in Israel's failure to perform what the prophet has commanded, either in commission or omission.

These are the two problems that presently confront our lives and knowing: we are broken people in a broken world, and we do the wrong things because of desire, stubbornness, or a mixture of both. Both of these cause us to get it wrong, but both are also accounted for and mitigated against in God's solution: His prophetic guidance of Israel and the transformation of our *being* in Jesus.

Now we will return to Kierkegaard's *Philosophical Fragments*, where humanity's *existence in error* is posited as one of Christianity's fundamental tenets. More specifically, we must consider Murray Rae's claim that Kierkegaard's working theory of knowledge (i.e., his epistemology) is one with close affinity to the Christian canon.[14] For Kierkegaard, the epistemic goal is to be "released from the bondage of untruth" and "to learn the Truth." This is not "a matter of assenting to a series of propositions *about*

---

12. For a spectacular inspection of the world's brokenness, see C. Plantinga, *Not the Way It's Suppose to Be*.

13. E.g., It would not be far-fetched to interpret Jesus as teaching that hatred and devaluation of humanity moves from the heart to actions of murder (Matt 5:21–22).

14. Rae, *Kierkegaard's Vision*, xi–xii.

God, but rather, existing 'before God.'"[15] Through the gift of faith from God alone, our very being transforms through penitent change (i.e., *metanoia*) by the revelation of the Truth of Christ.

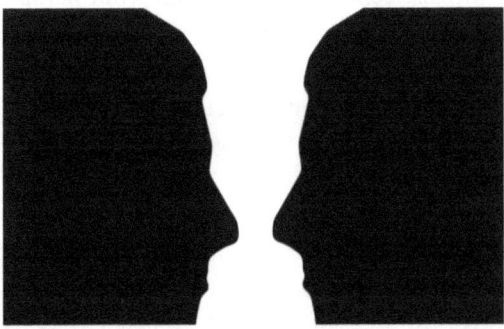

Rae examines Kierkegaard's *metanoia* transformation through the lens of Thomas Kuhn's well-worn *paradigm shift*. He suggests that "learning Christ" is not just learning principles or maxims, rather, it is transformative and incommensurate with the former way of existing. *Gestalt* psychology is known by most undergraduates through introductory psychology courses. But most of us understand the concept of *gestalt* by our experience of its renowned optical illusions. *Gestalt* is visually represented by those images where, at first glance, we see a candle stick. But then at some point, possibly after prompting, we see human profiles, face to face (see image above).[16] And then, just like that, we can flip back and forth, either seeing the image as a candlestick or two profiles. The same is true for the image of the young woman looking away or the profile of an old woman. It is two ways of seeing the same picture.

Rae says that Kierkegaard would not be satisfied with this description of human learning because it does not adequately capture our transformation through Christ. Unlike the concept of *gestalt*, we cannot flip back and forth between our past and transformed relationship with the object of knowledge, God Himself. Instead, because we are existentially transformed in our being when we learn Christ, we can only see through the new lenses of transformation.[17] Learning Christ is not a trick for seeing two things in one, but is like the paradigm shifts that occurred in the history

15. Rae, *Kierkegaard's Vision*, 213.
16. © Brocken Inaglory [CC-BY-SA-3.0], via Wikimedia Commons
17. Rae, *Kierkegaard's Vision*, 118–39.

of scientific exploration. Just as Newton's explanation of the cosmos does not make sense for us after Einstein, so too are creatures transformed by Christ through *metanoia*. Our knowledge of God and the world is radically transformed. Our existence is transformed from being in error to being in righteousness. Unlike the *gestalt*, where we can see it both ways, Kuhn's paradigm shift posits that the old way of seeing is incommensurable with the new. Not only will the two modes of existence not work simultaneously, but the old is transformed into the new, forever leaving it as an unserviceable remnant of history.

If transformation through *metanoia* is the solution, what is the problem with our knowledge according to Kierkegaard? We are not merely mistaken, but much for the worse, we *exist* in error. Our being exists in the bondage of untruthfulness and error which needs reclamation by a teacher, The Teacher.

> The teacher is then the god himself, who, in acting as an occasion, prompts the learner to be reminded that he is untruth and is that through his own fault. But this state—to be untruth and to be that through one's own fault, what can we call it? Let us call it *sin*.[18]

Through Rae's assessment of Kierkegaard, we find a view of human knowledge that is amenable to what we will demonstrate from the Scriptures. There are unmistakable signals in the texts of Scripture that self-deception and hasty desire intrudes or overcomes the characters' intended knowledge and upon which they are to subsequently act.[19] The notion that knowing is a transformational act surely fits the epistles' descriptions of what happens in Christian conversion. But a possible shortcoming of Kierkegaard's *Philosophical Fragments* is that it only describes the movement from untruthfulness (error) to truth (God) through repentance (*metanoia*). While this description is helpful, it does not account for the entirety of error (i.e., getting it wrong) and knowing (i.e., getting it) encountered in the Christian canon, most notably: Genesis 2–3.

One question emerges from Scripture that challenges Kierkegaard on this point: If knowing occurs within our being in a state of untruth, then what can be said about knowing in Genesis 2 before the error of Genesis 3? We will contend that a basic account of knowledge (i.e., getting it), free from sin and error, exists in Genesis 2. Affirming Kierkegaard's understanding, we

---

18. Kierkegaard, *Philosophical Fragments*, 15.

19. E.g., Pharaoh's myopia in Exodus (cf. What was shown to Pharaoh and what Pharaoh "sees": 9:16, 34) ; Saul's fear of the people in 1 Sam 15:24; etc.

How Should We Conceive of Knowledge and Error?

agree that the first couple moved from existence in truthfulness to existence in error. If we understand Kierkegaard to claim that conversion recoups our epistemic faculties, then we can sufficiently address the Fall and what was lost after humanity entered into sin. We lost the proper use of our faculties and the proper relationship to "the god,"[20] if holiness is the ultimate distinction between the god and man as Kierkegaard claims.[21] However, regarding Genesis 2–3, Kierkegaard's *Philosophical Fragments* lacks the discussion to substantiate how humanity transformed from truthfulness to error, the infamous move between what Ricoeur calls: the "supralapsarian state of innocence and an infralapsarian state of peccability."[22]

Without this accommodation—how we moved from being in Truth to being in error—the most significant instance of getting it wrong in Scripture is essentially annexed out of usefulness. This annex creates a further ambiguity, for it is not clear whether or not Kierkegaard adequately creates space in his argument for differentiating sinfulness writ large from a particular sin. In Kierkegaard's *Philosophical Fragments*, because error is ultimately rooted existentially, a discussion about how a particular sin causes error beyond a state of sinfulness eludes us.

Kierkegaard's work compels us to consider theological epistemology relative to humanity's being in error rather than mere mental mistakes. In this sense, we whole-heartedly endorse Kierkegaard's conclusions. But we also need to show how the Scriptures arrive at similar conclusions. His theological attempt at describing error and knowledge in existential terms appears largely successful, but because we cannot inspect his exposition of particular texts from Scripture, we cannot affirm his conclusions as entirely commensurate with ours. On these grounds, simple adaptation of Kierkegaard's theological approach is insufficient if that approach does not provide some theological exegesis upon which we can see his work.

---

20. "The god" is Kierkegaard's terminology.

21. "But if this god is to be absolutely different from a human being, this can have its basis not in that which man owes to the god (for to that extent they are akin) but in that which he owes to himself or in that which he himself has committed. What, then, is the difference? Indeed, what else but sin, since the difference, the absolute difference, must have been caused by the individual himself." Kierkegaard, *Philosophical Fragments*, 46–47.

22. Ricoeur, *The Symbolism of Evil*, 234.

Biblical Knowing

PRIVILEGING IN ORDER TO UNDERSTAND

So how will we approach the task of understanding knowledge in the Scriptures? Growing up in Oklahoma, when someone had taken on too much work, I would sometimes hear the exhoration, "Only mark off the field that you are willing to plow." We cannot tackle all the works written on knowledge and the Bible here. Neither will we do a word study on the term "know" (i.e., Hebrew: *yada* [ידע]; Greek: *gnosis* [γνοσις]). We are not going to give primacy to the philosophical views of knowledge, not even the supposedly Christian ones.[23]

What methods remain with which we can approach the issue of knowledge in the Scriptures? By side-stepping the above approaches, we are privileging another method that we hope yields insight beyond these well-worn paths into biblical epistemology. Word studies, wisdom literature, and the philosophical views of knowledge will all come into play within this investigation. However, we will focus on five major inroads and give some reasons why they offer us unique insight into the biblical view of knowledge and error, *getting it* versus *getting it wrong*.

Privileging the Diachronic, Not Synchronic

Generally speaking, a diachronic account is one that follows a trajectory through time (hence: *dia* and *chronos* roughly means "through time"). Synchronic accounts, on the other hand, tend to focus on a particular instance. If we were to paint current trends in Anglo-American philosophy, it would be a trustworthy approximation to say that knowledge is largely studied synchronically. This has caused no small amount of debate among contemporary philosophers because of the possible pitfalls of synchronically oriented studies.

For instance, it might seem reasonable to think about knowledge in terms of the question: What does so-and-so know with regards to a fact about the world? This is a synchronic question because it looks at an instance of knowledge without a exploration of the historical process leading up to it. Of course, this is not an entirely true depiction of philosophy, as many will argue that all synchronic examinations ultimately explain in

---

23. We will discuss the role of wisdom literature, to a lesser degree, within a broader view of biblical epistemology in chapter 6: "Scientific Epistemology, Wisdom, and the Epistles."

reference to historical development, whether they admit it or not. However, this generalization must suffice for now.

Philosophers have often sought to restate the modestly general question of, "How does someone know something," in terms of a knowing subject (abbreviated "S" for Subject) and the fact about the world (abbreviated "P" for Proposition). This basic construction of knowledge is then stated "S knows P." This is simple enough so far. As a working example, the philosopher Alvin Plantinga discusses how we could know that the clock reading 2:02 is correct when we read it.[24] Stated another way, how can S know that "it actually *is* 2:02" when they look at a clock that reads 2:02. After all, it could be the case that the clock battery died at 2:02 AM. As the saying goes, "Even a broken clock is correct twice a day." Pulling this together, we want to give philosophically valid reasons for affirming that "S knows P" where P represents "the time *actually is* 2:02 AM."

There are dozens of philosophical models for confirming something as simple as "S knows P," and we will not rehearse those attempts here. We only need to notice that these modes of examination primarily seek to validate statements such as "S knows P" and thus tend toward synchronic analysis. In doing this, they risk falling short of accurately describing all the phenomenally rich factors that engender, constrain, and mitigate the human process of knowing. In short, synchronic approaches might not help us *get it* when it comes to an accurate description of how humans were created to know the world.

Our reticence toward Anglo-American synchronic philosophy is not new. Some within the field have been critical of the narrowness of this way of thinking about knowledge. Philosopher Alvin Goldman collegially criticizes a fellow philosopher's depiction of real human knowers when he says: "[E]pistemic agents are often examined who have unlimited logical competence and no significant limits on their investigational resources."[25] Is the synchronic approach to knowledge positing how *real* knowers in this messy world come to know or are they being idealistic for the sake of clarity? Does this idealization then cause them to miss the forest for the trees? Jonathan Kvanvig, a virtue epistemologist, also critiques his fellow philosophers in the analytic tradition exactly because of their myopic "focus on a single belief of a single person at a single time and also to the

---

24. A. Plantinga, *Warranted Christian Belief*, 157–58.
25. Goldman, *Pathways to Knowledge*, 139.

fact that the object of a belief is presumed to be a discrete proposition."[26] To be clear, we are not condemning synchronic approaches as failures; that is not the point of this discussion. Rather, we are attempting to develop a view of knowledge from the Scriptures. When we look at how the Scriptures scrutinize the problems that attend knowing, they tend to be diachronically developed through a story. Frankly, synchronic techniques for thinking about knowledge have no way of gauging their own appreciation of a developing construct in an unfolding story. Without the safeguard of ensuring that they are faithful to what the Scriptures are rhetorically doing, then we must tentatively shelve these strictly synchronic methods for analyzing knowledge until we can test their fit with a biblically derived model.

Why do we advocate a diachronic approach? The simplest answer is: Narrative requires diachronic methods. The Scriptures are comprised, among other things, of narratives within the canonical narrative. A slightly more wordy answer ensues in the section below ("Privileging the Story of Scripture"), but as a matter of structure, narratives are primarily linear and occur over time by their nature. The wisdom literature and New Testament epistles will be brought back into our discussion after we have establish what the narratives are describing. Notwithstanding that treatment, wisdom literature is also diachronic in that there is an order and process to becoming wise, a claim which will need to be demonstrated in chapter 6.

Privileging the Story of Scripture

Claiming to privilege the story of Scripture most likely sounds rather pallid. After all, what kind of biblically faithful interpretation of knowledge would claim to neglect the stories of Scripture? There are several excellent studies of knowledge in biblical, theological, and Christian philosophical scholarship. How the present work differs is that the canonical story of Scripture will guide our pursuit. We will begin from the very first instance of human knowledge in Genesis 2–3 and work our way forward, observing how the Scriptures frame the problems and solutions to matters of knowledge within their narrative logic. This method of theological reading is generally called biblical theology, but for all the problems that attend that title, the modest statements above are all that we mean by it.

---

26. This pithy quote from Zagzebski is a summary of Kvanvig's position. Zagzebski, *Virtues of the Mind*, 44; Kvanvig, *The Intellectual Virtues*, 181–82.

How Should We Conceive of Knowledge and Error?

To advocate for a biblical theology of knowledge means that we will not organize or systematize epistemology across the canon. As stated above, we will not rely upon lexical studies (i.e., What could "know" [ידע] mean across these texts?) or word frequencies (i.e., Where does "know" [ידע] occur the most in the Hebrew Scriptures?) as a primary means of investigation, though lexicography and philology necessarily support our work.

The narrator's logical arrangement of conflict, tensions, and resolutions will constrain this study most significantly. We are reading the Tanakh (what Christians call the Old Testament) and New Testament, where matters of knowledge and error are actually present in the story, are relevant to the narrative's logic, and are persistent to further our understanding of the Scripture's epistemological concerns. But as much as is possible, the narrator is our authority to focus our attention to the salient features of the reality being described.

Privileging the Language of the Scriptures

Because we are privileging the story of Scripture, we also believe the Scriptures themselves, ancient as they may be, give us sufficient epistemological categories to describe adequately a present, relevant, and persistent system regarding, "biblical thinking about thinking."[27] We are concerned to focus on those areas where knowledge is actually present in the texts, by inference or direct language. We will identify these as conceptual and lexical connections respectively. But more than being present, knowing must be relevant, integral to the story. The narratives of interest are those which have something to say about knowledge. However, as we said above, we are not carrying out word studies or distribution analysis of *yada* (ידע) or *gnosis* (γνοσις), for instance. Rather, we will follow the narrator's terms and modes of description. To preview what this will look like, the Bible's systematic use of "see" and "hear" to evince concepts of knowledge has been noticed by many biblical scholars through the centuries. Hence, we will not shy away from examining that patterned use of sensory organs, even if it does not reflect the epistemological vocabulary *du jour*.

---

27. Carasik, *Theologies of the Mind*, 1.

Biblical Knowing

Privileging Ancient over Current

In that same spirit of analysis, we will attempt to read with current epistemological theories on the shelf, as it were. Although it cannot be helped that some current theories of knowing resemble what is occurring in the biblical narratives, we will try to note those similarities without importing the entire construct involved. Conversely, we will notice where the biblical modes of describing knowledge are at odds with current theories, even Christian epistemologies.

Privileging Israel's Errors

Most remarkably, we will not even privilege proper knowing in this study, whatever that might be. The reason is basic: the objective of proper knowledge is not always clear (or even articulable) in the Scriptures, but Israel's errors tend to be starkly appreciated by the narrators of Scripture. Moreover, the Scriptures just do not appear to be concerned with persons knowing objective facts, rather, Israel acts rightly in order to know God, creation, each other, and themselves. It's almost as if getting the process of knowing correct somehow ensures that the product of knowledge turns out better.

In this study, then, we will follow the process of knowing as it is clarified by the prophets and violated by Israel and others (e.g., Pharaoh, Balak, Saul, etc.) and note the product that ensues. We will argue that a thorough understanding of epistemological error will help lead us to proper knowledge. These errors are not flat, but have layers and degrees to which we must pay close attention. In the end, the prophets are far more concerned about the process, not the product. And so that is where we will focus.

WHAT KIND OF THEORY OF KNOWLEDGE DO WE HAVE?

One radical claim of this book is that we can discover a *general* theory of knowledge that is persistent in the minds of the authors of Scripture. I am using the concept *general* in opposition to *special*, as is done with the terms *general revelation* and *special revelation*. It should strike us as odd that the Bible would propose a general epistemology that applies to knowing everything, from scientific knowledge to legal and spiritual knowledge. Just because we believe there is a general view of knowledge in the Scriptures, we will not equivocate God as the object of our knowledge and the chemical periodic table as the object, for instance. However, in terms of process, the constitutive factors remain the same among these disparate objects of knowledge. The notable point of divergence between knowing God and knowing chemistry is in the authentication of those who speak authoritatively. We will discuss this in full further on in the book, but let me telegraph what I mean.

Not all pilots who have authoritative knowledge of flying have equal authentication to teach flying to others. Similarly, not all authoritative characters in Scripture have been authenticated to speak authoritatively for God.[28] This duality of authentication and authority works the same in medical schools, philosophy departments, golf academies, homes of toddlers, and anywhere learning happens. The difference between knowledge of automotive facts and knowledge in the Scripture, for the most part, is that prophets receive *special authentication* from God Himself. Where a mechanic or teacher receives *general* authentication, usually in the form of a license, prophet's receive *special* authentication. Signs and wonders serve to authenticate the prophet of God to Israel. However, the entire process by which knowledge occurs remains the same. The epistemological process is *general*, even though prophetic authentication is often *special*.[29]

Amazingly to us, the Hebrew Scriptures anticipate, accommodate, and even fund theories of scientific knowledge better than some current analytic theories. Toward the end of this book, we will turn our attention toward the scientific epistemology of Michael Polanyi and see how this could be the case. But we can first offer a renowned case of scientific error to begin our thinking about the role of authority and authentication in a famous scientific error.

THE ERRORS OF GALILEO AND KEPLER

If we are going to focus on knowing in light of error, then we cannot focus on propositions, the language used as a tool to confirm interpretations of experience. Rather, we must focus on the process meant to engender proper

---

28. For example, Old Testament scholar Walter Moberly has noticed that everything the serpent said to the woman was correct in some sense (Gen 3:1–6). She did gain knowledge and she did not die in the day that she ate of it. The serpent clearly had *some* authority on these matters, but he was not authorized to speak on behalf of YHWH. Moberly, "Did the Serpent Get It Right?"; See also: Geller, *Sacred Enigmas*, 161.

29. E.g., the revelation that Paul is an apostle, discussed above, came through ordinary (i.e., general) trust in Barnabas' testimony, not special signs.

Biblical Knowing

knowing. The importance of the process enables us to discern flat errors that are uninteresting (e.g., miscalculations, typos, grammatical mistakes, verbal stumbling while learning a new language, etc.) from errors in the process. We might even deign many of these flat errors to be unpreventable, due to simple human failures. But of interest to this study is when we make mistakes because we erred in some aspect of the epistemological process. As a particularly notorious example, it is not interesting that Galileo could not calculate celestial orbits because he did not account for them being elliptical, a simple conceptual mistake. What *is* interesting is *why* Galileo held onto the construct of circular orbits even though the observable celestial reality should have resisted that belief. The evidence over his head every night spoke otherwise about the circularity of orbits, but Galileo did not listen.

The error, as we assess it through the scope of history, was most likely due to a latent neo-Platonist metaphysic: the cosmos reflects the Platonic heavenly ideals.[30] Either way, it was not an unpreventable miscalculation, but a methodological error. Interestingly, not only did the night sky demand a hearing with Galileo, but Johannes Kepler had also presented Galileo with his theory of elliptical orbits and proofs to match. Nonetheless, Galileo maintained his conviction in circular orbits despite the voice of Kepler and the planets themselves. One of Galileo's biographers conclude: "Although he [Galileo] preached open-mindedness, he never lent an ear to Kepler's arguments about elliptical paths."[31]

This is an error of interest for we have one person appealing to another through instrumental means to view the same reality through a different lens. Kepler is an authoritative voice in this instance, though not necessarily authenticated to Galileo. He wants Galileo to use his calculations like an instrument, like a pair of spectacles, with which Galileo could then put the celestial reality into proper order (or at least, better order).

In this missed opportunity, an authoritative guide attempts to bring Galileo to see the cosmos with higher fidelity than Galileo's own heuristic instruments.[32] Kepler acted as an authoritative voice, he had a more accurate pair of spectacles (i.e., his calculations) with which to view the heavens. Galileo does not err because his calculations failed to explain, but because

30. Rowland, *Galileo's Mistake*, 35.

31. Shea and Artigas, *Galileo in Rome*, 26.

32. It just so happens that Kepler was closer to correct than Galileo, but not entirely accurate either.

How Should We Conceive of Knowledge and Error?

he never acknowledged either Kepler's calculations or the celestial observations that controverted his own calculations. It was not that Galileo was without knowledge of the heavenlies, but that what he knew was truncated or out of sorts because he was unwilling to listen to the authoritative voice of Kepler.

Moreover, Kepler also displayed his own error when he took Platonic ideals to be the prophetic voice to which he continued to listen. Polanyi surmises of Kelper's epistemic luck:

> [Kepler] thought that the solar distances of the six planets known to him corresponded to the sizes of the successive Platonic bodies, as measured by the radii of inscribed and circumscribed spheres. ... But though his view of reality lead Kepler astray in this case, it was close enough to the truth to guide him aright to the discovery of his three laws of planetary motion.[33]

Polanyi observes that while the passion of the scientist can correctly guide her, it can equally create an unwillingness to submit to an authority or external reality. These astronomical explorers were captivated with Platonic metaphysics. Galileo would not listen to Kepler's authority regarding orbits, but rather, held onto a particular ideal of circular orbits: an unscientific guess grasping onto Platonic metaphysics. Similarly, Kepler was listening to that same Platonic metaphysical authority as grounds for assessing particular observations of elliptical orbits. Both were confronted with the realities of observation, one which contradicted his own calculus (i.e., Galileo) and the other which happened to match his belief about metaphysical relations close enough (i.e., Kepler), like that broken clock that renders the correct time twice a day. Both men *got it wrong* to a consequential degree. The happenstance of Kepler's observations coinciding with Platonic ideals would eventually run out of empirical support in the history of astronomy.

How would we instruct these two astronomers if we were to guide them? Presumably, we would advise them to ditch their captivation with Platonism. In this instance, Platonic ideals act as an authoritative guide and astronomers were happy to use them, not to render a strictly scientific account,[34] but to give a metaphysical account of relations.

Why would perfectly circular orbits or radii-to-orbit relationships be preferred by Galileo and Kepler respectively? It is because they reflect a

---

33. Polanyi, *Personal Knowledge*, 143–44.

34. We are using the term "scientific" very loosely to mean an account that is strictly traceable to the scientific process.

theological reality. For them, metaphysical relations ultimately are funded in the divine nature as revealed in natural order. Unfortunately, the prophetic voice to whom they listened on matters of divinity and metaphysical relationships was Plato. Because they listened to the ancient Greek metaphysic, they committed an error of discerning proper authority, in reality, an error of authentication. This did not nullify their knowledge, but led them to know the cosmos in a way they did not actually intend to know it, further from the reality of planetary orbits.

SUMMARY

Above, we have considered the question: How should we conceive of knowledge and error? Our answer has been more methodological than substantive. Error is not insufficient information nor is it *being* wrong. To discover the Scriptures' conception of knowledge and error, we will move forward through the cannon privileging a diachronic account from the story and language of the Scriptures, not the present theories on knowledge. We will also look for narratives where knowledge is functionally present and relevant, but also persistent through the meta-narrative of Scripture. In approaching the question this way, we will find that error becomes a practicable inroad to begin answering the stated question: How should we conceive of knowledge?

None of the above is meant to be controversial. These are not radically new readings of the Scriptures or scientific history. But we should not be deceived into nodding along with the intuitive reasonableness of an epistemological process where authenticated authorities guide prospective knowers in light of a broad and confronting reality. Although we cannot tackle it until later, this proposal of epistemological process, where authority and authentication are paramount, is a far cry from the most current and popular theories of knowledge in Anglo-American academia, even those that attempt to represent Christianity. As we assess knowledge through the purview of the Scriptures, we must remember that the Scriptures might deliver a sharp critique of our post-Enlightenment view of knowledge, certainty, facts, and absolute facts.

Finally, we have given reasons from the history of science to understand that the process of knowing is *general*: functionally consistent for astronomers, factory workers, and Christians alike. Even within science and its renown revolutions (a.k.a. paradigm shifts), the issue is one of authority and authentication. So too we find that the Scriptures will expend significant effort in establishing authorities who will guide Israel to know so long as she enacts what is prophetically commanded. That is what we must now demonstrate.

NOTE ON METHOD

In the coming chapters, we will be following the notion of epistemology as it is unfolded in the Christian canon. We begin in Genesis 1 and work our way forward primarily through the historical texts of Israel, of which I include the New Testament texts. I will, however, have some brief interludes where a New Testament passage is briefly explored while in a chapter on the Tanakh. The reason for these excursions is to show that the epistemological problems of the New Testament are anticipated and scrutinized by the Tanakh's authors. These asides act as minor attempts to roll back the lasting impact of Marcion, who claimed the God of the Old Testament was fundamentally different then the God of the New Testament. These interludes uphold the conviction that there is not much new in the New Testament that has not already had a nuanced hearing in the Tanakh.

2

Knowledge in the Garden: Genesis 2

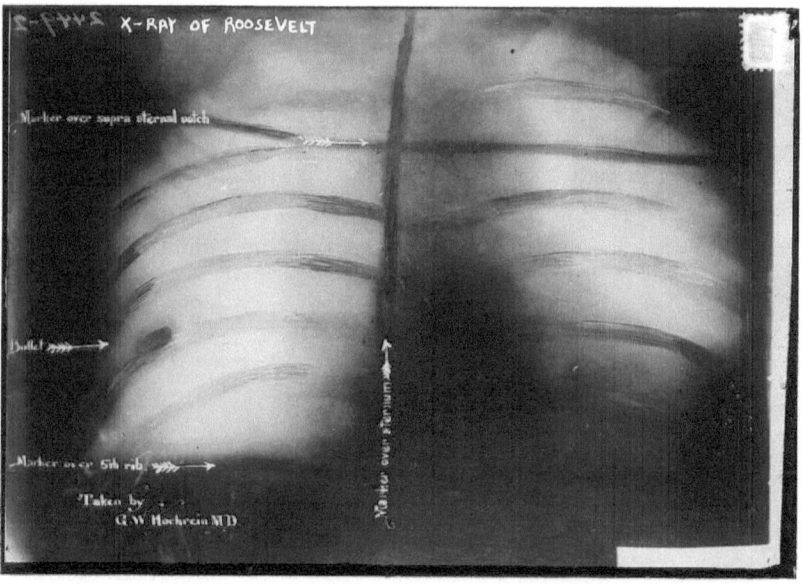

TAKE A LONG LOOK at this X-ray film.[1] In it, the bullet that wounded President Theodore Roosevelt can be seen. Actually, the bullet cannot be seen by just anyone. While anyone can see *something*, we want to know *exactly* what we are seeing. If it were not for the physician, Dr. Hochreim, trained to read radiographs who also knew the historical context of the X-ray film (i.e., it was to get a look inside Roosevelt's chest) and marked the film for us, we would only see the bare outline of what we presume to be someone's

1. Public domain image: Bain News Service, "X-Ray of Roosevelt [shows bullet]."

Knowledge in the Garden: Genesis 2

chest. Only by the guidance of Dr. Hochreim's marks and notations can we see it. The real test of our ability to read a radiograph is when we are presented with instances of X-rays that we have never seen and can accurately diagnose according to our ability to discern. But that level of skill to read X-rays requires hours of expert coaching without which we would not be able to see what is before us.

Likewise, Scripture records instances where characters are taught to see in a way that they would not have been able to do without the training. Man's discovery of woman as his proper mate is one such episode. Though there are many things going on in Genesis 2, we hope to evince a robust view of what knowing looked like before the egregious error of Genesis 3. What is suggested about knowing in Genesis 2 is clarified by its misuse in the error of Genesis 3—that knowing requires a guide, an interpreter, to teach us how to see.

THE COMPLEXITY OF THE TERM "KNOW"

When confronted by the broad use of "know" in the Hebrew Bible, we must consider whether or not there is a theory of knowing that can even accommodate the connotative range of the word itself. In the first four chapters of Genesis, the narrator employs "know" (ידע) to mean awareness of one's body, moral knowledge, and sexual intimacy. We will later offer Michael Polanyi's scientific epistemology as one capable of bringing all of these connotations under one epistemological roof, including what is often called propositional knowledge. But first, we must look at how the Scriptures are unfurling this matter of human knowledge in the foundational texts of Israel. We begin with the first instances of human knowing in Genesis 1–4, starting with the very beginning of creation.

What act of human knowing is described in Genesis 1? There are two ways in which Genesis 1 participates in the epistemological tapestry of Genesis 1–4. First, the initial command to humanity is to "be fruitful" (פרה). The concept of fruitfulness will be played upon over and again where Israel's knowledge is concerned, but more immediately in Genesis, it deals with sexual intimacy. When we later discover that knowing one's wife is a euphemism for sexual relationship, and have had the birds and bees explained to us, then we understand that human knowledge is portrayed in Genesis 1:28 as sexual activity. But sexuality cannot be the chief paradigm for knowing. While knowledge is a present idea in Genesis 1, the breadth

Biblical Knowing

of human knowing is not being employed. This passage is not explicitly epistemological because it fails the test of relevance.

Second, the woman's quest for knowledge in Genesis 3 is juxtaposed against the very things we see God doing in Genesis 1–2. In the beginning, it is God who repeatedly "saw" that His creation is good (טוב).[2] In Genesis 2, it is God who repeatedly "takes" things; specifically, the woman was built from the bone "taken" from the side of the man.[3] It is God who repeatedly "gives" light by the expanse of the heavens and "gives" plants for food.[4] The very first time we see humans "seeing," "taking," and "giving" is when the woman "sees" (ירה) the fruit, "takes" (לקח) it, and "gives" (נתן) it to her husband (Gen 3:6). While the cosmic creation account in Genesis 1 does not aim at fleshing out human knowing, it creates the narratival and lexical background for the more explicitly epistemological focus of Genesis 2–3.

GENESIS 2: KNOWLEDGE GUIDED BY GOD

If asked to identify the first instances of knowledge in the Christian Bible, most would head toward Genesis 3, where knowledge of good and evil explodes into the Garden in ways unanticipated by the reader. However, we propose here that a process of coming to know, a fundamentally epistemological process, is being described in Genesis 2 that then acts as contrast to Genesis 3.

Let us begin with a few points of evidence in favor of this position. First, the only command of YHWH Elohim to the man whom he just formed is to eat everything, but not of the tree of knowledge of good and evil. Hence, man's livelihood, "surely eat from of every tree" (Gen 2:16), was contingent on his avoidance of a particular sort of knowledge. While it's not entirely clear to the reader how a tree communicates knowledge of any sort,[5] it is clear that knowledge will play a central role in the narrative to come.

---

2. Cf. Gen 1:4, 10, 12, 18, 21, 25, 31; 2:19, and 3:6.

3. E.g., God "takes" and puts man in the garden (2:15), God "takes" the rib (2:21), and then there are four references to man being "taken" from the ground and woman being "taken" from man (2:22, 23; 3:19, 23).

4. Cf. Gen 1:17, 29, and 3:6.

5. Perhaps it is reasonable to infer that the other trees communicated something like "knowledge of covenantal relationship with YHWH."

Knowledge in the Garden: Genesis 2

Second, with knowledge now playing an active role in the narrative, YHWH Elohim declares something that He knows about the man's solitary situation: it is not good (לא טוב). This statement of incompleteness stands in opposition to cycles of creation present in Genesis 1 punctuated with the statements: "God saw that it was good (טוב)."[6]

What interests us is the process through which God resolves this tension. Notably, God does not fashion woman and commend her compatibility to the man. Instead, God leads the man through a process by which the man himself comes to know what *is* and what *is not* his appropriate mate, what Aristotle will later call the *genus* and *differentia* involved in a definition.[7] We see this epistemological process as the man's discovery, but we notice that it could not have occurred by the man in isolation. It is a process of discovery led by God himself in order to show the man what God has already said to be true. In other words, God brings the man to know what God Himself already knows by presenting the man with various animals which results in the man himself recognizing his aloneness, "But the man he did not find a helper fit for himself."[8] The reader is not privy to what the man saw when he surveyed his companionless situation; the reader does know what God saw: a not-good state.

Many have understood the ensuing naming sequence in Genesis 2:18–20 as an act of man's dominion over creation, a reification of the command in Genesis 1:28. Notwithstanding man's dominion, this episode must also be about the man's discovery. If so, then the act of naming animals was not merely a display of the man acting as potentate. Rather it is evidence of a man who is able to articulate his realization after he participates in a process of naming *animalia* presented to him in contiguity. This process culminates in the presentation of the woman. Hence the "at last" (הפעם) in the man's proclamation reveals that he now knows something similar to which YHWH Elohim knew when he previously said, "It is not good for man to be alone."

Karl Barth also sees Genesis 2 as a process of discovery (i.e., epistemology) and dominion expressed in terms of human freedom where he says:

6. Gen 1:4, 10, 12, 18, 21. Cf. "very good" (*tov meod*) Gen 1:31.

7. In Greek: genus (*genos*) and differentia (*diaphora*). See Aristotle, *Posterior Analytics* II.13.

8. Or as Cassuto effectively argues, "*but* (antithetic *Wāw*) as far as *man* was concerned, he did not find a creature worthy to be his helper and to be deemed his *counterpart* . . . , and hence to be called by a name . . ." Cassuto, *Genesis*, 133.

> He leaves it to man to discover, that only woman and not animals can be this helpmeet. Thus the climax of the history of creation coincides with this first act of human freedom. Man sees all kinds of animals. He exercises his superiority over them by giving them names. But he does not find in them a being like himself, a helpmeet. He is thus alone with them (even in his superiority), and therefore not good, not yet complete as man.[9]

Barth's conclusion must assume that the trajectory of this naming process has at least one *telos* besides exercising dominion: to have man discover who is his proper mate. In what appears to be the first epistemological act, the text gives the impression that God leads the man through the process of coming to know something and the man articulates that knowledge in its discovery. But what was the man meant to know: a proposition? The proposition that she is "bone of my bones" comes at a point of discovery, not to be confused with the thing discovered. In other words, it seems that because he now knows his proper mate via the epistemological process, he could then articulate with language something about what he now knows.[10] His knowledge appears to precede his utterance. His articulation gives the reader clues about what he now knows, upon which the narrator then rhetorically acts to stitch together the story with a matrimonial maxim (2:24–25). It appears that the man was meant to discover that this bone and flesh woman matched up to him somehow.

Interestingly, if the narratival conflict is the man's isolation and ignorance of a proper mate, then God uses the difference between woman and the animals to instruct what his mate *is not* in order to reveal who his mate *is*. But why use the *differentia* rather than the *genus*? Can the elements of the narrative help to plot out the motives of God? The conflict that drives this narrative forward is this tension between man's actual aloneness and God's declaration that his aloneness is not good. Man comes to know both the solitary problem and God's solution through participation within that process. The solitary problem is twofold: man is alone, and there are no other creatures suitable for him. God's remedy is not only woman, but wife and family (2:24–25).

---

9. Karl Barth, *Church Dogmatics* III/ 2, 291. While this study is not a Barthian analysis *per se*, we cite Barth, Calvin, et al. to show that these aspects of the text have been noticed by theologians who are also working exegetically.

10. This articulation after the fact is similar to Polanyi's claim that knowledge is antecedent to articulation: "We grope for words to tell what we know and our words hang together by these roots." Polanyi, *Personal Knowledge*, 102.

Knowledge in the Garden: Genesis 2

What was God doing in this scene of presenting animals to the man? Aside from Barth, several biblical scholars have also seen a process of discovery in this sequence.[11] Man's naming of animals does not exclude a simultaneous trajectory of the man taking dominion by naming the animals or expressing creaturely freedom. Nonetheless, the narrative's focus is on the man's discovery that woman is his only proper mate. If correct, this first instance of human epistemology requires a commitment to participate in this naming process that is led by YHWH Elohim Himself and is submitted to by the man.

An objection may be posed that explicit epistemological language is noticeably absent in 2:18–22. The commands were concerned with "knowledge of good and evil," and yet, we do not see any of the knowledge language (e.g., the verbal and nominal form of *yada*: ידע, דעת) in this section. We contend that the prohibition itself (2:17) centers on knowledge and the epistemological issue frames this particular act of coming to know. Stated otherwise, God commands the man, indicating the possibility of knowledge of good and evil (Gen 2:17), and then, we see the woman desiring knowledge which ends in error (Gen 3:1–6). In between the account of divine commands *about knowledge* and the account of the woman's quest *for knowledge*, there seems to be a proper epistemological process that offers a stark contrast to Genesis 3. Next, we will pursue an analysis of that first epistemological process and its constituent aspects. We will then focus on the error of Genesis 3.

Genesis 2: Six Questions about the Man's Knowledge

Considering this brief narrative of the man's formation, the commandments concerning food and the discovery of his "built" mate,[12] the manifold nature of his epistemological process can now be considered. Specifically, what appears to be a basic narrative about arch-humanity reveals more than a few layers of social, anthropological, and epistemological interaction. We must now answer six questions that strike us as being central to understanding the narrative of Genesis 2:15–25 as palpably describing an act of knowing:

---

11. See Cassuto, *Genesis*,128; Von Rad, *Genesis*, 80–83; Waltke and Fredricks, *Genesis*, 89; Barth, *CD* III/ 2, 291.

12. The term "built" is meant to reflect the Hebrew: בנה. Where the man was made (עשה) from the dust; the woman was "built" from man's bone.

Biblical Knowing

1. Is YHWH Elohim guiding the man in an epistemological process? If so, to what end?
2. What does naming the animals have to do with discovering the woman?
3. Through what instrumental means does the man know his proper mate?
4. Is the man's knowledge instantaneous?
5. What do eating and marriage have to do with knowing?
6. What role is the man to play in this epistemological process?

Is YHWH Elohim guiding the man to know? If so, to what end?

In Genesis 2, God appears to lead the man to know his proper mate. Notably, the man does not sit back and independently reason within the counsel of his mind to deduce the woman. There is no hint of an autonomous epistemological agent and that notion is quickly eschewed in the curses of the next episode. How does God draw out this realization in man? We should be mindful of Kierkegaard's critique of Platonic epistemology, where the notion of *maieusis* places the teacher as the midwife of the pupil's knowledge.[13] Platonic emphasis on reincarnate knowledge of the *forms* being birthed by the student is opposed to prophet-like guidance ending in proper knowledge. God is not the midwife that births knowledge which has been pre-seeded in man's pre-incarnate heavenly mind. Instead, we mean that God can coach the man to see what is already before him, as a physician could coach us to see the crucial particularities of an X-ray, which would otherwise appear to us as a two-dimensional duo-tone flummox. Man cannot discover autonomously, and he needs God to guide him in his discovery.

Further, if we believed that the man's naming of animals is man acting as autonomous agent, this would neglect the thrust of the narrative. God declares the incomplete nature of man's condition. God then presents the animals to the man as the only subject of "bring" (בוא). God orchestrates these contiguous presentations including the final presentation of the

---

13. Kierkegaard, *Philosophical Fragments*, 9–25; See also: Rae, *Kierkegaard's Vision*, 213–36.

creature "built" from the man's side whom he calls "woman," a name which the man claims to be etymologically derived from their embodied affinity.

The man does not act or discover independently of YHWH Elohim. Rather, the man sees who his proper mate is when guided by YHWH Elohim.[14] In this scenario, the man's epistemological process appears to be social, requiring more than one person in order to know.

What does naming the animals have to do with discovery of the woman?

Intriguingly, the epistemological process begins with animals, which are not meant to be man's companionship. The animals, as insufficient mates, seem to offer progressive insight by their difference to the eventual woman rather than seeing the mere animal itself. Because he was first presented with unfit mates, the animals, the man is able to "find" (מצא) his proper mate. It seems to suggests that if the order were reversed, man might not have been able to recognize the woman as his mate. Or at the least, her *fittedness* would not have been so obvious.[15]

What does naming the animals have to do with discovery of the woman? This process of learning-by-difference, where one can name both what something *is* and also what it *is not*, appears to increase the narrative's tension. However, the man's exclamation summarizes what he now knows because of his encounter with the woman and animals who are not woman. Because it is fundamental to this particular story of knowing, we become mindful of the basic principle of learning by difference.[16]

Through what instrumental means does the man know his proper mate?

The act of knowing demonstrated in the second chapter of Genesis appears to claim that embodied humans can know things about each other

---

14. Ricoeur sees this social aspect mirrored in Gen 3 where man's new knowledge is socially bound. *The Symbolism of Evil*, 234–35.

15. The sages offer an extreme interpretation of this learning by difference: "This teaches that Adam had intercourse with every beast and animal but found no satisfaction until he cohabited with Eve." Babylonian Talmud: Tractate Yevamoth 63a.

16. Further, it might be suggestive of a differential relationship that inheres to knowledge of good *and* evil. We notice that it is not "knowledge of good *or* evil."

without propositional analysis. Thus if we ask, "How does the man know this creature is his suitable mate?" the answer from the story is something other than a proposition, an axiom, or Kantian synthetic *a priori*.[17] The man's exclamation appears to derive from an embodied sense of fit, a notion we will explore more below.[18] It is difficult to imagine a way in which this knowledge could be formulated in the classic model of a *justified true belief*. The story itself conveys the instantaneous nature of realization, but only in the context of a repetitious cycle (הפעם) of naming (2:23). It is as if submitting to God's guidance and naming the animals primed him to know woman at sight. This knowledge of the *fittedness* of woman is both discoverable and revealed without an articulated propositional analysis. It is the man's own body that knows the reason for the exclamation "At last! Bone of my bone..."

The significance of such a trivial detail, the fleshiness of the man, cannot be overlooked. The knower is embodied. However, his *situatedness* is not an impediment to knowledge. The text does not portray the man's ignorance as sinful and embodied finitude is not an obstruction to knowing. There is no sense in the text that the man's historically-situated existence is a limitation nor is it contrasted to God's infinite nature as is so often supposed in the history of theology, especially onto-theology.[19] The man's perspective and ability are not looked down upon or accommodated as a weakness, but appear to be the embodied creatureliness that God has already declared "exceedingly good" (טוב מאד of 1:31).

If our understanding of ourself and the world is fundamentally "constitutive of our experience," as suggested by Maurice Merleau-Ponty and Charles Taylor,[20] then place, history, and perspectival *situatedness* are

---

17. Regarding knowledge, a synthetic *a priori* for Kant is something like "the *shortest* distance between two points is a line," where a less interesting instance of an analytic *a priori* would be "a distance between two points is a line." Craig Bartholomew has recently reminded us that while Kant focused on *a priori* knowledge, he also re-situated philosophical discussion in the body to make something akin to phenomenology even possible. Bartholomew, *Where Mortals Dwell*, 178–79.

18. This somatic sense of knowing is reified in the third and rare use of the verb "know" in Genesis to mean sexual intimacy (4:1). This could lead to all kinds of speculation about sexuality and is the sort of detail upon which Malul focuses an anthropological analysis of biblical epistemology in general. Malul, *Knowledge, Control and Sex*.

19. Although he has recently been rebuffed (i.e., Wolterstorff, "Philosophical Theology"), I believe Merold Westphal's comments about onto-theology remain apropos. See Westphal, "Overcoming Onto-theology"; "Taking Plantinga Seriously."

20. Knowing is not merely reduced to the body's sensory experience. In exploring

fundamental to the man's knowing.²¹ The suspicion that humanity's ignorance is due to finite embodiment or a fundamental weakness imports a negative connotation that is not required to support the story before the Fall.²² Contrary to analyses that propose the tree-knowledge as liberating, violating God's commandment does not need to have, "a positive function in removing human ignorance . . . the insight that one should not appear naked before YHWH Elohim."²³ Importantly for the current argument, this creatureliness appears to be at the center of man's dependence on God to know his environs and other creatures. It is the disposition of their fiduciary relationship. This not knowing is what puts man and God in a fiduciary relationship so that man cannot know without commitment to trust God. God must commit to helping the man know.

Through what instrumental means does the man know his proper mate? Man's embodiment appears central to his relationship with both YHWH Elohim and the woman, and his knowledge thereof.

Is the man's knowledge instantaneous?

Above, we claimed that the man's realization of his proper mate shows signs of being instantaneous. But is the realization (a eureka moment)²⁴ the same as instantaneous knowledge? The Qur'an describes this moment differently. It says that Allah took Adam aside after the creation and revealed to

---

Merleau-Ponty's argument from the body, Charles Taylor concludes: "On this view [embodiment being more than access to our senses], our perception of the world as that of an embodied agent is not a contingent fact we might discover empirically; rather our sense of ourselves as embodied agents is constitutive of our experience." Taylor, "Transcendental Arguments", 25.

21. This same *situatedness* might be the referent of Hans-Georg Gadamer's term for the interpreter: "historically-situated consciousness" (or in the loquacious German: *Wirkungsgeschichtliches Bewußtsein*).

22. Schellenberg, *Erkenntnis als Problem*, 240–53.

23. Contra Stordalen, Olson argues that the serpent actually kept the humans ignorant by mixing "truth and falsehood." Olson, "Truth and the Torah," 18–19. Stordalen's and Savran's analyses on Eden are generally unsatisfying because they start with conceptual similarities between texts and do not make necessary lexical connections. For instance, they both provide a parallel analysis of Gen 3 and Num 22 because both texts contain the rare event of a talking animal. Even though they sometimes come to similar and rough conclusions about the Eden narrative as the current thesis, the underlying reasons are divergent. Stordalen, *Echoes of Eden*, 229; Savran, "Beastly Speech."

24. Polanyi, *Personal Knowledge*, 129.; Meek calls it the "Oh, I see it! moment." *Longing to Know*, 46–51.

him the essence of all being. In one fell swoop, Adam received knowledge, which serves as the basis for him being the arch-prophet of Islam.[25] This may seem to be a peculiar variant of the Hebrew account of creation, but Calvin also wonders about the source of Adam's knowledge in Genesis 2. "It is demanded when Adam derived this knowledge [i.e., Bone of my bones] . . ." To which, Calvin concludes that the "whole course of affairs" was either secretly or verbally revealed to the man.[26]

But in Genesis 2, man comes to know by enacting a process, through indwelled participation. By indwelled participation, we mean that if something can be known in Genesis 2, it appears to be divulged through performing some action. Because this act of knowing is a process, it is inherently bound in place and history, not the metaphysical abstractions of space and time, which appear as inextricable features of creaturely knowing. Participation[27] in the act of knowing ends in discrete points of illumination, of revelation: Such as "Eureka!"[28] Perhaps it would have been a different story entirely if the discovery of woman was not the literary climax of the naming sequence. Enacting the process appears to create an expectation that something will be revealed. It involves a longing for a settlement, which means that knowing involves an initial conflict that seeks resolution. The process of disclosure is like a narrative, with a beginning, increasing tension, climax, and conclusion, even if the end of knowing is not a finality (*terminus in se*), but a doorway to further disclosures. Because embodiment is inherently entangled with discovery, knowing is therefore revealed *through* history. Accordingly, that discovery happens here through participating in YHWH Elohim's process, which we will explore in detail below.

The man knows *through* his body, but also *through* his experience analogically.[29] Because he is embodied, knowing has an analogical facet so

25. Qur'an, Surah 2:30–35.

26. Calvin, *Genesis*, vol. 1, 134–35.

27. By "indwelling," we mean something akin to "participation." But we are wary of the latter term due to its ubiquity in current theological discussions. While this book may bounce between these two terms, "indwell" allows us to shape the meaning more than "participate."

28. Although they are not mutually exclusive, we are not arguing for knowing as divine revelation, but simply that knowing is a "revelatory" process.

29. The choice of preposition here is never ideal. If we say that one knows *with* or *through* their body, the body then becomes a mere instrument and we have unintentionally reverted to some sort of Platonic dualism. This might be similar to the tension Buber

Knowledge in the Garden: Genesis 2

that man can know that he is on a path to knowing his proper mate. The man is aware that he is on the way to knowing his proper mate ("But for the man, he did not find a fit helper for himself," 2:20b) and embodying the process. The man must bodily participate in naming and evaluating the animals in order to find out who is his proper mate. We cannot miss the fact that assessing the animals and naming requires an embodied effort as the embodied similarity is what defines the man's knowledge (i.e., "bone of my bones"). Further, the process by which he comes to know is a rite of passage, which he must indwell and indwelling means that we metaphorically embody the process.[30]

Awareness that one is on a path to knowing speaks to the non-stative nature of knowledge: that it is ripe with hope and expectation that must come to fruition in some recognizable way. This awareness of one's location within the epistemological process renders confidence that one is moving towards the goal, which is knowing.[31] To help us understand the notion of epistemological location, we can turn to recent studies in analogical reasoning. For instance, when we depict knowledge as a journey, we are employing a form of analogical reasoning meant to explain the connection between our actual experience of traveling and an awareness of location in a process.

---

is articulating, "Those who experience do not participate in the world. For the experience is 'in them' and not between them and the world." Buber, *I and Thou*, 56. What we want to affirm is that the body is part and parcel of the act of knowing in the Pentateuch which is why notions like Brain-In-Vat (BIV) arguments are not applicable here. For a brief summary of the basic BIV argument see Huemer, "Direct Realism and the Brain-in-a-Vat Argument." If forced to chose from current epistemological work, one could commend Nagel's notion that the "what-its-like" feature of reality is known *through/with/as* an embodied being. Nagel, "What Is It Like To Be A Bat?".

30. I am indebted to Esther Meek for her reading of Polanyi's indwelled sensibility and placing it at the center of his epistemology in her thesis. "'Recalled to Life': Contact with Reality."

31. Awareness of one's epistemic "location" in coming to know something is discussed by Polanyi, *The Tacit Dimension*.

Biblical Knowing

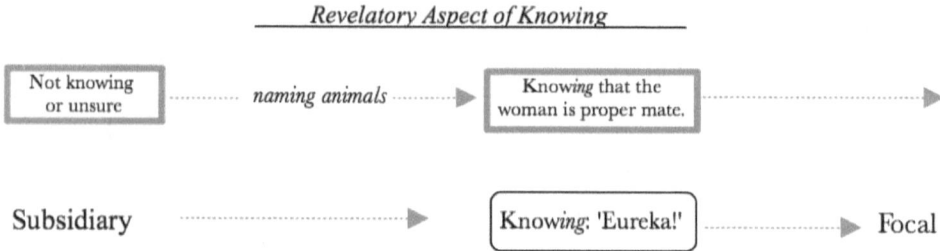

Analogical reasoning allows us to rationalize from within a construct we could only gain through an embodied experience.[32] For example, we can understand the meaning of a phrase such as "career path" only because we have physically moved our bodies down an actual path from Point A to Point B at some point in our life. The physical experience becomes our way of understanding the relatedness between the concepts of career and path. Without the concrete experienced reality of traveling a path, the phrase "career path" is vacuous.[33]

Additionally, Michael Polanyi calls the awareness that we are on our way toward knowing to be "tacit awareness," where one is conscious of the process that is inherently embodied. In Genesis 2, man's focus shifts *from* the immediate particularities of all the animals being presented *toward* the sequential expectation that wants to find a proper mate.[34] This focused movement from the particularities to the coherence of a pattern is ultimately realized in a point of illumination: "At last, bone of my bones..." (see *Figure* 2 above).[35]

---

32. For more on this, see Johnson, "Some Constraints on Embodied Analogical Understanding," 28–33; Lakoff and Johnson, *Metaphors We Live By*; Also, Polanyi deems the awareness to be "tacit awareness" where the awareness process is inherently embodied. Polanyi, *Personal Knowledge*, 69–124 passim.

33. Cf. Johnson, "Some Constraints on Embodied Analogical Understanding," 28–33.

34. Polanyi, "Tacit Inference."

35. Cf. Polanyi, *Personal Knowledge*, 63.

Knowledge in the Garden: Genesis 2

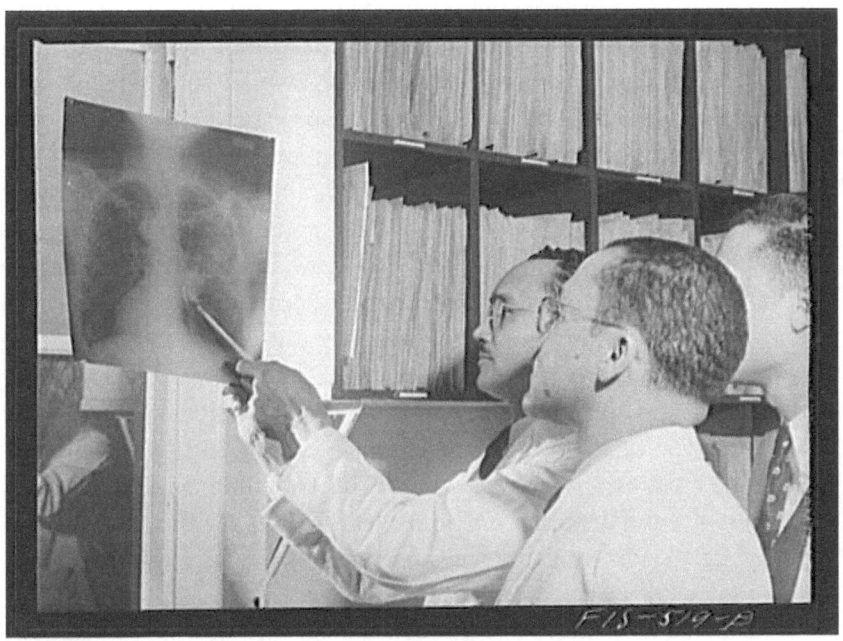

Returning to a prior example, X-rays provide us with an overwhelming amount of visual particularities (e.g., the duo-tone flummox of a chest X-ray; see image above).[36] However, we expect that physicians have had to gain the skill of knowing how to see through that visual mess and cohere very focused patterns in that two-dimensional film. We also expect that as they participated in the process of learning how to read those films, they had a sense that they were gaining the knack for seeing something as subtle as a collapsed lung or a lodged bullet, even if they could not yet see it. And at some point in that process of inspecting films and listening to the voice of their trainers, they had a moment of discovery, where they went from not being able to see a collapsed lung on an X-ray, to being able to spot instances of it on new X-rays they had never seen before. Michael Polanyi describes illumination as, "the leap by which the logical gap is crossed. It is the plunge by which we gain a foothold at another shore of reality."[37]

Looked at conversely, if the man in Genesis 2 never found a proper mate, then the story would have to go in a different direction. But, the

36. Public domain image: Jack Delano, "Chicago, Illinois. Provident Hospital. Dr. B. W. Anthony discussing an x-ray negative with two interns."

37. *Personal Knowledge*, 123. Likewise, Meek makes Polanyi's "illumination" more graspable as the "Oh! I see it!" moment. *Longing to Know*, 46–50.

Biblical Knowing

reader's awareness that man must come to know his proper mate is situated in the necessity of resolving the central conflict of the narrative. The point is that the account in Genesis 2 not only suggests that man comes to know woman as his proper mate, but that he is also aware that this knowing is a quest and he intentionally participates by embodying that quest.

Second, "embodying a quest" is just another way of saying that he enacts the process of knowing itself by participation.[38] Because man appears to know through his body and is aware of the movement from *not knowing* toward *knowing*, we say that knowledge is revelatory. This term simply acknowledges that a situated creature comes to know through a process that unfurls in a particular place and personal history, not the nebulous abstractions of space and time. It makes knowing a fundamentally historical function. It also acknowledges that man was in ignorance about his situation and his relatedness to others before the error of Genesis 3. Ignorance and error are not equivalent matters for this story and that is why basic errors of ignorance are not interesting for our purposes (e.g., stumbling while learning language).

Looking at Genesis 2–3 through the lens of knowing as historically revealed demonstrates that man must commit to know in fiduciary relationship with an authenticated prophetic guide. Through enacting this epistemological process, what is hidden becomes revealed. Or more specifically, what was known by YHWH Elohim is made known to the man.

Is the man's knowledge instantaneous? We are prepared to say, "No." Because man participates in a quest to know through place, history, relationship, and his body, we will argue that Genesis 2 portrays knowing as historically-disclosed, not instantaneous.

What do eating and marriage have to do with knowing?

The difference between *knowing about* and *knowing* will become stark in the narratives of Exodus. But in Genesis 2, the decided difference between *knowing about* and *knowing* is that proper knowing seems to be revealed in sacramental engagement, where one acts in accordance with what one knows. For the man, because he now knows his proper mate, the narrator makes the rhetorical move to matrimony as the implication of this knowledge. Knowing woman as a proper mate (2:23) looks as though it is sacramentally exercised through leaving family and cleaving to his mate

---

38. See "indwelling" in Meek, *Longing to Know*, 90–95.

(2:24). The narrative indicates a direct relationship between the couple's knowledge and their sacramental actions.

By "sacramental," we mean nothing more than has been traditionally construed in the Reformed and Roman Catholic traditions where embodied actions are mediated through outward visible signs that are united to the thing signified.[39] Calvin explains that the role of sacramental action in the garden is epistemic (i.e., it acknowledges something known):

> [Re 2:9] He intended, therefore, that man, as often as he tasted the fruit of that tree, should remember whence he received his life, in order that he might acknowledge that he lives not by his own power, but by the kindness of God alone; and that life is not (as they commonly speak) an intrinsic good, but proceeds from God.[40]

However, sacramental does not mean that it is merely symbolic, because it relates humanity with YHWH Elohim by some sort of union. In a similar way, Barth treats the sacramental nature of humanity's participation: "As the tree of life was to mediate life to man as a reward for obedience by its enjoyment, so the tree of knowledge was to give man a right use of freedom by its avoidance."[41] And, "The tree of life is the symbol and sacrament of the eternal life promised to the perfectly obedient man and accruing to him as a reward."[42]

Why use the term sacramental? Because it captures the inevitable human action that symbolically represents knowledge. For instance, because we have the skill that enables us to know that "$2 + 2 = 4$,"[43] we can sacramentally exercise that skill by adding two pieces of pie to the two that we already have in order to reach a total of four. This trite and provisional example becomes less parochial when one considers the possibility that all

---

39. The general features of a "sacramental" view across Christian theology is that God must author the action, the action must refer to the relationship between humanity and God, and the sacramental action must acknowledge some aspect of that relationship. All three aspects appear present in the garden episode. For a post-Vatican II exploration of the relationship between symbol and sacrament, see Rahner, *Theological Investigations*, vol. IV. For an example of contemporary Reformed treatment of sacraments, see Berkof, *Systematic Theology*, 616.

40. Calvin, *Genesis*, vol. I, 55.

41. Barth, *CD*, III/1, 285.

42. Barth, *CD*, IV/1, 59.

43. Notice that we did not say, "Because I *know that* '$2 + 2 = 4$' . . . ," rather it is due to the adeptness of knowing.

Biblical Knowing

human activity is embedded in and expressive of our skilled knowing.[44] In order to know good and evil, whatever that may mean, the man and woman must commission that quest by eating the fruit of prohibition. This notion of the physical commissioning of knowledge is not alien to the epistemological process, but inherent in the semantic range of "know" (ידע) itself.[45] To know one's wife in these first chapters of Genesis comes to fullness in a sacramental act, to be sexually intimate with her (e.g., Gen 4:1, 17, 25).

There are inherent difficulties with the notion that knowledge not only requires participation in order to know, but is also symbolically acted out. How do the sacramental act and the knowledge correspond?[46] Or, how is it that eating fruit has anything to do with knowledge of good and evil?[47] If knowing is embodied and comes to fruition in sacramental acts, then the reader must consider both facets in order to correctly assess what is meant to be known. Stated otherwise, the sacramental act is either arbitrary, or it reveals a layer of sophistication beyond the simple relationship between the knower, the known, and the prophet-like voice who guides the knower.[48]

One could imagine that God could have put red and green buttons in the middle of the garden with the instruction to push the green button to accept YHWH Elohim's authority in order to know properly. However, the sacramental act of eating fruit does not appear arbitrary or button-like. Rather, it is enmeshed in the whole act of creation and care for YHWH Elohim's creatures.[49] In short: we do not believe that the narrative presents it as coincidental that the command to "surely eat from every tree" is controverted by the eating of the one and only forbidden tree.

What do eating and marriage have to do with knowing? Our argument is that knowing has physicality and is ultimately expressed in humanity's

---

44. Polanyi, *Personal Knowledge*, 49–68.

45. Carasik reminds us that in a very few instances, ידע contains within it the idea, via its sexual connotation, of "coming closer to." *Theologies*, 20.

46. Or even less conspicuous: How is it that matrimony is the *sequitur* of knowing that the man is no longer alone and woman is his proper mate?

47. For a discussion of the role of food in Gen 2–3, see: MacDonald, *Not Bread Alone*, 2, 11; "*Food and Diet in the Priestly Material of the Pentateuch*." Kenneth Stone argues that sexuality and food should not be separated in this narrative. *Practicing Safer Texts*, 25–27.

48. Marjorie Grene explores the sophistication of this relationship in scientific observation: *The Knower and the Known*.

49. Kenneth Stone sees both sexuality and food bound into the creation narrative, not accidental to it. *Practicing Safer Texts*, 27.

Knowledge in the Garden: Genesis 2

actions. Indeed, we cannot ever confidently assess another's knowledge until we see it expressed in actions. How could one be confident of a surgeon's knowledge without the actual act of surgery?[50] The same applies to the theoretical physicist whose calculi must eventually come to physical expression or we doubt them as authentic incidences of skilled knowing. Throughout the Scriptures, we will see that the knowledge urged to the reader as normative and proper is the kind upon which one must act. Additionally, as in the garden, sacramental action exhibits either proper participation in the epistemological process or error. Hence, knowing the woman's suitability is not captured only by the proposition, "She is bone of my bone . . ." The man's knowing is sacramentally expressed in matrimony and the union of their flesh.

What role is the man to play in this process of knowing?

This social aspect of the process reveals more structure than the mere plurality of persons in the garden. As YHWH Elohim is the authoritative guide for the man in this sequence, it appears that the man is meant to be an authoritative voice to the woman. This term, authoritative guide, simply means that we yield to the knower who can guide us to know, as the master craftsman is the authoritative guide to the apprentice. This does not mean that we must ordain the man as a prophet.[51] But for now, we observe that the man is privy to YHWH Elohim's counsel in ways that the woman is not.

Further, we must answer how the man's position of privy plays out in the whole story of Genesis 2–3. Eventually, when the office of prophet is fulfilled in Moses, this aspect of authoritative guidance takes on a new emphasis. But for these basic purposes, we will restrict ourselves to say that epistemological guidance is prophetic-like, although it does not require the title "prophet."[52] It does require that we understand this guidance to be some type of authority that is given by means of privy, and that authority is meant to guide others in knowing. Similar to how we think of prophets, the man relates to the woman the commandments of God that he heard. This

---

50. Polanyi, *Personal Knowledge*, 92.

51. Although we will see significant affinities between the man's authoritative role and that of later prophets.

52. Some prophets refused the title (e.g., Amos 7:14) and some prophetic functions were seen as non-prophetic (e.g., the parables and poetic prose of Ezek 33:32). Gordon, "Where Have All the Prophets Gone." See also Overholt, "Prophecy."

is commensurate with R. W. L. Moberly's overarching concept of prophet where he focuses upon Paul's statement, "the word of God that you heard from us" (1 Thess 2:13).[53]

In Genesis 2, these are the three prophet-like features that we observe specifically in the man's relationship to the woman: 1) private authority, 2) public authentication, and 3) fiducial binding through commitment to the symbolic message and its recipients.[54] In order to address these aspect of the man's unique role, we must look at the interplay between the narratives of Genesis 2 and 3.

Private Authority

First, asserting that the notion of authority is present in Genesis 2 simply means that one of the parties in the epistemological process has insight where another does not.[55] A structure exists to the social dimension where the man's knowledge is authoritatively guided. More generally, knowers must be directed by an authoritative source, in the first case God to man.[56] Man is given the commands about the tree of knowledge of good and evil before woman is "built" (2:15–17). The man then presumably takes the role of authority in this particular aspect. Much like Moses, the man's prior proximity to YHWH Elohim appears to act as the basis for his authority.[57]

If we restrict ourselves to the narrative at hand, the man is coming to know *something*, and by presenting the animals and eventually the woman, YHWH Elohim is the authoritative guide in his process of coming to know. Consequently, these socio-epistemological roles must be understood in order to make the narrative coherent. For unless we see God as someone

---

53. Or, "Thus, the *nāvi'* is in essence one who speaks for God." Moberly, *Prophecy and Discernment*, 2, 4.

54. "Sacramental" overlaps here with the notion of "symbolic."

55. In the literature on epistemology of trust, the distinction is made between "fundamental" and "derivative" authority where the former is a "blind" epistemic right and the latter is based upon one's reasons to believe in the authority of another. Foley, "Egoism in Epistemology." We are not arguing for a fundamental authority, but that there are reasons to view one's authority derivatively based on their authentication. Goldman, *Pathways to Knowledge*, 139–63.

56. See further: Meek, "Learning to See."

57. "Moses' prophetic role is explicitly based upon his proximity to God, his standing in the divine presence." Moberly, *Prophecy*, 9. See also: Eichrodt, *Theology of the Old Testament*, vol. 1, 344.

Knowledge in the Garden: Genesis 2

guiding the man through the process of coming to know, then God's actions might appear haphazard. In other words, the man's "at last" (הפעם) makes sense of YHWH Elohim's "not good" (לא טוב) only if the man's *naming* (קרא) and *not finding* (לא מצא) are directed by God for a specific epistemological effect: man knowing woman as his proper mate. So Karl Barth claims: "The whole story aims at this exclamation [At last!]."[58]

This discussion of prophet-like authority should not be taken as an indication that we have now reverted to a *special* epistemology against a *general* epistemology. In all cultures, religious, professional, scientific, or otherwise, what we are calling prophet-like authority recognizes that beyond the plurality of opinions, there are authoritative guides. These are generally recognized as gradations where ability to discern can range from common to connoisseur.[59] But even beyond authority, guides must be authenticated as well.

Public Authentication

Authentication, or accreditation, is taking someone who can authoritatively guide others and officially recognizing their authority to do that work. My son, when he was five years old, might have known best how to defuse land mines or direct air traffic over London Heathrow airspace. Nevertheless, he is not authenticated to act in such a capacity. Certainly, in training for such crucial tasks, we want those who are both authoritative *and authenticated* to guide us. Nevertheless, these terms need not be spiritualized or specialized to religious epistemological contexts. Authentication simply means that trust must be furnished in the act of knowing, which will ultimately be expressed in the fiduciary aspect of prophet-like direction.

The strongest evidence of the man's authentication comes after the violation of the commandment, his implicit authority is later found out in his relationship with the woman in the consequences of The Fall. The authentication of the man as the authoritative voice is presumed in the discourse of YHWH Elohim, specifically in the indictment of man (3:17). Only the man is sought out in the masculine singular (3:9, לו איכה). Once found, God speaks to the man alone, in the masculine singular (3:11). And God recollects the broken commandment, referenced only in the masculine singular (3:17b). The prophet-like authentication of the man's authority

---

58. Barth, *CD*, III/1, 291.
59. Polanyi, *Personal Knowledge*, 54–55.

appears as the understood social structure prior to what happens in Genesis 3. This presumed authentication is borne out publicly in the final scene where the man's privy to divine counsel (e.g., "Do not eat . . .") becomes the measure of judgement for all involved (3:17b).

While we would not propose that the man is openly authenticated in the Genesis 2, his accreditation to speak on behalf of YHWH Elohim is publicly presumed in Genesis 3. As we move into the Pentateuch, we will see that authentication takes center stage in the epistemological process of Israel and those outside Israel.

Fiducial Binding

YHWH Elohim authoritatively guides the man to know the woman. But a fiduciary relationship between God and the man must also exist. By fiduciary, we mean that knowing requires an obliged commitment between the knower and the prophet-like voice in order to know what is being shown to him.[60] Both parties must commit and the one coming to know must submit. It is not unreasonable to think that if the man or God had given up commitment to the process in Genesis 2, then knowing would not have occurred or would have been contorted and diminished. Just as if we wanted to learn to see a collapsed lung on an X-ray, we must submit to an authority, someone who has insight. Further, we must submit to an authenticated authority so that we do not get duped. Both parties must commit to the epistemological process of the apprentice. A failure on fiduciary grounds of either party becomes destructive to the act of knowing itself.[61]

No doubt the question has been raised in our minds as to why we are using the formal distinction of prophet here in Genesis 2, when authority to speak truth becomes complicated in Genesis 3. The serpent's authority in Genesis 3 illustrates the problem with placing authority as paramount in guiding others to know. The serpent has some form of discernible authority as the reader proceeds. Walter Moberly has pointed out that everything the

---

60. On the "binding authority of his will," see Patrick, *The Rhetoric of Revelation*, 54–57.

61. Although I am borrowing this concept of the "fiduciary dimension" from Polanyi, my use is somewhat broader. For him, "fiduciary" generally refers to the commitment to the act of knowing itself, not always the external voice to which one submits *in order to know*. *Personal Knowledge*, passim.

serpent says comes to fruition: Their eyes *were* opened, they *were* like God, and they did not "surely die in that day."[62]

However, the question posed by the text is not about the serpent's authority, but his authentication: Who has the right to speak on behalf of YHWH Elohim? When stated this way, theologians have generally recognized that only prophets speak on behalf of YHWH Elohim.[63] While we do not want to import the entire construct of the Israelite prophet into this analysis of God and the man's roles, we do recognize that the man functions in analogous ways to those who will be called prophets. But even more, the man's authority needs to be differentiated from the authority that the serpent shares. We will explore this further below in seeking to discover the error of Genesis 3.

After finding this epistemological process to be social, we asked: What role does the man play in this social process? On the grounds of private authority, public authentication, and fiducial binding of the man to the sacramentally symbolic commands of YHWH Elohim and the woman, we would offer that the man is meant to act authoritatively in the scenes of Genesis 2–3, and it is on account of his prophet-like role that he receives indictment from YHWH Elohim (3:17).

SUMMARY

We have asked and answered six questions that are central to understanding the narrative of Genesis 2:15–25 for epistemic features:

1. Is YHWH Elohim guiding the man in an epistemological process? If so, to what end? *The man sees who his proper mate is when guided by YHWH Elohim.*

2. What does naming the animals have to do with discovering the woman? *The naming sequence reveals that the man is trying to find his mate and that he can distinguish between what she* is *and* is not.

3. Through what instrumental means does the man know his proper mate? *The man comes to know through his bodily participation in the process and analogical embodying the quest to find his mate.*

4. Is the man's knowledge instantaneous? *No, it comes at the climax of the process of discovery.*

---

62. Moberly, "Did the Serpent Get It Right?" 161.
63. "Thus, the *nāvi'* is in essence *one who speaks for God*." Moberly, *Prophecy*, 2, 4.

Biblical Knowing

5. What do eating and marriage have to do with knowing? *The sacramental actions taken in eating mean to function as submission to know creation the way YHWH Elohim intends. In other words, the sacramental participation in eating from all but the one tree indicates that the man is submitted to the process. Marriage then indicates that he understands the suitability of his proper mate.*

6. What role is the man to play in this epistemological process? *As a knower submitted to YHWH Elohim, the man can then lead the woman to know creation and Creator alike.*

The answers to these questions then help us to understand how knowing is described apart from any specifically epistemological terms. It also acts as contrast to what occurs in the next scene of knowing: Genesis 3.

3

Error in the Garden: Genesis 3

1

It must be admitted at the outset: Pursuing an abstract idea like knowledge in the Edenic account of the Fall is audacious. A prominent Christian philosopher once warned me that any attempt to derive a philosophical view *from* the Scriptures is a fundamentally asinine attempt. Before we attempt this particular asinine feat from the error in the Garden, let us first consider a direct implication of knowing in the Fall which happened on the top of a mountain: The Transfiguration of Jesus.

The Transfiguration accounts that come to us through the Synoptic Gospels are uniform in most of their narrative details. In Mark, the Transfiguration comes midway through the book, both a high point in the story

1. Public domain image: Duccio di Buoninsegna, "The Transfiguration."

Biblical Knowing

and geographically.[2] A primary question shapes our investigation: If the Transfiguration acts as the high point of Mark's Gospel, why does God only give one rudimentary instruction: "Listen to him." Of all the things that could have been shown, spoken, or even revealed to the disciples, why this one simple command that echoes Deuteronomy 18?[3] This singular command raises all sorts of questions: Were the disciples not listening to Jesus prior to this point? Why "listen"? Why not, "Look at what he shows you"? Taking the long view of the canon, is it not precisely because the apostles listened to Jesus that we have surviving Gospel narratives?

From the surface, this divine command to listen seems askew of everything that has happened up to this point in the story. The disciples seem to have been listening to Jesus, to some extent immediately prior to the Transfiguration. Peter even proclaims Jesus to be the Christ, although vaingloriously, indicating that Peter heard something correctly (Mark 8:27–30). Why, then, does God have to remind the disciples to "listen to him [Jesus]"?

As we will contend below, listening takes priority in the epistemological process. In short, by listening to Jesus, they will then be able see what Jesus shows them. We will eventually head back up to this mountain top in chapter 5 to see what Mark's Gospel is trying to show us. For now, we must shelve this riddle and head down to the Garden of Eden with this basic mountain-top principle in mind: When God descends from the heavens and chooses to say just one thing to the founders of the church of Jesus Christ, He reifies these words from Deuteronomy, "Listen to him." Now, we must consider how the infamous account of the humanity's Fall prioritizes listening in order to know.

KNOWLEDGE IN THE GARDEN

Having tantalized us with an enigmatic tidbit from the Transfiguration, a larger question looms: Is there one principled account of knowing (i.e., an epistemology) in the Scriptures that accounts for the variegated texts of the Hebrew Bible, much less the New Testament? We have made the case in

---

2. Re: Mark 9:2–13. Kelber writes, "Structurally, its place is precisely at mid-point of the gospel. Topologically, its locale is the only 'high mountain' in the gospel.... Dramatically, it stages God's attestation of his Son in opposition to Peter's vainglorious Christos [re: Mark 8:29]." *The Kingdom in Mark*, 85.

3. Cf. LXX Deut 18:15; Mark 9:7.

Error in the Garden: Genesis 3

the previous chapter that knowledge is a process, where an authenticated authority leads the knower to the known through a fiducially bound relationship, and both must be committed to the process. Knowledge can come through the body and our embodiment even shapes and enables our understanding of abstract concepts, such as the way in which the man's journey to knowing his proper mate includes animals. Or, where knowledge is used to represent sexual intimacy (e.g., Gen 4:1, 17, 25), the construct *two things becoming one* can only be known somatically, through the body.[4]

We also saw that the process of discovery (i.e., the epistemological process) involved the analysis of *what it is not* (i.e., *differentia*) in order to lead the man to know *what it is* (i.e., *genus*). In a similar vein, we now consider the possibility that in Genesis 2–3, we have two juxtaposed stories describing epistemological process: one that ends in knowledge and one that ends in error. As we've said in the first chapter, error and knowledge are not a two opposite poles of a continuum. So we should not conceive of it according to Figure 3.1.

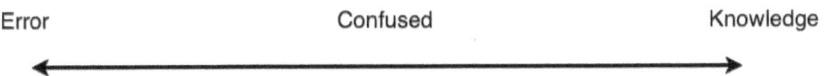

Instead, we should conceive of knowledge and error as two types of epistemological outcomes, so that error is a form of knowledge—erroneous knowledge—contingent upon which authorities we heed (see Figure 3.2).

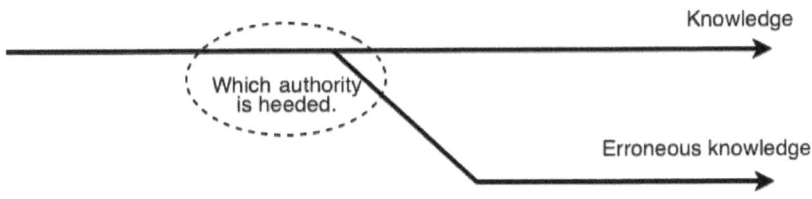

Now we must show the work as to why this model of epistemological process reflects what happens in the primeval account of humanity's error in Genesis 3.

---

4. Lakoff and Johnson make the case that all our constructs find their origins in our embodiment. Lakoff and Johnson, *Metaphors We Live By*.

What Went Wrong?

I used to work as a computer network technician for a large stock brokerage firm and whenever we had a major network failure we would eventually gather together for what was termed a "postmortem." The postmortem was a meeting where everyone involved was called into a single conference room to review the timeline of events, corrective actions taken, and analyses that were generated. Then, we would try to determine how to prevent a similar failure in the future. It was like a crime scene investigation, but nerdier, and with the intent of having a proactive resolution to prevent future network outages. It is natural, when things do not work as expected, to ask the question: What went wrong and how can we prevent this from reoccurring?

So if we perform a postmortem on the Garden narrative of Genesis 3, we seek to answer: What went wrong? In the process of the postmortem, we will need to sharpen the question a bit more. We will not ask "When did the first sin occur?," but rather, "Where or how did the first couple get it wrong?" Or stated otherwise: What is the error of Genesis 3? The answer is surprisingly found coming from the mouth (anthropomorphically) of YHWH Elohim Himself. In short, we will argue below that this is the error: By listening to the woman, the man listened to the voice of the serpent and acted upon its direction. As will be seen below, the role of an authoritative interpreter in guiding others toward knowledge will be central, even primary, in a biblical depiction of epistemology.

To make this case, we will have to deal with four aspects of the story that, when taken together, argue for Genesis 3:17 as the diagnosis of error: 1) the narrative's structure, 2) the literary opposition of verbal action, 3) the rhetorical force of "listening to the voice," and 4) the heightening of sacramental actions.

Knowledge of Good and Evil

Before launching into the story, we should pause and consider our silence about the most obviously epistemological object in this story: the tree of *knowledge* of good and evil. Many have tried to work out the exact content of this knowledge of good and evil, despite the fact that Genesis 3 leaves it largely unexamined.

Error in the Garden: Genesis 3

What is the object of knowledge in reference to good and evil? The story does not dwell on knowledge as an object.[5] Instead, it offers indications of the nature of the error in only one instance: Genesis 3:17. For Gerhard von Rad, however, the phrase "is not at all used only in the moral sense, not even especially in the moral sense."[6] Even though he admits to the sexual and relational nature of knowing in the meaning of "knowledge" (ידע), von Rad espouses what later became a generally accepted interpretation of "knowledge of good and evil": "omniscience in the widest sense of the word."[7] R. W. L. Moberly finds agreement with James Barr and others when he argues that the text itself provides the meaning, namely *moral autonomy*: "one decides right and wrong for oneself rather than in obedience to divine Torah."[8] Barth recognizes both the moral agency of the term while holding onto the sexually laden context, but he does not allow that the grandeur of sin can be merely equated to sexual corruption.[9]

Methodologically, Malcolm Clark argues that prevailing views of the content of the knowledge of good and evil, specifically von Rad's, need not frame the discussion.[10] Even more, Claus Westermann shifts the understanding away from objective knowledge toward knowledge as a skill, even an ethical skill:

---

5. For instance of an analysis that does focus on the content knowledge of good and evil, Schellenberg finds that the Gen 2–3 narrative deals mainly with knowledge of good and evil that makes man like god. In turn, this disparity must be balanced, after the Fall, by the negative outcome that these new knowers can no longer be near God. Hence, Schellenberg's choice to center her analysis on the content of knowledge of good and evil ends up detracting from the narratival thrust of Gen 2–3. Schellenberg, *Erkenntnis als Problem*, 240–53. For a recent and astute treatment of "knowledge of good and evil" without any recourse to the broader epistemological structure; see Peels, "The Effects of Sin," 50–56.

6. Von Rad, *Genesis*, 79.

7. The sexual connotation of "know" (ידע), "is right in so far as the verb *yd'* ('to know') never signifies purely intellectual knowing, but rather an 'experiencing,' a 'becoming acquainted with' . . ." Von Rad, *Genesis*, 79.

8. Moberly, "Serpent," 23–24; In his recent book, Moberly chooses to reflect more upon the "heart of the interpretation of this narrative" (re: YHWH's authority) instead of the content of knowledge. Moberly, *The Theology of the Book of Genesis*, 70–78; Barr believes that "the power of rational and especially ethical discrimination is meant." *The Garden of Eden*, 62.

9. Barth, *CD*, III/1, 285–86.

10. "[T]here has been in my experience a tendency for students to accept uncritically the statement that the basic meaning of knowledge of good and evil is 'omniscience.'" Clark, "A Legal Background."

> The expression "to know good and evil" is to be understood as a whole. It would be misunderstanding to divide it into a verb "to know" with an object "good and evil." It is a whole and as such describes a particular way of knowing. This way of knowing is not a knowledge of some thing, of an object, as it is very often explained; it is rather a functional knowledge. "Good and evil" does not mean something that is good or evil in itself, but what is good or evil for humans, i.e., what is useful or harmful. If "the knowledge" is functional and concerned with mastering one's existence, then the meaning of "good and evil" is explained. There is no question of an isolated object which is good or evil in itself.[11]

Following Clark's methodological lead, whatever "knowledge of good and evil" might mean, we must not restrict our work to the prior explanations in order to make sense of the narrative. Further, per Westermann, we are not constrained to working out knowledge as an object rather than a skill, disposition, or adeptness.[12] The narrative does not require us to define knowledge in terms of objective content or skill because clarifying that knowledge-content does not resolve the narratival tension of Genesis 3. The tension of the plot resolves when the story reconciles whose voice is being listened to, not what knowledge has now come to the couple.[13] Thus, we will not center our analysis on the content of the objective "knowledge of good and evil," because the narrative appears to be ambiguous about its content.

The Narratival Structure of Genesis 3

By deferring to the logic of the narrative, we are showing deference to the authority of the narrator's construal of events. Of the many things that could be said, these characters, this setting, and this plot is put forward as defining the human predicament. Where does the logic of the narrative lead the reader? If the story's conflict was stated as "the serpent offers a different interpretation to which the couple might listen," then the narrative climaxes when the fruit is eaten. The resolution is the vindication of the serpent's interpretation as being largely correct, but completely out of sorts with what YHWH Elohim expects of the Garden community.

11. Westermann, *Genesis*, 241.
12. Von Rad hints at this too where he says, "To know in the ancient world is always to be able as well." *Genesis*, 86.
13. Moberly, *Genesis*, 78.

Error in the Garden: Genesis 3

The action that moves the plot between that initial conflict and its resolution is terse. The piling up of verbs indicates a hastened narrative tempo. The serpent proposes an alternative version of the tree of knowledge of good and evil. And after some confusion about the actual commands of YHWH,[14] the woman hastily responds: she *saw*, she *took*, she *ate*, she *gave*, and finally, he *ate*. Then, as the serpent had predicted: 1) They did not die in that day, 2) their eyes were opened, and 3) they were like YHWH. Again, Moberly notes that phenomenologically, what the serpent said, appears to be true so as far as it goes.[15]

WHAT WAS THE ERROR OF GENESIS 3?

If we have appropriately sketched out a view of knowing in Genesis 2, then error must violate one or more of these six aspects of knowing. Humanity's first error in Genesis 3 uniquely stands in the middle of a seemingly undisturbed epistemic disposition. Because the actions of the woman and

---

14. The woman replies to the serpent by offering the commandment given to the man as her own with modifications. As many modern commentators rightly point out, we should be cautious in asserting motives solely based upon the modified wording of the woman's response. However, the woman unmistakably revises the conditional prohibition given to the man: "*neither shall you touch it*, lest you die." This raises the question for the reader as to where the communicative act through the man broke down. Due to the narratival silence surrounding the transmission of the commandment, it is difficult to surmise where this modified version is to be sourced. Ancient commentators were not hesitant to fill the gap with different versions of how this command appears in this form in the mouth of the woman. One solution in the Rabbinic material is to have the man, unsure of the woman's ability to keep the command, append this *halakhic* command to the original: "neither shall you touch it!" *The Fathers of Rabbi Nathan* in Anderson, *Genesis*, 78. See also MacDonald where he argues for Eve's halakhic addition as commensurate with Levitical code, if the fruit is regarded as sanctum. "Food and Diet in the Priestly Material of the Pentateuch," 24.

Gary Anderson believes that the modification is at the heart of understanding this story. "Did Adam misinform her, or did she willfully alter the wording? The answers to these questions are absolutely necessary in order to determine who is to blame for the fall." Anderson, *Genesis*, 19. In his recent text, *Sin*, Gary Anderson begins with the fact that Adam and Eve *did sin* rather than the nature of their sin. Anderson, *Sin*, 137–40. As we will show, the story itself reveals who is to blame without any reference to Anderson's questions. The story intimates that one way or another the woman entered the conversation with the serpent with a confusion about the arrangement between God, humanity, and the tree of knowledge of good and evil.

15. Moberly, "Serpent."

man are centered around a desire for knowledge, we must look carefully at the attendant circumstances.[16]

In short, the woman coming to know good and evil follows the same epistemological trajectory as the man coming to know the woman as his fit mate in Genesis 2. The attempt at knowing in Genesis 3 impinges upon several aspects of epistemological process, but the concern of YHWH Elohim appears to center upon authority and authentication.

The error of the woman could be mistakenly summed up as a push for autonomy.[17] For instance, Daniel Treier believes that autonomy is the problem in his analysis of Genesis 2–3. He does not, however, treat the inherent difficulty with that assertion, namely, that the man and woman submitted to the serpent's interpretation of the situation. Basically, the couple's actions against God cannot be distilled down to autonomy if submission is integral to the act.

This study generally agrees with Treier's analysis if he means that autonomy is the outcome, but not the process. But this examination hopes to show that the push for autonomy is not offered as a primary motivation in the narrative. We will use five approaches that will unveil the error as being induced by the serpent. First, we will examine in the story's empirical indications of error: structural, lexical, rhetorical, and sacramental. Second, the man is found guilty of listening to the wrong prophet. Third, the man fails to act as the prophetic voice. Fourth, the narrative indicates the woman's error by failing to discern the proper authority. And finally, the story emphasizes humanity's failure to enact the prophetic message.

The Error Portrayed in the Narrative

First, a literary analysis of Genesis 3 itself evinces four indications concerning the nature and source of error: a) the story's structure, b) the terminology of Genesis 1–3, c) the rhetoric of the "listen to the voice," and d) sacramental actions.

---

16. Some like Schellenberg and Stordalen do not want to leap to the conclusion that knowledge of good and evil was a necessarily bad thing.

17. Treier, *Virtue*, 36–40.

Error in the Garden: Genesis 3

Structure

Particular narrative emphases within the story offer insight into what went wrong. The reader presumes that the woman is built to know creation and creatures as does her mate. Devotion to humanity's nature (1:26), directives (1:28), and prohibitions (2:17) appears requisite in order to know the created order and function within it.

The error can only occur along certain boundaries within humanity's relationship within creation and YHWH Elohim. As the story unfolds in chapter 3, it is immediately apparent which boundary is being scrutinized. In the opening lines, the serpent is granted status by the narrator as "more crafty" (ערום) than all the animals.[18] The serpent questions the woman, cutting to the central conditions of the couple's relationship with the Creator. He refers to the Creator as Elohim, not YHWH Elohim.[19] In asking the woman, "Did God say . . . ," the serpent must be understood to be asking, "What do you believe God said per what the man told you?" The woman offers a revised version of the commandment given to the man, adding: "neither shall you touch it, lest you die." Where did the communication with the man break down? The story is silent about how the man communicated the commandment to the woman, making the source of misstatement difficult to locate. Ancient commentators were not hesitant to fill the gap with different versions of how these words came to be spoken by this woman. One suggestion from rabbinic literature is that the man thought the woman would be unable to obey, so he appended this *halakhic* command to the original: "neither shall you touch it!"

The serpent then flatly contradicts the command known to the woman (with the Hebrew infinitive absolute), "You will not *surely die*" (לא־מות תמתון). The serpent's refutation of the consequence of death is based on the epistemological disparity between the humans and God: "For God knows . . . you will be like God, knowing good and evil" (Gen 3:5).

---

18. The "craftiness" (ארום) of the serpent is surely a word play on "nakedness" (ארומים), which connects the actions of Gen 2–3 more closely. See Rudman, "A Little Knowledge," 461–66. As Barth notes: "the nakedness of the first human pair in the garden before and after the fall" is an unmistakable point of continuity, but "nakedness" does not capture the extent of the affair. *CD*, III/1, 285–86.

19. It has been widely noted that the woman's appropriation of "Elohim" (אלהים) instead of the prior moniker "YHWH Elohim" (יהוה אלהים) is indicative of the serpent's rhetorical sway on the woman (3:3). This absence of the full name is noticeable where is the full name has been used both before and after this passage in Gen 2–4.

Importantly for the reader, if the serpent meant to be persuasive, then his rhetoric was not meant to be deductively logical.

The ensuing discourse, about the difference between Elohim's knowledge and the couple's knowledge, does not logically follow from the serpent's initial arguments. His refutation concerning death by disobedience does not logically correspond to what God knows. In other words, the serpent is not making an argument, but rather a declaration, which means that the couple are not being persuaded, but having to choose under whose authoritative interpretation they will submit. In fact, the only way the serpent's words can act persuasively is if they are taken in blind trust, having no way to authenticate them besides the act of eating the fruit. The narrative sequence is then terse, bluntly informing us that "she saw that the tree was good," its fruit was "desirable for wisdom," and she "took," "ate," and "gave to her husband."

Terminological Contrasts

The terms employed also offer more subtle indications of error. The subject of the action verbs shift appreciably from YHWH Elohim (Gen 1–2) to the woman (Gen 3). In the first three chapters, YHWH Elohim is the only subject of the verb "to see" (ראה) used eight times in Genesis 1–3 up until the woman "saw the tree was good for food" (3:6).[20] The irony, which re-enforces the idea that the serpent is interpreting the trees differently for her, is that God had initially planted the trees, which are all described as "pleasant to the sight and good for food..." (Gen 2:9). Even more, God specifically "saw that it was good" seven times in reference to what he had created in chapter 1. But it was not merely seeing that was occurring here.

Considering the role of prophetic authority in the epistemological process, the woman did not *see* "that the tree was good for food, . . . a delight to the eyes, . . . was to be desired to make one wise" until she *listened* to the authority of the serpent. It was in *listening* that she *saw* and it was through the serpent's hermeneutical lens that she *saw*. In other words, it is not clear from the narrative that any of this was self-evident to the man or woman before the serpent arrives on scene. She saw something in those trees which she might not have been able to see without the prophetic voice of the serpent intruding (more on this below). Further, YHWH Elohim is the only implied or direct subject of the verb "take" (לקח) in Genesis

20. Cf. Gen 1:4, 10, 12, 18, 21, 25, 31, and 2:19.

Error in the Garden: Genesis 3

2–3, until we see the woman "took of its fruit and ate" (3:6). Where God is seen as the one taking, it is now the woman taking. We will discuss the sacramental implications of this below. Indeed, these two chapters have the highest concentration of the use of "take" (לקח) and "see" (ראה) with God as the subject in the entire Tanakh.

Rhetoric

After the garden violation, YHWH Elohim indicts the man alone with the words, "because you listened to the voice of your wife...." (כי שמעת לקול אשתך). The rhetoric of this phrase is used in four narratives within Genesis: the man and woman (3:17), Abram and Sarai (16:2; 21:12), Jacob and Rebekah (27:8, 13, 43), and Joseph with Potiphar's wife (39:10). These incidences focus on a man (i.e., Adam, Abram, and Jacob) listening to the voice of a woman with specifically negative outcomes. Or, in the case of Joseph, a man refuses to listen to Potiphar's wife seeking to adulterate her marriage through him and is valorized within the story for so doing.

The rhetorical force of the phrase "because you listened to the voice of your wife" should not be missed. Much of the story of Israel will be dichotomized by whether or not they are listening to the voice of YHWH through His prophets. Indeed, Genesis' account of Sarai's plan for Abram is so lexically similar to Genesis 3 that Werner Berg and Gordon Wenham view it as a direct parallel, saying, "By employing quite similar formulations and an identical sequence of events in Gen 3:6b and 16:3–4a, the author makes it clear that for him both narratives describe comparable events, that they are both accounts of a fall."[21]

	Genesis 3	Genesis 16	Genesis 27
"listen to the voice"	שמעת לקול 17	ושמע... לקול 2	שמע בקולי 8, 13, 43
"and took"	ותקח 6	ותקח 3	וקח 9
"and gave"	ותתן 6	ותתן 3	ותתן 17
"to her husband"	לאשה 6	אשה 3 (dir. ending)	לי 9 ("to him")

In the book of Genesis, this indictment by YHWH Elohim is neither a casual phrase nor a subtle indication of patriarchal misogyny, but the employment of a phrase particularly pregnant with connections to Israel's covenant faithfulness throughout Genesis and beyond. It is a cue to the

---

21. Berg, "Der Sündenfall Abrahams.", quoted in Wenham, *Genesis 1–15*, 8.

Biblical Knowing

careful reader of the Tanakh that something dire has just happened or will happen in reference to divine promises implicit and explicit. In this case, the breaking of conditions in Eden, which ends in exile from the Garden.[22]

Sacramental Actions

Humanity's deeds indicate to the reader that error has been enacted. Punctiliar action is at the center of the story: taking (לקח), eating (אכל), and giving (נתן), but they must be situated within the narrative. "Taking" is only done by God at this point. Genesis 2–3 contains six of the thirty-two occasions in the Tanakh where God is the implied or direct subject of the verbal form "take" (לקח).[23] The fact that woman "takes" is in contraposition to God's actions (3:6).[24] Later, the possibility of man *taking* from the tree of life was deemed a negative action by God (3:22). *Taking* was not the action that led to sin, but it provokes the reader to ask why she is now *taking*, and whether this will be a good or bad thing? Essentially, the action serves to heighten the narrative tension in the immediate story; namely: What will come of this act of *taking*?

Likewise, "eating" occurs twenty-one times in this literary unit with four instances in the commands of chapter 2 (2:16–17) and seventeen occurrences in chapter 3 (passim). The story itself demands that "eating" not be taken as the action of sin. Rather, both *taking* and *eating* act metaphorically (i.e., sacramentally) to reveal what is happening in humanity's commitments to YHWH Elohim throughout this pericope.

This is all to say that the progression of the verbs in the story indicate a movement only in the woman's interior relation to her mate and their God. This interior movement, from trusting God to trusting the serpent, ends in sacramental acts. She *listens* to the serpent. Because she listened, she *saw* the fruit, she *desired* wisdom, she *took*, she *ate*, and she *gave*. These sacramental acts appear to consummate the error; however, outward indications cannot be confused with the error itself, as fever should not be

---

22. For an extended discussion of the "listen to the voice" motif in Genesis, see Johnson, "Error and Epistemological Process."

23. E.g., God "takes" and puts man in the garden (2:15), God "takes" the rib (2:21), and then there are four references to man being "taken" from the ground and woman being "taken" from man (2:22, 23; 3:19, 23).

24. This lexical connection is explored by Rudman, "A Little Knowledge is a Dangerous Thing," 465.

confused with viral infection. Indeed, God does not accept these actions as exculpatory when the man himself simultaneously accuses both God and woman by saying, "The woman whom You [YHWH Elohim] gave ... she gave ... and I *ate*" (3:12). The action verbs demonstrate sacramental signs that point to internal relationships, like all sacramental actions. Here in Genesis 3, the narratival structure, terms, rhetoric and sacraments suggest that humanity is acting in contraposition to YHWH Elohim's actions in creation.

The Error as Listening to the Wrong Person

The four literary indications above draw out the question latent in the error: Who should the woman trust?[25] The story gives no reason to believe that she should trust anyone other than YHWH Elohim and the man as both are faithful to evince trust. Mark E. Biddle's understanding of Genesis 3 may stretch into a psycho-analysis beyond the text, but he rightly highlights the centrality of trust:

> Thus, the serpent insinuated that the God who had created them, who had planted the rich and luxuriant garden to provide for them, and who walked with them daily had intentionally and deceptively withheld from them the best gift of all. Adam and Eve disobeyed God because, in their *mistrust,* they *feared* that God might not have provided the best. ... Key for the story of human sin, however, is the fact that Eve extended the serpent's logic on her own, enumerating only the potential benefits to be gained from the forbidden fruit: it appeared to be nourishing, it was aesthetically pleasing, and it promised to make her and her husband wise like the very deity.[26]

Prior to the serpent's arrival, the story gives no evidence of a breach of trust by the man, no reason for the woman to shift her trust from the authoritative and authenticated voice of the man to the unauthenticated voice of the serpent. Whether or not the serpent speaks authoritatively, it is the woman's shift of trust that is pictured negatively. But that is what she does

25. Theologians have long struggled with the statements of Paul in Rom 5 and 1 Tim 2 concerning who to blame. The *problem* is parsed along the lines of "all have sinned in Adam" or "the woman was deceived" respectively. I will show here that the focus of the text itself is ultimately Adam's failure, which lends modest support to Anderson's conclusion that Rom 5 has primacy in interpreting 1 Tim 2. Anderson, *Genesis*, 99–116.

26. Biddle, *Missing the Mark*, 12–13.

Biblical Knowing

(3:13, זאת עשׂית) in what we can only assume is a blind hope for knowing something in the future that is better than her knowledge in the now.[27] In this sense, the error is found in ambition, an eschatological hope of knowing something more or different, both of which are ironically achieved.[28] This hope of knowing apart from obeying YHWH Elohim then shows that the couple took the interpretation of the serpent as authoritative, which reveals that the problem was their epistemological disparity with YHWH Elohim.

R. W. L. Moberly returns our attention to the central point of Genesis 3 as one concerned with accreditation, what does one do when a different voice conflicts with YHWH Elohim's commands:

> At the heart of the interpretation of this narrative lies a decision about the weight to be given to the discrepancy between what God says about the forbidden fruit, "when you eat of it you will die" (2:17), and what the snake says—"you will not die" (3:4).[29]

As well, Moberly intimates that seeing is a function of listening to and embodying a view of reality that had not been previously considered:

> When the woman looks again at the prohibited tree, seeing it with fresh eyes in the light of the serpent's words, all she can see is that everything about it looks desirable; so why should there be a problem with it?[30]

Examining the man's role lends credence to the view that the failure to recognize and participate in the message of the authorized and accredited voice (i.e., the man's voice) leads to error. The woman blunders by shifting her trust to a non-authenticated voice, someone to whom the narrative yields no reason for trusting. Faithfulness to the message and life according to the man's guidance has done her no harm, so far as the reader knows. The man is her authenticated authority, speaking God's words to her.[31]

---

27. The only hint that God indicts the woman comes from His questions about her actions, "What is this you have done?" The "doing" implicates her trust of an unauthenticated voice whose authority is negligible given its lack of authentication.

28. So Ricoeur finds that error is something like an improperly contextualized knowledge: "The concept of original sin is false knowledge..." And, "*The defeat of knowledge* is the other side of working toward the recovery of meaning." *The Conflict of Interpretations*, 270.

29. Moberly, *Genesis*, 78.

30. Ibid., 80.

31. This, however, raises another problem that will have to be discussed in regards to

Error in the Garden: Genesis 3

Strangely, the measure of a prophet's veracity found in Deuteronomy 13 and 18 is seemingly met by the serpent's words, which seem to map faithfully onto what ensues the Fall. Everything the serpent claims actually comes true: their eyes were opened, they did not die in that day, and they were like God (cf. Gen 3:22).[32] Yet we still see that the man and woman should not recognize the serpent's words as reputably prophetic. The point is that the authentication of a prophet cannot be based merely on the accuracy of their prophecy. Just as Deuteronomy 13 later instructs Israel, predictive power is to be ignored if anyone leads Israel to follow instructions that contradict YHWH's directives. Although the serpent's words were faithful to reality in abstraction, they are not the full reality in the actual sense in which they must now be lived out by the man and woman.[33] As Barr observes:

> The tree of knowledge is characterized several times in precisely this way, as the tree of knowledge of good and evil, and that good and evil are the products of its fruit is made plain not only by the declarations of the snake beforehand but also by those of the deity himself afterwards (Genesis 3.22).[34]

In other words, the serpent's statements are true propositions, but they do not find satisfaction in the lived-out truth of the matter. At this juncture, we must attend to the possibility of an implicit caution regarding the reduction of reality to propositional statements.

The man's role in this affair also offers indications of the same error. The story provides some signs of his error when it switches abruptly to the man's participation. We find out that this seemingly isolated conversation is actually attended by the man. The text simply states that, "she also gave some [fruit] to her husband *who was with her*, and he ate" (3:6). But the strongest indicators of error are again in the chastisement of the man later in the chapter, regardless that he was with her or not. God first asks the woman, "What is this you have done (זאת עשית)?" As the victim of deceit, she blames the serpent. After rebuking and cursing the serpent for having "done this" (עשית זאת), God addresses the woman, and then finally the man. But God's discourse to the man is unique in that God explicitly says

---

the formal prophets of Israel: namely, that a formal prophet should be judged by whether the prophet's words come to pass (Deut 18:15–22).

32. Moberly, "Serpent."
33. Ibid.
34. Barr, *Eden*, 61.

why the man is being cursed. The serpent's curse is because he has "done this" (3:14). But to the man he says, "Because you have listened to the voice of your wife and have eaten of the tree of which I commanded you, 'You shall not eat of it,' cursed is the ground . . ." (3:17).

The concern is not about the action of eating, but rather about the man shifting his trust away from YHWH Elohim to his wife, who by implication, is listening to the voice of the serpent. Further, the language is explicit that God is concerned about who received the commands. Again when God comes into the garden, he is only calling for the man in second person masculine singular. When God chastises the man, he recalls specifically that he commanded only the man, again using second person masculine singular to reference the command: "you shall not eat . . ."

God searches for, questions, and indicts only the man in this scene—speaking in the second person masculine singular. It is clear to any reader of the Hebrew that the man is being held especially accountable for what has happened based on the command given to him when he was still alone in the Garden. In short order, the admonishment of God to the man is centered on shifting his trust to the woman who was listening to the serpent. Both actions, listening to his wife and eating from that tree, indict the woman for stepping into the place of God's commands with her serpentine interpretation. Being the accredited voice of YHWH in the Garden does not ensure faithfulness, as we will also see in future prophets.[35] We will soon return to the motif of "listening to the voice" in order to affirm its centrality in this narrative.

The Error as a Failure of an Authority

Besides indications of the woman's error and the man's error of listening to the serpent through the woman, there are also indications of prophetic failure to which we have already alluded. In the first place, God looks for man and after sorting out what he now knows, God responds with a peculiar question for modern ears: "*Who told you* that you were naked?" Notice that God does not ask: How did you deduce this knowledge? Rather, God presumes that someone else was involved; that a different voice had been heeded. In other words, it is not that the prophetic voice has been compromised through Adam's corruption, rather that another voice is being listened to.

35. A facile example is the story about the "man of God" in 1 Kgs 13.

Error in the Garden: Genesis 3

God's question indicates that there was only one accredited voice in the garden, which was the man. As soon as humanity has violated the only negative command, God assumes an unauthenticated voice has intruded. Again, God does not talk to the woman, and he only acknowledges her error as a thing she has done, reversing the words "this" (זאת) and "you have done" (עשית) with which he chastised the serpent (3:13–14).[36]

As well, God never acknowledges the woman's misstatement of the command as He singularly focuses on the man's violation of the original commandment, which was given to the man alone. All things considered, the narrative reads as if it does not matter whether the woman has misconstrued, added, altered, or received a modified form of God's commandment. The narrator's only concern with the man's indiscretion focuses on listening to the woman who is listening to the serpent. It should be noted that the other emphasis is the future relationship between descendants of the woman and serpent. If this analysis is correct, that future enmity could be anticipating the same kind of tension observed in the Paradise narrative: strife between two prophetic voices.

God's discrete concern is the man's failure to be the authoritative voice, what Albert Wolters might term his "(mis)direction."[37] Man's failure to be the authoritative voice forces the question not dealt with directly in the text, which is: If man was with woman and failed by listening to her, what should he have done? The man is the only one in the triad who could actually recall the command of God and who understood that the woman corrupted the command in her retelling of it, regardless of whether she added to the command "neither shall you touch it lest you die." The failure for which God chastens him might be the failure to speak. If this is the source of his error, then it was not enough for him to know the true command, but he must also reject what is false and speak what he knows. Instead, the authoritative voice is inverted so that the woman is listening with desire to an unaccredited prophet. Even worse, the one who knows what God said, who should be acting as an authoritative guide, is listening to the woman who is listening to the serpent.

With this understanding, against the background of a proper epistemology in Genesis 2, the error of Genesis 3 becomes stark. God's upbraid of the man appears necessary and the relative silence toward both the serpent

---

36. Similarly, Aaron is questioned with similar words and tone by Moses after the worshipping of the golden calf (Exod 32:21).

37. Wolters, *Creation Regained*, 50.

and the woman is made coherent within the narrative. The serpent and the woman, while problematic, were not God's immediate concern.

If this is an accurate read, then the error cannot be the desire or search for autonomy apart from God or man, although these elements play their role in the totality of actions. Rather, the error is the shift *from* trusting the voice of God through the man accredited as the authority *to* the voice of the serpent.

The Error as Failure to Discern the Authenticated Voice

We claimed in the previous chapter that the epistemology described in Genesis 2 has six aspects It is: 1) social, 2) prophetically-induced, 3) differentiated, 4) embodied, 5) participatory and revelatory, and 6) sacramental. Thus far, we have only focused on knowing as being prophetically-induced by means of an authoritative knower. "Prophetically-induced" means that knowing is not only social, but there is a hierarchy to that social dimension as well. Structure includes authoritative guides who are necessary to the epistemological process, and which must be authenticated and fiducially-bound to the process as well.

Here in Genesis 3, we see that knowing maintains all six aspects. It is social in that the entire epistemological scenario is inextricably grounded in the interaction between the participants. It is differentiated in that good knowing can be distinguished from improper knowing only after one participates in obedience and disobedience.[38]

It is embodied in that humanity's newly acquired knowledge is directly referenced to their relationship with their bodies. Their somatic knowledge is stated bluntly and without comment other than its juxtaposition to their nakedness at the end of chapter 2: "Then the eyes of both were opened, and they knew that they were naked" (וידעו צי עירומם).[39] This knowledge caused some sort of disjunct so that they saw themselves in a way that made them react somatically. They cringed, exclusively an epistemological action of an embodied person. Although, being disembodied would not have prevented the error, it is revealing in that they can only see themselves and creation in relation to their embodied experience. Humanity cannot come to this

---

38. Deut 1:39 describes children who have no "knowledge of good and evil" as people who will obey YHWH, specifically contrasting them against those who "would not listen, but rebelled against the command of YHWH" (Deut 1:43).

39. Compare Gen 2:25 and 3:7.

knowledge of good and evil until they actually eat the fruit of prohibition. Humanity's knowledge is not stative, but it is the ability to say what they previously did not know in terms of what they have come to know. In other words, they can now say: "We were afraid because we were naked"; an articulation (like all affirmations of knowing) that happens because they now know.

The couple does not seem to have access to knowledge of good and evil apart from breaking the fiduciary bond between YHWH Elohim and themselves. Because they are creatures, they must be in a fiduciary relationship with their creator in order to keep the commands. It is participatory and revelatory in that the man and woman come to know something that they could not know apart from undergoing the process of shifting their trust to the serpent and enacting his words. We have already discussed the way in which eating the fruit acts as a sacrament in their knowledge. Even though we could imagine that the emphasis might be placed on the woman's decision to take and eat as the error, we maintain that *taking* and *eating* act only as the outward sacramental signs of the interior error. This insistence that the actions not be confused with the error has a lingering effect for Christian theology. For these exact actions, *taking* and *eating*, are sacramentally reversed in the ordinance of Christian communion.[40]

All six aspects of epistemological process are exhibited in the error of Genesis 3, but it is only in the woman's failure to discern the man's voice as an authentic authority that we find explicit narrative warrant to claim that she has committed an error. Even though her error is not directly indicted by God, clarity concerning her participation in the error is required in order to discern exactly how the man's error manifests itself. She follows the wrong prophetic voice, and her knowledge proceeds from her submission to the serpent. *Who* serves as our authoritative voice becomes the threshold to *what* we can know.

The Error as Failure to Enact

Finally, the failure to enact the instruction of God leads the woman to know something that in actuality she did not want to know. *Knowing about* the commandments is not equivalent to *knowing* by inhabiting the commandments. The woman *knew about* the commands and even had extralegal

---

40. Compare the use of "take" and "eat" in the Septuagint's version of Gen 3:6 with Matt 26:26 (λάβετε and φάγετε respectively, in the LXX and NT).

apparatus in place to protect her (i.e., "neither shall you touch it, lest you die."), if one takes her addendum to be an intentional rule surrounding the tree, a *halakhah*. But *knowing* appears to be something else, something that requires committed participation beyond acquaintance.

Again, what proviso could prevent such an error? We might speculatively assume there was also something to be known through enacting the commands of God. Faithfully living out the commands, eating from all the trees, and not eating from that one tree would have avoided the error. Even so, knowing does not merely aim at avoiding error. Unfortunately, the first couple's proper epistemological process is obfuscated to the reader by the events of chapter 3. Hence, we can only offer vague notions about what they could have known, such as: knowing what it is like to live in direct community with YHWH Elohim and one's fit mate. It does not seem like too large a leap to say that God intended them to know through the faithful garden community, but not by rejecting the authoritative and authenticated voice.

This qualification about what could be known through enacting the YHWH Elohim's injunctions prepares us for what we see in the rest of the Tanakh. As with Genesis 2–3, we cannot always suggest in detail what exactly is meant to be known through trusting participation in the prophets' instructions, but the ramifications point toward tendencies in knowing. We cannot always say what knowing is meant to be, but we can often identify what it is not.

SUMMARY

The focus of Genesis 2–3 on guidance, listening to accredited authorities, embodying their instruction, which leads to seeing and therefore knowing puts the Edenic model of knowing as an outlier among contemporary epistemologies. The matter we must now pursue is: what does the rest of Christian Scripture do with this epistemological model? Is it ignored or treated as a special instance? We hope to demonstrate that what we find here in Genesis 2–3 becomes the epistemological brick and mortar with which the Pentateuch builds further epistemological accounts and which the Tanakh and New Testament model themselves upon.

4

Erroneous Knowing in Exodus and Beyond

SO FAR, WE HAVE attempted to show that the canon is concerned to portray an epistemological process at the very outset of humanity's history. What does the Tanakh then do with this view of knowing throughout its texts? Stated otherwise, is the epistemological process of Genesis 2–3 unique or normative? We contend below that Scripture recounts Israel's errors in terms of Genesis 2–3, where knowing is contingent upon which authority is being heeded, and then whether or not the knower participates in the prescribed route to knowledge (e.g., not eating the fruit of prohibition). Proper knowing happens when one both listens to the accredited authority and follows their directions.

Recalling that our goal was to follow the intentional descriptions of knowing in Scripture, Exodus is informative for several reasons. First, in Exodus, we are able to clearly distinguish knowing and error from each along several lines: knowers who refuse to listen to the authenticated authority and knowers who listen yet fail to embody the authority's instructions to the degree required. As we examine instances of accurate and erroneous knowing in the historical books of the Tanakh, we will distinguish errors of the first and second orders respectively.

EXODUS

Exodus is first in a series of canonical books that are predicated on the death of a main figure: Joseph.[1] Remembering our discussion of biblical

---

1. Deuteronomy is predicated on the impending death of Moses. So too, Joshua

Biblical Knowing

theological method in chapter 1, we are continuing forward in the story of Israel to see how the authors of Scripture unfold and nuance the epistemological process. Although the Abrahamic covenant is clearly pushing this story forward, knowledge of Joseph—followed by the Pharaoh's death to whom Joseph's authority was accredited and the ignorance created in the ensuing centuries—creates one of the primary tensions to be resolved in Exodus. The question before us in Exodus is: How does one come to properly know? Let us take a brief excursion into the New Testament to evince the importance of brute seeing that will come to the fore in Exodus.

2

---

begins with the death of Moses and Judges partially derives its literary conflict from the death of Joshua.

2. Public domain image: Rembrandt van Rijn "The Baptism of the Ethiopian Chamberlain."

The Problem of Brute Seeing

> So Philip ran to him and heard him reading Isaiah the prophet and asked, "Do you understand what you are reading?" And he said, "How can I, unless someone guides me?" And he invited Philip to come up and sit with him. . . . Then Philip opened his mouth, and beginning with this Scripture he told him the good news about Jesus. (Acts 8:30–31, 35)

Exodus contains some of the most brute and brutal examples of humans witnessing YHWH's direct and objective actions on the earth—as opposed to Israel's inability to witness what occurs in the heavens. In the world of Enlightenment philosophy, there has been an ongoing debate as to what counts as evidence toward a belief. The question centers on how we view evidence and what counts as evidence. Can we see the evidence immediately before our eyes? Stated more colloquially: Is seeing believing? In the following pages, we affirm that the Tanakh is very interested in this question and generally answers in the negative: bare seeing is *not* believing. Just as the Ethiopian reading the words of the Isaiah scroll knew how the language functioned grammatically and had a sense of the text's referents, he needed an authority to guide him to know. His question is suggestive: "How can I [understand] unless someone guides me?"

Exodus, Deuteronomy, Joshua, et al. address the problem that seeing requires authoritative guidance, authority which is presumably authenticated to Israel. We will observe that Israel often saw something, but did not see what it meant. In other words, brute witness of an event does not equal understanding. Although knowing is often represented by the Hebrew and Greek terms for seeing (Hebrew: ראה; Greek: εἶδος), we must be savvy readers of narrative and attentive to the lexicography in order to understand when "seeing" means something like "merely witnessing" as opposed to "understanding."

Telling Israel What to See! Exodus 14

We want to begin by considering an elucidating moment in the collective knowledge of Israel on the far shores of the Red Sea. "Israel saw the great power that YHWH used against the Egyptians, so the people feared YHWH and they believed (ויאמינו) in YHWH and in His servant Moses" (Exod 14:31). In this summary, the reader can finally discern the trust that

God meant to ensure from the beginning of the Exodus narrative: Specifically, we will focus on three aspects of the first half of Exodus:

1. the knowledge plot of Exodus 1–14,
2. the inability of Pharaoh to understand the brutal acts of YHWH, and
3. the epistemic functions behind the innocuous phrase "Israel saw . . ."

Most basically, the presumption of brute sight—seeing something as it is, without any interpretation required—creates a difficulty given what has occurred in Exodus 1–14. To demonstrate this difficulty, we must return to the knowledge plot, which requires a look at the beginning of Exodus and the pharaoh's participation in that plot.

The Knowledge Plot (Exodus 1–14)

First, from the beginning of Exodus, the historical setting is stated in epistemological terms and it acts as the narratival conflict to be resolved (Exod 1:8–22). Because a new Pharaoh does not know Joseph (לא ידע עת יוסף, Exod 1:8), which we take to be metonymy for the history of Hebrew-Egpyt relations, the numerous Hebrews are conscripted for slave labor, reversing the situation of Joseph at the end of Genesis, when YHWH conscripted Egypt through the prophetic authority of Joseph thus protecting the Egyptians and Israelites from famine. Now Pharaoh does not discern Egypt's relationship to YHWH through Joseph's descendants and protects his own interest by enslaving them. Pharaoh's ignorance and the enslavement of Israel will be resolved through Moses: A pharaoh will know Joseph's descendants by means of their relationship to YHWH and the Hebrew slaves will be liberated.

In Exodus, the plight of the Hebrew people must be resolved in a plot that is intertwined with the epistemological process of two nations. Merely surveying the repetition of "know" (ידע) reveals a conscientious effort to frame God's actions not only in terms of liberation, but in terms of knowledge. Considering who will know what through whom in the first half of Exodus, an almost-rhythmic employment appears, over a dozen occurrences of "know" (ידע).[3] This rhythm forces us to look for the possibility

---

3. Briefly, it is worth demonstrating that the concern of YHWH's actions can be seen by looking at ידע with either the Israelites, YHWH, or Egypt as the object of the verb "know": Cf. Israelites as direct object: Exod 1:8; 3:7; 6:3. YHWH as direct object: Exod 5:2; 6:7; 7:5, 17; 8:10, 22; 9:14, 29; 10:2; 11:7; 14:4, 18. Egypt as direct object: Exod 9:30.

of epistemological process as a resolution to the opening dilemma: "there arose a new king over Egypt, who did not know Joseph" (1:8). This initial conflict and eventual resolution through a subsequent pharaoh is what we are calling the knowledge plot.

Pharaoh's Myopia

Second, the pharaoh of Exodus is unable to see the brutish plagues as clues to knowing that YHWH is the God of Israel, one of the stated goals of this epistemological journey. The plagues were meant to *show* (ראה) Pharaoh evidence of God's power. God kills the livestock of Egypt, "in order to show (ראה) you [Pharaoh] My power . . ." (9:16b). Yet, the narrative focuses in on Pharaoh's myopia. Instead of *seeing* God's power, Exodus says, "But when Pharaoh *saw* (ראה) that the rain and the hail and the thunder *had ceased*, he sinned yet again and hardened his heart . . ." (9:34).

The brute evidence of God's acts in the epistemological process cannot be seen by Pharaoh himself. In other words, it appears that Moses means to help interpret these events for Pharaoh, connecting the dots in order to see that God is not just some god about whom Pharaoh can know things. Instead, Pharaoh's knowledge of YHWH must come *through these Israelites*. Further, Pharaoh must participate, submitting to the instructions of the prophet, in order to see who YHWH is and what is the nature of Egypt's relationship to YHWH. In other words, there is an epistemological process being put in place in the narrative of Exodus 1–14 that is bent on answering Pharaoh's initial question: "Who is this YHWH that I should listen to his voice. I do not know him . . ." (Exod 5:2).

Due to his refusal to listen to the voice of Moses, Pharaoh cannot discern how these events are all related; he does not see the dots connecting. The pattern does not cohere for him, and hence, the things that he comes to know *about* God are not in proper perspective or context. Pharaoh can only see YHWH as an outside oppressor who is destroying Egypt. As a demonstration of this, Pharaoh's myopia is focused on the hail *ceasing*, not the hail itself as a symbol of something grander, such as YHWH's power. In short, because Pharaoh does not listen and obey, he does not see or know properly. His knowledge is truncated, out of sorts with a transcendent knowledge of reality meant to be revealed. Hence, seeing is not a brute epistemological function. Evidence—even the most extraordinary evidence—is not self-interpreting.

Biblical Knowing

Now we are in position to understand that if the Pharaoh could not correctly interpret the most plain acts of YHWH without the help of an authoritative interpreter, then how much more does the Ethiopian in Acts need an authority to makes sense of Isaiah's reference to the Messiah. We can now clearly see that all actions require interpretation, a guide who sees the significance of the particulars and can comprehend how they cohere within the whole. This will not be the last time that a prophet must interpret plagues and famine. And elsewhere in the Tanakh, Israel herself will require prophetic insight in order to understand the hardships they experience (e.g., Hos 8; Joel 1; Hag 1, etc.).

How "Israel Saw"

Third, if there is an intentional knowledge plot as part of Exodus' narrative, and the pharaoh has shown us that brute seeing does not lead to correct knowledge, then we should discover a contrast when Israel listens to Moses' interpretive guidance. Here, we turn to the end of the liberation saga at Exodus 14.

The presumption we are resisting is that Israel could merely see the evidence of the Egyptian bodies washing up on the shore and through this brute evidence alone, understand her relationship to YHWH. We propose that this would be a problematic understanding of the Exodus narrative. If the above is an accurate depiction of Pharaoh's error, then something quite different should be observed in the narrative for those who do listen to the voice of the prophet.

Before the Israelites cross the Red Sea and see the Egyptians pursue them, YHWH uses Moses to invoke their *seeing* in order to believe (ימונה). Like the serpent who prepared the man and woman to see the fruit as a portal to concealed knowledge, Moses prepares Israel about what she will see in the exodus. The only route by which Israel can know the veracity of Moses' claims in 14:13 is to embody the actions of crossing the sea and then to "see the salvation ... which he will work for you today" (14:13). The only course within the narrative logic for Israel to understand that this particular god was going to fight Egypt on their behalf, was by listening to Moses' words beforehand (14:13), fleeing through the Red Sea, and then reflecting back on the dead Egyptian bodies in light of what they had heard and performed. This is precisely what the narrator portrays in the symmetry between Exod 14:13 and 14:30–31:

Exodus 14:13	Exodus 14:30–31
And Moses said to the people, *Fear* not, stand firm, and *see* the salvation of YHWH, which *he will work* for you today. For the Egyptians whom you *see* today, you shall never *see* again.	Thus YHWH saved Israel that day from the hand of the Egyptians, and Israel *saw* the Egyptians dead on the seashore. Israel *saw* the great power that YHWH *worked* against the Egyptians, so the people *feared* YHWH, and they believed in YHWH and in His servant Moses.

After the destruction of the Egyptians, the text portrays Israel's reaction to what she has just seen (14:13) in the reverse order of the prophet's declaration (14:30–31).[4] The effect of their seeing is unmistakable. Seeing dead Egyptians is not brute or self-interpreting evidence. Rather, it was because they listened to the voice of Moses prior to crossing and enacted his instructions that they were able to see the exodus in relation to God's actions. It was an epistemological process.

We simply want to highlight the constitutive aspects of the knowledge plot as it plays out for both Israel and Egypt. Both groups come to very specific knowledge of God: Israel, by submitting to Moses' authority, and Egypt, by refusing to submit. But the text is adamant that both epistemological processes end in some kind of knowledge, thus informing the reader that there are better and worse types of knowledge per Exodus. The story focuses on the integral factors of each.

Knowledge is depicted as a process by which an authority is accredited and that authority's voice is heeded in order to see what is being shown. Moreover, heeding Moses' voice is not equivalent to mental or logical assent. Rather, heeding requires participation in the embodied story of YHWH's plan for Israel, just as proper knowing could have only been enacted in Eden by eating all except for the fruit of prohibition. Knowledge is not portrayed as an object that one attains, but it is akin to a path that a subject can enter (or refuse to enter). Knowing is integral to the overarching plot of Exodus, and we assess its characters based upon how they participate in that epistemological process.

---

4. Re Exod 14:13 "fear not," "he will work," and "see" compared to "Israel saw," "YHWH worked," and "Israel feared YHWH" in 14:30–31.

FIRST AND SECOND ORDER ERRORS IN EXODUS

It is now appropriate to introduce a construct that has unfolded in Exodus, something commensurable with but not previously clarified in Genesis. Namely, YHWH's stated intention is for Pharaoh and Israel "to know," yet the difference between their knowledge appears to be categorical.

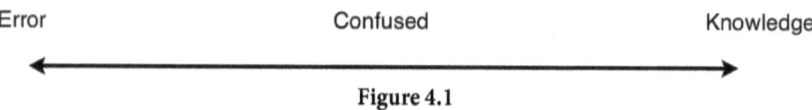

Figure 4.1

So far we have advocated that one epistemological process contains two distinct ends: Israel knowing YHWH as her god and Egypt knowing *about* YHWH who is Israel's god. We have emphasized that both Egypt and Israel end up with some kind of knowledge. As previously stated, it appears that knowing and error are not at two opposite poles on a continuum where one can either know or be in error or somewhere in between (see *Figure* 4.1). With Pharaoh in Exodus, for instance, he errs in the initial step of listening to the accredited prophet. But that error ends in a knowledge distinct from what the Israelites knew. So what can we say about the knowledge gained through error?

If proper epistemological process requires listening to the authenticated authority and enacting his instruction in order to see what the authority is showing us (i.e., to come to know), then error can occur in either of these phases of the process. Failure to acknowledge the authenticated prophet is a first-order error since it has priority in knowing. The second order error is that of acknowledging the authenticated prophet, but failing to participate in the instruction to the degree required (See Figure 4.2).

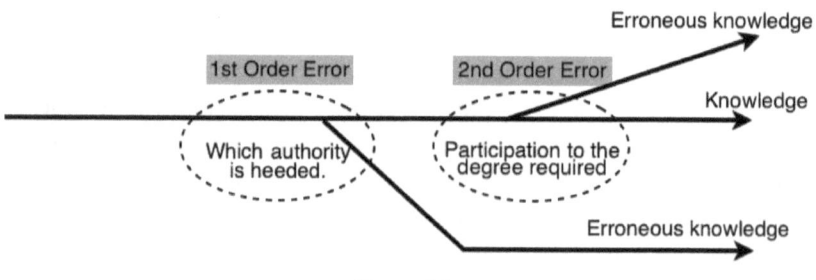

Figure 4.2

Erroneous Knowing in Exodus and Beyond

In Exodus, Pharaoh's obduracy illustrates that errors of the first order do not necessarily lead to errors of the second order. In the first half of Exodus, the knowledge of YHWH as Israel's god is internal to Israel's covenant through Abraham, Isaac, and Jacob. Pharaoh and Egypt will know *about* YHWH external to that covenant, not because Pharaoh is a non-Hebrew, but perhaps because Pharaoh would not acknowledge Moses as prophet, nor YHWH as god. In other words, Pharaoh's first-order error makes the second order of error irrelevant. Pharaoh could not enact the instructions of an authority to which he was not already listening.

The concern for Israel appears to be that they would know YHWH within that covenant, where one party is fiducially-bound to the other.[5] The first order error divides *knowing* YHWH from *knowing about* YHWH.[6] The desire to know YHWH appears to reverse the error of Genesis 3. In the garden, judging by their surprise, the man and the woman of Genesis 3 appear to believe that they would *know about* good and evil as a matter external to them rather than *know* good and evil within a fiducially binding relationship to their new knowledge. Eschewing for the moment the possibility of divine causation in the hardening of Pharaoh's heart,[7] Exodus suggests that rejection of the authenticated prophet will terminably bind one into erroneous knowledge. Thus, one can never actually *know X*, but only *know about X*.[8]

---

5. Cf. Exod 2:4; 6:4–5.

6. The difference could be pictured as coming *to know things about* one's spouse versus knowing one's spouse in fiducially binding ways.

7. Discussion of YHWH hardening Pharaoh's heart might focus on two facets in Christian theology. First, the verb "harden" is in the *hiphil* imperfect with YHWH as the subject and Pharaoh's heart as the object (Exod 7:3). This indicates causation. But second, the actual mechanism may be more nuanced than direct causation. The mirror image of this in the Gospel narratives is the disciples of Jesus (Mark 6:52; 8:17), the Jewish leaders (Mark 3:5), and the crowds following him (paraphrase of Isa 6:10 in John 12:40) all being described as having "hardened hearts." Lexically, the phrase "hardened heart" is not formulaic and several verbs (קשח, חזק, אמץ + לב) are conflated to the one Septuagintal rendition that is repeated from the LXX into the NT as "harden heart" (i.e., σκληρυνω καρδια). We will later argue that the hardened hearts of Jesus' disciples also entail the circumcision of hearts prescribed in the covenant renewal of Deuteronomy 29–30.

8. This confusion between *knowing* and *knowing about* is replete in the history of philosophy and the sciences. Where atomistic tendencies in reductionisms and positivisms of all sorts seek to *know* via *knowing about* par excellence. Likewise, many tropes in postmodern thought seek to *know about* without ever clarifying what authenticates one authoritative voice over another. Taylor offers a similar critique of epistemology as disengaged, atomized, and founded in "instrumental reason," see Taylor, "Overcoming Epistemology," 1–19.

This problem, discerning which voice to listen to, will be taken up in full in the teaching of Deuteronomy.[9] For now, we observe the text's concern to recognize the difference between those who *know about* YHWH versus those who *know* YHWH. For Pharaoh, the shift of trust is decidedly back onto himself and away from Moses. Pharaoh does not argue theologically that the Egyptian gods (e.g., *Ra, Horus,* et al.) are the legitimate gods to whom he should listen. The narrative indicates only that Pharaoh's heart is the center of the multiple decisions to refuse YHWH's authority through Moses.

Importantly, Pharaoh's error is of the first order: rejecting the authenticated prophet where it could be argued that accreditation was plentiful. His knowledge then corresponds to his rejection of Moses as prophet. Pharaoh and Egypt would come to know dreadful things *about* YHWH and Israel due to his first-order error. But insofar as Israel listens to Moses and enacts his instruction, she comes to know YHWH *as her god*. The error of the second order, not enacting the commands of the prophet, follows directly from Pharaoh's prior error of rejecting Moses and YHWH.

Why Should Israel Listen to the Voice of Moses?

The answer to this question seems obvious: They should listen to Moses because *God* authenticates him to Israel. However, there are serious questions about his authentication that must be considered in order to understand later canonical texts (e.g., Deut 29:4). Regarding Israel's prophets, Moses is generally deemed to be the standard-bearer of a prophet's authentication. Indeed, Moses' ability to speak authoritatively on behalf of YHWH impinged upon his authentication to Israel (Exod 4).[10]

Here, we consider a notable problem with prophetic authentication that has not yet been considered: the paradoxical employment of signs and wonders. The question of interest is: How does seeing a sign actually authenticate a prophet? A conundrum follows directly from our answer. The process of authenticating a prophet requires provisional trust in the

---

9. For a detailed analysis, see Johnson, "Error and Epistemological Process," 110–33.

10. Moberly's text *Prophecy and Discernment* meant to dredge up this discussion in a canon-wide argument for considering the role of prophecy in Christian theology. More recently, Briggs has re-invited discussion of Moberly's 2006 text in an effort to make prophecy a more central focus of theological reading. Moberly, *Prophecy and Discernment*. Briggs, "Review Article: On Christian Theological Interpretation of Scripture."

prophet in order to understand the means of authentication (i.e., the signs and wonders). However, the authentication process is the very thing meant to instill the trust required in order to understand the means. But this appears to be a circular argument.

In Exodus 4, Moses has received his authority from YHWH and been authenticated to the Israelites (Exod 4:29–31). Nevertheless, the question of Israel's need for authenticating evidence is raised by Moses himself and accommodated by YHWH. From the initial authentication of Moses to Israel's elders and beyond, the reader understands that Israel ought to respond by acknowledging the signs and wonders of Moses.

Why should Israel acknowledge that Moses is YHWH's prophet? So that they can see what YHWH is showing them. Of particular interest, the authentication of Moses appears to result from Israel's direct observation of the signs and wonders that Moses performs.[11] Because Israel *sees* (ראה) the signs produced by Moses, their seeing leads to trusting Moses. But how does Israel know where she should look in order to see what YHWH wants her to see? In short, Israel must listen to Moses in order to see the signs that give her the reasons to listen to Moses, in order to see that YHWH is Israel's God. This problem of circularity will be addressed below.

However, if Israel can only have insight by listening to the voice of an authenticated prophet and participating in his instruction, how is authentication itself efficacious? Going back to Moses and the elders of Israel (Exod 4:27–31), the means of authentication in Exodus 4 are an Israelite witnessing a sign and simultaneously having Moses interpret what the Israelites are seeing (4:29–31). In other words, if Moses had not ever mumbled a word about YHWH who sent him to the enslaved Israelites, then Moses' signs, which were meant to authenticate him, would have little effect. The signs themselves are not self-interpreting.

By way of exploring this premise, if we could ask ancient Israelites why they believe Moses is the prophet, we expect that they would say that it was because they had seen the signs (staff-to-snake, water-to-blood). But if we pushed them to justify how a staff turning into a snake is evidence that Moses is YHWH's prophet, we presume that they would be forced to admit, "*Because Moses said that* the staff-snake miracle was evidence that 'Moses is YHWH's prophet.'"

---

11. E.g., Deut 7:18; Remembrance of historical instances of *seeing* is then invoked as the basis for indwelling future prophetic instruction in Deuteronomy and beyond.

Biblical Knowing

If we are to claim the signs and wonders as evidence of YHWH's work through Moses, then there has to be something else added into the equation. That *something* must be that YHWH allows some to see the signs as evidence and others not to see, even worse, some are blinded. This issue appears boldly stated in the hardening of Pharaoh's heart, but it also appears in the theology of Deuteronomy, Isaiah, and even Mark's Gospel, which will be discussed in the coming chapter.[12] For now, we must face what seems to be a paradoxical story of a prophet authenticated either by naivete or by YHWH himself allowing people to enter the epistemological process in order that they might see what the prophet is showing them. Lacking an explanation to the conundrum, we will have to wait until Deuteronomy's discussion of how future prophets will be authenticated to Israel after Moses dies.

What Is It? Exodus 16

After exiting Egypt, avoiding an error of the first order is paramount, the Israelites must listen to Moses. But there is also a pressing logistical problem that increases the narrative tension: the need for water and food. After the people grumble, the bitter waters of Marah are sweetened by Moses (15:22–27). The instructions that follow the healed-water miracle at Marah contain the first of the "listen diligently to the voice" statements in the strongly-worded infinitive absolute (שמוע תשמע לקול). Listen diligently to what? This "listen diligently" is focused on: doing what is right, giving ear to his commandments, keeping all his statutes which reminds the reader of garden language again (15:26).[13] YHWH then tells Moses that he will send miraculous food to test whether or not they had *diligently listened* (16:4). The instructions for reaping the food are given in stages as they come to the Sabbath. Later, the final regulation about double-gathering the food is given (16:22–26).

Notably, the stated purpose in this whole affair is that Israel, "shall know that I am YHWH your god" (16:12). This trajectory of events depends

---

12. Deut 29:3–4; Isa 6:9–10.

13. Although he takes it to be Deuteronomistic, Mettinger sees a parallel between the garden narrative and Exod 15:26. "We recognize the Deuteronomistic phrase for obedience to the law, "listening to the voice of YHWH," and we also note the variation in the preposition, . . . with exactly the same preposition as in Gen 3:17." Mettinger, *The Eden Narrative*, 53–54.

Erroneous Knowing in Exodus and Beyond

upon the Israelites *listening diligently* (שמוע תשמע) to the voice of Moses and *doing* (עשה) exactly as YHWH has commanded. But we should notice what lies at the core of the story. YHWH listens to the grumbling of the Israelites, and his reaction is noticeably reflective of the garden narrative, which we could paraphrase: Eat your fill, but under certain conditions.

YHWH *gives* bread for them to *take* and *eat* (16:16). They are to *see* this action as a way of *knowing* YHWH as their god (16:5, 12, 29).[14] In contrast, the woman *saw* the fruit that could make her *like* god (כאלהים), *takes* it, *eats* it, and *gives* it to the man. In the garden error, their eyes are opened to *see* and they *know* their wrong doing. Here in Exodus 16, the Israelites are encouraged to *take* (לקח) and *eat* (אכל) all that YHWH *gives* (נתן) by *listening diligently to the voice* (שמע תשמע לקול) of Moses who makes them *know* (ידע) that they are in an obligatory relationship with YHWH *as their god* (יהוה אלהיך).[15]

Whether or not this is meant to be a reverse image of Genesis 3, one aspect is plainly repeated in their error. Knowing is directly related to "listening diligently to the voice of YHWH" (15:26) and hence, enacting Moses' prescriptions to the degree required. This relation is clarified when the narrator later laments the only conflict addressed in the story, "But they did not listen to Moses . . ." (16:20).

At first blush, it appears that YHWH expects Israel to see something by means of Moses and the manna provided. On the contrary, Moses and manna are not enough to connect the dots for some of the people: "When the people of Israel saw it they said . . . 'What is it?'" (16:15). Once more, the stated purpose of this sequence was so that Israel "shall know" (16:12). Because "they did not listen to Moses" when they went in search of manna on the Sabbath, they did not know something being shown to them. Although they saw the manna, they did not see the grander reality: knowing YHWH as their god meant relationship with conditions (i.e., covenant). In turn, YHWH's response here aims at their failure to see.

As was the case with Moses' signs of authentication, the mere event of manna falling does not appear sufficient to know that which YHWH is showing them. Rather, this reality of manna must be interpreted to them by the voice of Moses. The point is this: Brute seeing is not believing as there

---

14. Although Fretheim explains the manna and quail as entirely natural phenomena, he still ascribes the entire event's purpose to the "so that they shall know" clauses of 16:6, 12. Fretheim, *Exodus*, 182–83.

15. Exod 16:9–21.

is no self-interpreted seeing in these texts. Although the Israelites listened to the voice of Moses, avoiding an error of the first order, they failed to perform his instructions to the degree required, an error of the second order. Just like the one tree in the garden, the plagues, and now the manna, seeing only becomes knowing when one listens to the authenticated prophet and participates properly in his instruction in order to see what is being shown. How else could the woman know which tree is of interest? How else could the Pharaoh understand the plagues beyond his own magicians' interpretations? How else could Israel understand the significance of flaky dew on the ground?

What Does a Golden Calf Bring Israel to Know? Exodus 32

Upon the heels of Israel's submission to Moses before he goes up on Mount Sinai (Exod 20–31), the error of the Golden Calf appears without warning. The reader now understands that the Israelites have every reason to fear YHWH and believe Moses according to what they had seen (i.e., 14:31). And yet, at the end of the Sinai law-giving sequence, Moses goes up on the mountain. On account of the fact that "we do not know what has become of him [Moses]" (32:1), we read the people's request of Aaron to "make for us gods (אלהים)." Then Aaron *took* gold that the people *gave* and made a golden calf saying: "These are your gods (אלה אלהיך), O Israel, who brought you up out of the land of Egypt" (32:4).

This error is sacramentalized through Aaron's proclamation of a feast the next day.[16] The feast is to YHWH, a confusion in the story which might be resolved if the reader considers YHWH and the golden calf to be the referents of *these*, in the people's statement: "these are your gods."[17] The Israelites offered burnt and peace offerings with the narrator's note that, "the people sat down to eat and drink and rose up to play," an error so gross that Moses later calls it a "great sin."[18] It begs for comparison to Genesis 3,

---

16. In their repentance, Moses sacramentally reciprocates their deed by making them consume the crushed idol (Exod 32:20).

17. Many commentators see the plural pronoun "these" in 32:24 as a redacted indictment against the statues at Dan and Bethel. Aaron's words are mimeographed in the voice of Jeroboam saying, "Behold your gods, O Israel, who brought you up out of the land of Egypt" (1 Kgs 12:28b). E.g., Noth, *Exodus*, 246. However, Davies notes that the plural pronoun is supported where the "great sin" (Exod 32:21) refers to the already pluralized "gods" (Exod 32:23). Davies, *Exodus*, 230.

18. "Rose up to play doubtlessly refers to sexual orgies (see Gen 26:8)..." Noth, *Exodus*, 248.

Erroneous Knowing in Exodus and Beyond

because both are monumental errors within their own narratives. Whether or not these two stories are meant to be connected, both errors share lexical and narratival connections that remain between them.

In YHWH's discourse to man in the garden and Moses at Sinai, YHWH draws attention to their errors in parallel terms; that "which I commanded you [sing.]" and that "which I commanded them" respectively.[19] Both errors are sacramentally commissioned by eating.[20] Both errors involve complicit parties, the man and Aaron respectively, both of whom were commissioned to act as the authoritative voice. Like the bountiful fruit in the garden, what YHWH intended for their copious good was now their instrument to sacramentally disobey him. The gold was a gift to the Israelites, given as a part of their liberation (3:21–22). But the gold was to be used as an offering to make the elements of the sacramental worship in the Tabernacle (Exod 25). Further, they have already been directly commanded not to make gods from the gold they took from Egypt (20:23). Upon confrontation, Moses asked Aaron alone the question that is reminiscent of YHWH's question to Eve, "What did this people do . . ?" (מה עשה).[21] Aaron's answer to Moses also shares the rhetoric of the man's blame shifting and the woman's victimhood: "So they gave it to me, and I threw it [gold] into the fire, and out came this calf" (32:24). Finally, the failure to listen to the voice of the authenticated prophet led eventually to death, which is symbolically represented by a sword in both accounts (cf. Gen 2:24; Exod 32:27).[22]

Davies also observes a conceptual connection between Genesis 3 and Exodus 32:

> The people under the wrong leader worshipped the wrong God at the wrong altar with the right confession and sacrifice but in a sexual orgy. The serpent in the garden (Gen. 3), the sin at Sinai (Ex. 32), and Satan at the Last Supper (John 13:27) are three illustrations of how sin rears its head amid sacred occasions.[23]

If all the actions of YHWH up to this point were meant for Israel to know YHWH as her god and Moses as her prophet, then the people's worship of the golden calf flatly frustrates all of YHWH's efforts. Israel's request

---

19. Compare the indictment of man in Gen 3:17 "the tree which I commanded you" (העץ אשר צויתיך) and "the way which I commanded you" in Exod 32:8 (הדרך אשר צויתים).
20. Compare Gen 2:17; 3:6; Exod 32:6.
21. Cf. YHWH's question of Eve. Gen 3:13: מה זות עשית.
22. Cf. Gen 3:24.
23. Davies, *Exodus*, 231.

for a god at Sinai reflects a deep misunderstanding about the connection between Israel, Moses, and YHWH. Much like the woman in the garden, they have no reason not to listen to the voice of YHWH through Moses' authoritative voice, *since the very reason they are waiting impatiently at the base of this mountain is because listening to the voice of Moses has thus far kept them alive and out of Egypt.*

This error cannot be confused with ignorance or partial knowing. The Israelites' out-of-sorts interpretation fails to enact the prophetic counsel specifically authenticated for their guidance. In place of that authenticated voice, they commission their error through a self-trusting interpretation. This misguided interpretation is eventually sacramentally commissioned by making the calf and feasting[24] in offering to the god it symbolizes.[25]

How does Israel get *from* crossing the Red Sea by Moses' guidance *to* bowing down to a self-made idol? The answer can only come through her rejection of some of YHWH's commands through Moses. But more precariously, the Israelites foisted their own interpretative sight onto their present reality, a pattern to be repeated often in the story of Israel. This is an error of the second order, failing to participate in Moses' injunctions. We have already observed these two epistemological movements: rejecting the prophet and accepting fallacious interpretations of current situations. Both errors appear to be driven by fear of abandonment or desire for something more and better. We saw this same pattern in the desire of the woman in the garden toward a romantic view of wisdom, in Sarai's hope for children through Hagar, and in Rebekah's desire to make the "older serve the younger." This pattern of error helps to explain why the Israelites can find no safe harbor in partial understanding or plain ignorance. Error is not a matter of what they misunderstood, but rather what they did according to their self-authenticated interpretation of their present reality (32:21). And, this self-authentication of understanding has been typically rooted by the biblical authors in the motifs of fear and desire.

---

24. Although Noth is fairly sure of the immoral nature of this ambiguous saying, MacDonald (and 1 Cor 10:7) is skeptical of this reading in light of Judg 9:7, 1 Sam 30:16, and Gen 26:8 itself. MacDonald, "Recasting the Golden Calf," 36.

25. "The earnestness of the people in the prosecution of their error is again set forth;" Calvin, *Four Last Books of Moses*, vol. 3, 253.

Summary of Exodus

Because knowing is portrayed as risky in Exodus, requiring one to enact the prophetic instructions before seeing the outcomes, knowing necessarily involves historical *situatedness* and cannot be exhausted by mere verbal confession. Knowing, in Exodus, can be affirmed only as tentative because we are historically situated, not knowing the end of the story or sequence of events but simultaneously requiring trust in order to know. But even this is problematic as all affirmations of knowledge, even Peter's infamous confession of Christ in the Gospels, can be rooted in better or worse knowing. Therefore, confessions about what we know, in and of themselves, are indistinguishable in their superficial details from proper knowing. We will encounter this dichotomy between confession and knowing beyond Exodus, even in the words of the apostles.

Exodus is concerned with knowing properly. Proper is the operative term here. First order error necessarily leads to truncated and erroneous knowledge because it refuses the authority of the accredited guide. Second order error looms where the authority of the guide is not enacted in order to know.

Numbers

Numbers further unfolds and reifies prior epistemological constructs from the exodus, where the issue of authentication is directly addressed in the two confrontation accounts of Numbers 12 and 16. The book of Numbers offers the reader a unique view into authority and authentication in knowing, the most confounding of which is the report of a prophet from outside Israel who speaks on behalf of YHWH (Num 22–24).[26] Yet, for the sake of brevity, we must survey two accounts that are direct reports of who can lead Israel to know properly in Numbers 12 and 16.

Aaron and Miriam's Rebellion

Numbers 12 is a rich nexus of several aspects of proper epistemological process. At stake is the authentication of Moses to speak uniquely on behalf of YHWH. This uniqueness then becomes the basis for further

---

26. For an exegetical account of epistemology and Balaam in Numbers 22–24, see Johnson, "Error and Epistemological Process," 99–108.

teaching about future prophets, who cannot violate the prophetic authority of Moses. While this narrative has discrete epistemological concerns—YHWH speaks peculiarly through Moses and not so with Miriam and Aaron—the implications are manifest through Jesus, the apostles, and to the present.

The initial complaint betrays the duplicity of Aaron's and Miriam's later question. They object together (Num 12:2): "Has YHWH indeed spoken only through Moses? Has He not spoken through us also?" Moses' marriage to a Cushite reportedly launches their investigation of Moses' unique authority to speak on behalf of YHWH (Num 12:1–2). YHWH hears their question, "Has YHWH spoken only through Moses?" (12:3), and calls Aaron and Miriam out in order to definitively answer them (12:5). YHWH begins, "Listen to my words:

> If there is a prophet among you, I YHWH make myself known to him in a vision; I speak with him in a dream. Not so with my servant Moses. . . . With him, I speak mouth to mouth, clearly and not in riddles, and he beholds the form of YHWH. (Num 12:6–8)

Unmissable is the fact that YHWH wants to authenticate the authority of Moses to guide Israel based on the clarity of knowing that Moses has over and above Aaron or Miriam. Because Moses listens directly to YHWH—the presumed meaning of the colloquialism "mouth to mouth"—he sees (ומראה) that which he needs to know in order to guide Israel. Because Moses knows by means of apprenticing under YHWH's unambiguous counsel (12:8), he comes to hold special authentication above any other prophets in the history of Israel.[27]

To add emphasis that this scene aims at prophetic authentication, Miriam is subject to the very sign that authenticated Moses to Israel in Exodus 4: leprosy. Whereas Moses controlled leprosy as an object of his authentication, Miriam was an unwilling subject of the horror of leprosy (Num 12:12).

Korah's Rebellion

Briefly, the account of Korah's rebellion against Moses centers on the controversy of holiness, whether or not YHWH circumscribes Israel's access

---

27. Jumping forward in the history of Israel, the Gospel narratives portray Jesus similarly to YHWH, choosing to speak in riddles to some, but plainly to his disciples so that they would know "the secret of the kingdom of God" (Mark 4:1–20).

to Himself (Num 16:1–40). Although the controversy was not focused on knowing *per se*, it evinces distinct aspects of the epistemological process. The narrator seems intent on framing the narrative epistemologically. The complaint is charged and Moses responds with a clear and objective test to evince both his own authority and Korah's impoverished theology. Note Moses' justification: "[Y]ou shall know that YHWH has sent me to do all these works . . ." (Num 16:28) and "if YHWH creates something new, . . . then you shall know that these men have despised YHWH" (Num 16:30).

YHWH, through Moses, is guiding Israel to definitive points of knowing. The matter of who has the authority to interpret YHWH's directives is at stake. These scenes in Numbers point us to an extreme emphasis on accrediting the authorities who can guide Israel to know YHWH and her covenant with Him better, rather than worse.

Deuteronomy

Anticipating the crisis caused by the impending loss of the Prophet of Israel, Deuteronomy revisits old epistemological themes by re-employing Edenic images and language to warn the young conquerors of Canaan about how to properly know the promises given to Abraham, warnings explicitly meant to help Israel avoid *getting it wrong*. These warnings also promise future prophets who will guide Israel inasmuch as they listen to the prophet's voice and that prophet is circumscribed by Moses' teaching. Finally in Deuteronomy, another epistemic diagnosis is made about the manifold errors that Israel has made under Moses (Deut 29:2–4), Israel's lack of "heart to know or eyes to see or ears to listen" (Deut 29:4). This diagnoses will be re-iterated by both Isaiah and Jesus of Nazareth.

Reading through the Scriptures canonically, the rhetoric of the teaching in Deuteronomy moves back to a past event in order to give instruction for Israel's future. Below, we will look at three key places in Deuteronomic teaching because they are determinative for Israel's epistemological process from Joshua through Jesus and the apostles. Regarding the future of Israel's prophetic voices, we will examine the two passages concerning authentication and authority of future prophets in Deuteronomy 13 and 18. Then we will address an epistemologically perplexing and influential passage in Deuteronomy 29, where the epistemological organs are cited: heart, eyes, and ears.

Biblical Knowing

Deuteronomy 13: Israel's Future Prophets

> If a prophet or a dreamer of dreams arises among you and gives you a sign or a wonder, and the sign or wonder that he tells you comes to pass, and if he says, "Let us go after other gods," which you have not known, "and let us serve them," you shall not listen to the words of that prophet or that dreamer of dreams. For YHWH your God is testing you, to know whether you love YHWH your God with all your heart and with all your soul. You shall walk after YHWH your God and fear him and keep his commandments and obey his voice, and you shall serve him and hold fast to him. (Deut 13:1–4)

The twin matters of authority and authentication persists into the teaching of Deuteronomy. The argument of Deuteronomy 13 concerns the straying of Israel from "these words" in the Torah, otherwise known as the Pentateuch, and specifically the ones being commanded "today."[28] The burden of this teaching on a "prophet or dreamer" is to address Israel's desire to cling to YHWH as opposed to other gods. Gordon McConville observes, "The point here is not to warn against certain types of official [i.e., prophet] as such, but only in so far as they [sic] aim to seduce Israel to the worship of other gods."[29] This passage is most concerned with whether or not a) prophecies/dreams come to pass and then b) the content of a prophet's exhortation. The means of authentication (prophecy coming to pass) are ignored if the content is unorthodox according to the present teaching of Moses.

It appears as if special means of authentication only act as an entrée to considering the content of the prophecy compared to the current teaching of Moses. So Duane Christensen says, "Even if the credentials of the prophet in question are impeccable, if the intention is to draw the people away to the service of other gods, that fact alone is sufficient to prove that the person is a false prophet."[30] If this is the case, then the special authentication of Moses as Israel's prophet (Exod 3–34) must necessarily form the basis of any future prophetic authentication, because the grounds for judging all future prophets and prophecies is rooted in Moses' authentication. This compels us even more to clarify the paradox of Moses' own

---

28. See O'Dowd for the significance of "today" (היום) in the rhetoric of Deuteronomy. *The Wisdom of Torah*, 32.

29. McConville, *Deuteronomy*, 236.

30. Christensen, *Deuteronomy* 1:1—21:9, 272.

authentication that we saw in Exodus where the Israelites believed the signs because Moses told them what the signs meant. Deuteronomy establishes the boundaries within which all future prophets and prophecy must operate. Violating those boundaries and/or encouraging others to do the same is a capital crime (13:5).

Even though this is all rather uncontroversial, we observe that authentication of the prophetic voice who speaks on behalf of YHWH will always require special means of authentication. The only way to consider whether or not a prophet's words are from YHWH is to wait for the prophecy to manifest in history and compare them to the Law that Israel received through Moses. *Both of these steps in the process are special, as opposed to general, means of authentication.* Even the Scriptures of Moses follow the same path of authentication. From within the Pentateuch's own narrative, there is nothing generally authenticating about the books of Moses in their giving, their reception, or their immediate provenance by Israel. These are all special or extraordinary, for lack of a better term.

The Pentateuch itself is part and parcel with the Moses' life as a special redemptive-historical series of events retold. These Torah-making events are as entangled in the signs to Pharaoh (Exod 4–12) as they are with the later signs to Israel herself (e.g., the glory of YHWH over the tabernacle; Exod 40:34f.), without which the internal coherence of its own teaching might be threatened.[31] Consequently, both the words of a future prophet and the Pentateuch, by which those words are compared, exhibit special authentication in that they are extraordinary. But like Pharaoh, and Israel herself, not everyone sees the extraordinary events the same way. Only by the primacy of listening to Moses' prophetic voice can Israel see what YHWH is doing in her own history, specifically by listening to Moses' prophetic voice in the Pentateuch, which authenticates all future prophets and prophecies.

---

31. Vasholz argues extensively for this point on Mosaic authentication: "We will continue to develop the position that the rationale for accepting writings as authoritative, i.e., canonical, resides in the observation of contemporary eyewitnesses of some kind of manifestation of God's approval of the authors of Scripture." Vasholz, *The Old Testament Canon in the Old Testament Church*, 20–33.

Biblical Knowing

Deuteronomy 18: Future False Prophecies

> YHWH your God will raise up for you a prophet like me from among you, from your brothers—it is to him you shall listen. . . . I will raise up for them a prophet like you from among their brothers. And I will put my words in his mouth, and he shall speak to them all that I command him. And whoever will not listen to my words that he shall speak in my name, I myself will require it of him. But the prophet who presumes to speak a word in my name that I have not commanded him to speak, or who speaks in the name of other gods, that same prophet shall die. And if you say in your heart, "How may we know the word that YHWH has not spoken?"—when a prophet speaks in the name of YHWH, if the word does not come to pass or come true, that is a word that YHWH has not spoken; the prophet has spoken it presumptuously. You need not be afraid of him. (Deut 18:15–22)

The question presented by the above is: Does the coherence of the Pentateuch's scheme of prophetic authentication jibe with what we actually find in the historical narratives? This pursuit of coherence must begin in Deuteronomy 18, where we find the promise of future prophets who will be authenticated, including Jesus himself.

Unlike the rest of the Pentateuch, Deuteronomy shifts from listening to Moses' voice "today" toward listening to "these words and commandments," as Moses will eventually die in the wilderness. Nevertheless, the tone is positive in nature, starting with the promise that YHWH will raise up a prophet and "to him you shall listen" (18:15). YHWH promises to put his words in the prophet's mouth and warns against anyone who "will not listen to my words that he shall speak in my name" (18:19). Then the special means of authentication are given in anticipation of the natural question: "How may we know the word that YHWH has not spoken" (18:21).[32] There is one way to discern the actual words of YHWH in a prophet's mouth: the foretelling of future events. The exact nature of this can only be seen in subsequent episodes. This type of foretelling might not be a punctiliar incident, but rather a pattern of special authentication.

---

32. Miller, alongside others, observes that the list of so-called "abominable practices" that is immediately prior to this episode (18:9–14) enumerates practices that would have been commonly employed to discern the will of the gods. "The list is long enough to indicate clearly that *all* the customary ways of discerning the divine will or plan by magic or divination are rejected." Miller, *Deuteronomy*, 151.

Erroneous Knowing in Exodus and Beyond

Either way, Deuteronomy 18 emphasizes the words of the prophet, not merely whatever the authenticated prophet may say. Even more, this passage gives comfort and warning—comfort that YHWH will not forsake Israel regarding her need for prophets and warning that not every statement from a prophet's mouth must necessarily be heeded just because it proceeds prophetically. Recalling the prior discussion surrounding Moses' own authentication in Exodus, it is not a patent or perspicuous affair. Trust must be initially furnished and they must "listen to the voice" of a future prophet in order to see whether or not he has spoken presumptuously. For Israel (as for us today), epistemological ventures inherently involve risk, even ventures of divine communication with special authentication. No solution to the paradox has yet been found by examining Moses' authentication itself or his instruction for future authentication. We are still left having to trust the interpretation of a prophet's signs based on the prophet's instructions about how we should understand the signs. The paradox continues in this circle and so we must now turn to a plausible resolution found in the covenant renewal of Deuteronomy 29.

Deuteronomy 29: The Gift of Epistemological Organs

Following up on the structure of knowing by listening and then seeing, Deuteronomy 29 serves to introduce the covenant renewal by explaining Israel's epistemological problem up to this point in the story. Like Deuteronomy 4, Moses calls Israel to remember what YHWH did "before your eyes" (29:2 [MT 29:1]) and the signs and wonders "that your eyes saw" (29:3 [MT 29:2]). Then comes the reason for the forty years of wandering: "But to this day YHWH has not given you a heart to know, nor eyes to see, nor ears to listen."

What is the nature of the relationship between knowing, seeing, and hearing as it is ordered in 29:4 [MT 29:3]. Given the correspondence between these three elements posited in this book so far, we should be suspect of reading these three as hendiadys, equally interpreting each other. Rather, they may form a reverse order. In other words, Israel has not known *because* she has not seen what YHWH was showing her *because* she was not listening to the voice of the prophet. That certainly would be a fair summary of Israel's history to this point, however one interprets this particular saying.

Biblical Knowing

As evidence of the proposed reading above, in the text leading up the triplet of heart/eyes/ears (29:2–3 [MT 29:1–2]), there are only references to what Israel has seen.[33] Therefore, we could easily make sense as to why Deuteronomy says the Israelites do not have "eyes to see." But why does this saying also contain "a heart to know"[34] and "ears to listen"? This can be resolved if we consider the diverse use of "see" as it is employed throughout. Sight can mean "witness" in 29:2–3, but here in 29:4, it means something like "insight," interpreting appropriately what one has seen. Recognizing that "eyes to see" means insight also avoids the incoherence of a flat reading. Otherwise, we would be forced to render something like, "You saw X and you saw Y, but YHWH didn't give you eyes to see anything."[35]

Richard Nelson takes this verse to mean that Israel can finally obey the command of YHWH: He says, "Now that Moses has promulgated the law and encouraged obedience to it, . . . it [Israel] can obey the covenant" (v. 9 [MT 8]).[36] However, Nelson's understanding will not be sufficient because we have already suggested that Deuteronomy teaches that Israel must listen/obey in order to see what YHWH is showing her. Nelson appears to argue that because Israel can now see, she can then obey the commandments of Moses. But listening and obedience are not what Israel can do with her new "eyes to see." Listening and obeying enables her eyes to see![37]

This arrangement of knowing, seeing, and hearing will be picked up again most notably by the prophet Isaiah and then again in regular employ for the Synoptic Gospels. Consequently, establishing its significance in the Pentateuch will have implications beyond the Pentateuch and Tanakh. Deuteronomy calls Israel to see by listening to the prophet and therefore know what God is showing her.

---

33. "You have seen all that YHWH did before your eyes . . . the great trials that your eyes saw . . . [MT 29:1–2]."

34. Cf. 4:35: לדעת.

35. N.B. By my count, 40 percent (26/65) of the instances of "see" (ראה) in Deuteronomy connote "insight" beyond what one is physically seeing.

36. Nelson, *Deuteronomy*, 340.

37. Along similar lines, Braulik argues that Israel's wisdom is not her law, but her indwelling of the law. Braulik. *Deuteronomy*, 9.

The Missing Ingredient

What is most important for the current argument is that Moses assesses Israel's lack of sight in Deuteronomy 29 as a lack of epistemological organs given to her by YHWH. Now we have a candidate for resolving the paradox that we encountered in Exodus. We argued that the narrative logic appeared to describe a circularity of trust in the prophetic interpretation of the signs that were meant to instill trust in the prophet. In Deuteronomy 29, we have Moses telling Israel that understanding comes when YHWH gives understanding, a point made more poignant if one reads on into Deuteronomy 30. By implication, then, the Israelite elders in Exodus 4:29–31 believed because they listened to YHWH who allowed them to see and thus know that YHWH had sent Moses to them.

Implications for Theological Reading

Interestingly, the only other arrangement of heart, eyes, and ears in the Tanakh is Isaiah 6:9–10, which is then cited by Jesus in similar circumstances to those we have discussed above. In Isaiah, the hopefulness for a circumcised and understanding heart has evaporated almost entirely (cf. Deut 30:6). Instead, Israel's eyes will be blinded and their ears will be deafened by the prophetic voice of Isaiah.

The implications of this reading are manifest. As was the case with Israel in Deuteronomy 29, it is God who restores the sight and enables the blind to see. It is something *given* to the Israelites that allows them to see, not something within themselves. It is not a rational nor autonomous grasping of the events at hand, but a gift of the heart to know *because* they now have the eyes to see *because* they were given the ears to listen.

For Deuteronomy, as was anticipated in the conundrum of Moses' authority in Exodus, if we are left to our own wits in the authentication of the prophets, then it seems that we end with a paradoxical process or naïve trust in whatever prophetic voice comes our way. However, it appears that the Pentateuch's way around this conundrum is to reveal that it is God who gives the requisite sight to see, not our own rational faculties acting alone. And that sight comes from first listening to the authenticated prophetic voice through our "ears to hear."

Biblical Knowing

Synthesis from the Pentateuch

This brief sample from the Pentateuch is meant to establish an objective epistemological contention with which any theology must be confronted. Not only is knowledge present in core narratives of the Pentateuch, but also highly relevant, right at the center of the story. It appears that some epistemological tropes persist between these disparate texts. Most notably:

1. There is a socio-prophetic role in knowing where authorities are established and the intended knowers either submit to or reject those authorities;
2. Knowing is a diachronic process, not a punctiliar moment in the narrative's logic, although it often comes to heightened points of illumination (e.g., Gen 2:23; Exod 14:31; Deut 4:35);
3. Knowledge requires the embodiment of instructions given by the authenticated authorities;
4. The Pentateuchal description of knowledge is focused on the subjective apprehension of it rather than an objectivist account about something called knowledge.

Joshua and Israel's Future Prophets

Finally, after the death of Moses, we must trace the use of this epistemological process in the remaining historical books of the Tanakh: Joshua, Judges, Samuel, and Kings. Because of the shift in narratival focus, the problem of knowledge is presumed more than explored in these texts. Yet the epistemological priorities remain and are employed in key passages of Israel's and Judah's histories.

This trend of authority, authentication, and participation in order to know continues into the remainder of the historical texts of the Tanakh, but more sparsely. We will briefly highlight a few of these instances that follow the motif. Of immediate interest, we see that Joshua does not pass the prophetic authentication test as it is laid down in Deuteronomy 13 and 18. Instead, his authority appears to be authenticated through the public succession ceremony via hand-leaning rite (Num 27:12–23, Deut 31:1–8).[38] It

---

38. Joshua's authority appears to have been initially gained through a public "hand-leaning" rite rather than the criteria of Deut 13 and 18. See Milgrom and Sklar on the possible meaning of "hand-leaning" rituals. Milgrom, *Leviticus 1–16*, 151; Sklar, *Sin, Impurity, Sacrifice, Atonement*, 183.

Erroneous Knowing in Exodus and Beyond

is not until Joshua 4 that we see his prophetic instruction in a testable form. If his directive to cross the Jordan is from YHWH, then they should be able to pass and authentication is implicit (Josh 4:1–7). However, Israel must submit to his authority in this matter in order to find out if these words are true. For this reason, we must affirm that the succession from Moses to Joshua carries with it the authentication for him to act as YHWH's prophet. Indeed, the final words of Deuteronomy attest to the reason for Joshua's authority (34:9): "And Joshua the son of Nun was full of the spirit of wisdom, for Moses had laid his hands on him. So the people of Israel listened to him and did as YHWH had commanded Moses."

The text of Joshua continues to indicate the people's errors in the "listen to the voice" (שמע קול) motif already observed. Two instances merit consideration. In the retelling of Israel's former error of wandering in the wilderness, Joshua 5:6 describes that error: "... because they did not listen to the voice of YHWH." In consequence, Israel's inability to "see the land" flows from this failure to listen.[39] Toward the end of Joshua, the tribes of Israel that remain east of the Jordan (Reubenites, Gadites, and half of Manasseh) are commended because they "have kept all that Moses the servant of YHWH commanded you and listened to my [Joshua's] voice..." (22:2). Then, the Deuteronomic counsel is given: "be very careful to do the commandments," "to love YHWH your god," "walk in his ways," "keep his commandments," and "cling to him and serve him with all your heart and ... soul" (cf. Deut 30:15–20; Josh 22:5). The result of this counsel is that these tribes were blessed by Joshua and returned to their land with abundance (22:7–8).

We merely want to point out that listening to the voice of the prophet in Joshua is accompanied by the Deuteronomic (and Edenic) language of blessing and fruitful abundance while disobedience carries the language of perishing and dearth. Also worth mentioning, the narrator indicates that listening to Joshua and enacting his instruction leads to knowledge. Rahab *knows of* YHWH's covenant with Israel by listening to the report and then acting appropriately by taking in the spies (Josh 2). Consequently, Rahab herself knows YHWH's covenant itself when the walls of Jericho come down and her household is spared and lives long in the land with Israel (6:22–25). Submitting to and enacting the spies' instructions, with prevenient reasons

---

39. "For the people of Israel walked forty years in the wilderness, until all the nation, ... perished, because they did not listen to the voice of YHWH; YHWH swore to them that he would not let them see the land that YHWH had sworn to their fathers to give to us, a land flowing with milk and honey" (Josh 5:6).

Biblical Knowing

to trust them, leads her to that knowledge—something that is impossible to confirm at the very point where she acts on the instructions.

In Joshua 3, the instructions "that you [all] may know the way by which you shall go" must be heeded and enacted in order to know (Josh 3:4). They also needed to know that their God is living and among them and will inconceivably dispossess Canaan's inhabitants. The only way to bridge that gap in knowledge is not by facts about God, but to follow the priests across the river just as Joshua has instructed them. The consequence is stated clearly: "By this you shall know that the living God is among you, and that He will assuredly dispossess from before you the Canaanite, the Hittite, . . ." (Josh 3:10). And as the inexperienced Israelites re-enacted the Red Sea crossing over the dry bed of the Jordan River, their submission to Joshua and requisite actions are meant to instruct outsiders as well: "that all the peoples of the earth may know that the hand of YHWH is mighty" (Josh 4:24).

Joshua's narrator continues to presume and employ the patterned discussion of knowing. In order to know well—in this case, to know the covenant promises well—Israel must listen to the accredited prophet and perform his instructions. Proper knowing does not occur apart from the avoidance of first and second order errors. Those who fail to listen or act, come to a definitive knowledge, but their knowing is truncated or it is of the covenant curses (e.g., Achan; Joshua 7:10–26)—the very aspect of the covenant that we do not want to know.

Judges and the Man of God

Judges is unique in the Hebrew canon in that it opens with a historical summary and then a preview of what one is about to read. In its second chapter, there is a précis of the cycle of error that Israel will repeat over and again within this one text. This is initiated by the angel of YHWH (מלאך יהוה) going up to speak to the people at Bochin (Judg 2:1). On behalf of YHWH, the angel decries to all of Israel that by making covenants with the inhabitants of Canaan and failing to tear down their altars (Judg 2:2) they have not "listened to my voice." Then, in identical language to YHWH's query of the woman in the garden, YHWH asks Israel, "What is this you have done (מא זאת עשיתם)."[40] This becomes a real and specific warning given at the end of Joshua:

40. Compare Judg 2:2 to Gen 3:13: מא זאת עשית.

Erroneous Knowing in Exodus and Beyond

> [B]ut you shall cling to YHWH your god. ... Be very careful, therefore, to love YHWH your God. For if you turn back and cling to the remnant of these nations remaining among you and make marriages with them ... know for certain that YHWH your God will no longer drive out these nations before you, but they shall be a snare and a trap for you, a whip on your sides and thorns in your eyes, until you perish from off this good ground that YHWH your God has given you. (Josh 23:11–13)

Therefore, YHWH makes the Canaanites a snare to Israel and a "thing in their side" (לצדים).[41] Once more, the very thing that is meant to be a blessing to Israel (e.g., dispossession, good land, freedom from idolatry, etc.) becomes her oppressor.

The greatest indication of error to come in the book of Judges is the description of the next generation: "And there arose another generation after them who did not know YHWH or the work that he had done for Israel" (Judg 2:10). At the fore of Deuteronomy, the next generation does not know "good and evil" (Deut 1:39). In Judges, this next generation "did not know YHWH" and "did evil in the sight of YHWH" (Judg 2:10–11). The terse addendum that neither did they know the "work he had done for Israel" portends something much greater than naivete or flat ignorance (cf. Exod 14:13, 31). Almost every plea for Israel to listen to the voice of YHWH thus far has been accompanied by an appeal to consider that which YHWH has done for Israel. On what basis could these pleas now be made if they no longer knew "work he had done for Israel"?

The cycle of Israel's error in Judges is plainly established from it's beginning:

1. The Israelites syncretize with the Canaanite gods they have failed to dispossess (2:11–13).
2. YHWH hands them over to their "plunderers" (2:14–15).
3. The Israelites cry out to YHWH.
4. YHWH raises up a judge who liberates the people (2:16–18).
5. The judge dies (2:19).
6. The people revert to syncretism (2:19).
7. The cycle repeats.

---

41. Cf. the warnings and fore-tellings about other nations as a "snare": Exod 10:7; 23:33; 34:12; Deut 7:16; Josh 23:13.

YHWH's anger at Israel's error is again associated with her failure to listen: "Because this people have transgressed my covenant . . . and have not listened to my voice, I will no longer drive out . . . the nations . . ." (2:20–21). This repetition is explored in the Midianite oppression of Israel. In Judges 6, we find that when Israel cries out to YHWH, he sent a prophet who pleaded with Israel on the basis on YHWH's past actions. "[I] brought you out of the house of bondage . . . delivered you . . . drove them out before you and gave you their land . . . *but you have not listened to my voice.*" Once more, within the cycle of the Judges stories, Israel's cry for help due to her own error is assessed with the indictment of the "listen to the voice" (שמע קול) motif.

Samuels and Kings

First Samuel, in its early chapters, is also invested in evincing the authority of Samuel as Israel's prophet. His authentication before Israel is obscured to the reader (3:19–21), but the reader and Eli are certainly privy to YHWH's call. We find it beyond coincidence that the term for listen/hear (שמע) becomes the verb around which his authority is manifested. The double meaning of his name plays off his childhood call where Hannah is "heard by God" (1:20) and Samuel is the only one who "hears God" (3:4–21). But the author is certainly aware to establish confidence that this was a public authentication that went beyond his private call as all "from Dan to Beersheba knew that Samuel was established as a prophet of YHWH" (3:20).

Error becomes most pointed in the person of Saul and the "listen to the voice" (שמע קול) motif is employed. First, before Saul enters the scene, the motif is used to describe the exchange between Samuel and the people of Israel. We see an inversion of the motif that resembles Genesis 16 where Samuel, like Abram with Sarai, is commanded to "listen to the voice of the people" concerning their juvenile desire for a king (8:7, 9). In his stern warnings to Israel against rejecting YHWH as their king, the author indicates their folly with: "But the people refused to listen to the voice of Samuel" (8:19). YHWH once again instructs Samuel to "listen to their voice" (8:22), even in their error to assign for themselves a king instead of YHWH.

Second, we see the "listen to the voice" (שמע קול) motif exercised in Saul's folly. Beginning with Samuel's private exhortation to Saul, he warns him to "listen to the words of YHWH" concerning what to do with the

Amalekites. In failing to indwell the instructions of YHWH via Samuel, Saul is obdurate to admit his error. The sequence begins with Samuel's interrogative:

> Why then did you not listen to the voice of YHWH? (15:19)?
>
> I have listened to the voice of YHWH. (15:20)
>
> Has YHWH as great delight in burnt offerings and sacrifices as in listening to the voice of YHWH? (15:22)
>
> I have sinned . . . because I feared the people and listened to their voice. (15:24)

Finally, two instances of interest are found in 1 Kings 20 and 2 Kings 18. We must only make mention here that in the story of Ahab fighting Ben-hadad of Syria in First Kings, Ben-hadad is said to have erroneously "listened to their voice" when his servants circumscribed YHWH's power to the hills and not the valleys (1 Kgs 20:23–25). In 2 Kings we find the terse explanation as to why Samaria and Israel were carried into exile stated, "because they did not listen to the voice of YHWH their God . . ." (2 Kgs 18:12).

CONCLUSIONS

Although the frequency of the "listen to the voice of" motif lessens in the historical books after Deuteronomy, the significance of its employment cannot be understated. In defining the Israelite response to post-Mosaic prophets (Deut 34:9; Josh 5:6; 1 Sam 8:19), the cycles of error are specifically framed in epistemological terms in Judges (Judg 2) and even the stated reason for the exile of Judah (2 Kgs 18:12). The authors regularly employ the idea that knowing was preceded by listening to the voice of the prophet who was clearly accredited to Israel and to the reader.

The reason for this shift in focus might be just as easily explained by the focus of the narratives. Genesis opens with its priority on knowledge of spouse and proper relationship to YHWH. Exodus concentrates its narratival emphasis on describing who knows what and how, picturing entire nations as singular epistemic characters in the story. These empire-shaking events aim at the Egyptians so that they will know YHWH's relationship to Israel and so that Israel will know YHWH is her God. The reinforcement of that knowing is regular and intentional in the following story of Israel's wandering and settlement in Canaan. After Joshua's conquest, what used to be a singular character called "the Israelites" is now a dispersed and disparate group. Judges opens with an epistemological diagnosis as well, but then the knowledge arc is not explicitly articulated throughout.

This is all to say that epistemology, like many theological constructs in the Tanakh, is pursued in the Garden and throughout the Pentateuch, and then presumed to be roughly normative from that point on. As a rough analogy, there is no ceremony or clearly articulated construct for marriage in the Tanakh. However, monogamous marriage is propounded through the creation narrative as essential to humanity's normative existence in Eden and then can only inferred through the Levitical code and beyond. If proper knowing and the ramifications of improper epistemological procedure are clarified in Genesis 2–3, then it should not surprise the reader that discerned knowing is only examined in key instances where it often makes the difference between life and death (cf. Deut 29:2–4; 30:15–20).

5

Knowing under the Prophet-Messiah: Mark, Luke, and John

IN THE PRIOR CHAPTERS, we have offered a view of knowing as a process that begins with listening to accredited authorities and then enacting their directions in order to see. Submission and praxis are not novel concepts in the history of Judaism or Christianity (or any religion for that matter). However, the idea that accredited authorities, process, and embodied participation form the centerpiece of all proper knowing is a more radical proposition.

In the coming chapters, we will argue that the biblical epistemology we are exploring here is fully commensurate with Polanyi's scientific epistemology. Hence, Scripture's description of knowing is not limited to interacting with religious epistemology, but it is conversant with knowing physics, medicine, family, and skills. The goal up to this point was to demonstrate that the Scriptures care about knowing and knowing well. Epistemology is a persistent, not tangential, concern, and its prominence in these ancient Jewish texts (including the New Testament) will be necessarily instructive for how we think about physics, family, and our particular focus: theology. More specifically, our theology might need to submit to the way of knowing prescribed in Scripture. If so, then Christian discussions about epistemology in general and theological method in particular must reckon their fittedness or variance to Scripture's epistemological process.

What about the wisdom literature of Israel? When most people think about Scripture and knowledge, they instantly go to the Proverbs, Ecclesiastes, or Job. After all, the stated purpose of these texts is the pursuit of wisdom. We cannot yet articulate an epistemological model of wisdom literature because we are concerned to first engage the historical texts of

Israel. Later, we will address wisdom literature in tandem with the epistles because both presume the mode of wisdom instruction. The specific reasons for this will be pursued in the next chapter.

Having examined the foundational texts of Israel's canon and some of the epistemological tropes in its historical texts, we now turn our attention to the foundational and historical texts of the New Testament, itself a collection of ancient Jewish texts. These texts focus Israel's attention to the promised Messiah, employing the very texts of the Tanakh that we have already examined. In this chapter, we will make a very modest contribution to the study of Markan epistemology: what Jesus wants his disciples to know and how. The disciples are portrayed as dolts. They get it wrong quite often and falter in their understanding up through the founding of the early church. Again, our goal is to show that epistemological process is central to the work of Jesus and that the process proceeds from a Tanakhic understanding of knowledge, possibly even Edenic and Deuteronomic. Again, we will find that the utmost priority in the disciples' knowledge is placed upon listening to Jesus as their accredited authority and then embodying the actions he prescribes. Without both facets, they cannot know the "secret of the kingdom of God" promised to them at the outset of the process (Mark 4:10).

Some brief comments about Lukan and Johannine epistemology are warranted, even if they are only cursory. In both gospels, we will attend to the narrator's own awareness of the narrative as an epistemological process, where the narrator is the accredited authority and the reader must participate in order to see that which he is showing the reader.

MARKAN EPISTEMOLOGY[1]

Why are the Disciples' Hearts Hardened?

By the time the reader arrives at Mark 8, we have seen the disciples characterized as confused, confounded, resistant, and rarely submitted to Jesus' instructions. In utter frustration, which the narrator fosters in the audience as well, Jesus interrogates the disciples:

---

1. A full length discussion, including lexical and exegetical support, can be found in my PhD thesis. See Johnson, "Error and Epistemological Process," 134–69.

Knowing under the Prophet-Messiah: Mark, Luke, and John

> Do you not yet perceive or understand? Are your hearts hardened? Having eyes do you not see, and having ears do you not hear? And do you not remember? (Mark 8:17–18)

When Jesus asks if the disciples' "hearts are hardened" any reader of the Christian canon immediately summons the other instances of a hardened heart: the pharaoh of Exodus (7:13) and also the Israelites (1 Sam 6:6). Although the phrase "hard heart" is not a direct citation from the Septuagint, it begs that comparison.[2] The narrator does not clarify which parallel is being drawn upon, whether the disciples are more like the pharaoh of Exodus or the wandering Israelites. Whichever comparison is intended, neither is meant to be favorable.

What is most puzzling is that only the pharisees (3:5) and the disciples (6:52; 8:17) are described as having a hardened heart in Mark's Gospel, yet the disciples are the very ones who are promised to know the "mystery (μυστήριον) of the kingdom of God" (4:11). How do we explain this? We must consider the epistemological goal for the disciples, and more importantly, the process by which they are meant to embody in order to see what is being shown to them and therefore know the secret of the kingdom of God.

What is the Epistemic Goal for the Disciples?

In brief, we contend that Jesus is leading his disciples to know how all of his own particular actions cohere into a broader view of the cosmos called something like "the kingdom of God." Specifically, they need to discern how the miracles, commands, suffering, and crucifixion all fit into that mysterious "kingdom of God" framework just as the Israelites needed to understand how plagues, manna, and holiness cohered to the theocratic kingdom of YHWH. What we find in Mark is a depiction of disciples who, like the Israelites in the Tanakh, are initially resistant and obdurate to the epistemological process, but Mark leaves the reader with hope that they will know it eventually. Quite simply, the epistemic goal is stated at the outset of the process by employing two previous paradigms found in the Tanakh: Deuteronomy 29 and Isaiah 6:9. After giving the cryptic parable

---

2. In the Septuagint, Exodus uses σκληρύνω (e.g., 4:21, 7:3) and βαρύνω (e.g., 9:7, 34) to describe Pharaoh's heart where Mark uses πωρόω to describe "hardening," a word which does not appear in the Septuagint.

Biblical Knowing

about the seed sown onto different types of soil (Mark 4:1–10), Jesus promises his disciples:

> And he said to them, "To you has been given the secret of the kingdom of God, but for those outside everything is in parables, so that
> "they may indeed see but not perceive,
> and may indeed hear but not understand,
> lest they should turn and be forgiven." (Mark 4:11–12)

First, Jesus speaks in parables so that some will not understand (cf. Mark 4:12; Isa 6:9–10). But second, he speaks plainly to his disciples so that they would know the objective: *the secret of the kingdom of God* (cf. Deut 29:2–4, 29; Mark 4:13–34). This epistemic objective, stated as ambiguously as possible, must be put in the context of the entirety of Mark.[3]

Some scholars have viewed the disciples' epistemological grasping of the "secret of the kingdom of God" as being illustrated to the reader in the successive two-stage healing of the blind man at Bethsaida. Indeed, many have proposed that the two-stage healing at Bethsaida is a paradigm for the disciples' understanding (8:22–26), going from fuzzy vision to clarity over time.[4] The disciples are on the cusp of seeing and knowing the kingdom of God, even if not clearly. Kelly Iverson comments on the significance of the miracle having two distinct phases:

> The two-stage healing of the blind man (8.22–26) symbolizes the possibility for the restoration of the disciples' vision. They are no longer blind as Peter's confession makes clear but neither do they have full sight. . . . The two-stage healing of the blind man suggests that the movement from blindness to sight, from misunderstanding to understanding, is possible, but the disciples must await a second restorative touch that brings clarity of vision.[5]

This movement from blindness to sight, from *getting it wrong* to *getting it*, adjourns with another healing blind man healed: Bartimaeus. Many Mark scholars have noticed the literary symmetry of the blind healings in

---

3. We will not rely on a particular view of the ending of Mark here. However, the ending would have slightly different impacts on how decisively we should view the epistemological goal being accomplished. In other words, are the disciples left floundering in Mark's Gospel, not yet knowing about the resurrection. Or, does the resurrection account act as the resolution to their misunderstanding of the kingdom of God?

4. Matera, "The Incomprehension of the Disciples," 167–71.

5. Iverson, *Gentiles*, 121.

Knowing under the Prophet-Messiah: Mark, Luke, and John

Mark chapters 8 and 10. Specifically, the second healing account—which is commissioned by Jesus' question to Bartimaeus, "What do you want me to do for you" (10:46–52)—mirrors a witless request from disciples James and John: "Teacher, we want You to do for us whatever we ask of You" (10:35–45). At this point in Mark's narrative, the reader begins to suspect that Mark is using blindness to metaphorically implicate the disciples' inability to grasp the mystery of the kingdom of God.

Focusing on the disciples' ability to see the promised mystery, we observe the two stage healing at Bethsaida (8:22–26) followed by the hollow confession of Peter (8:27–30). Then, following the Transfiguration, we observe a blind request for power ensuing Jesus' question to James and John, "What do you want me to do for you (10:36)?" The response of James and John shows that at least two of the chief disciples do not understand how the kingdom functions, the very point of the epistemological process stated in Mark 4:11. Finally, Jesus questions Blind Bartimaeus with the identical question posed to James and John: "What do you want me to do for you (10:51)?"[6] But Bartimaeus asks for sight, not power, which some have taken to be an implicit critique of the disciples' obtuseness to the kingdom of God.

In short, sight is an epistemic faculty being developed in the disciples despite their resistance. But it is their responsibility to acknowledge Jesus as their prophet by enacting his instructions in order to see what he is showing them. Their lack of comprehension is mitigated by either their failure to listen or their failure to participate.

How Do the Disciples Come to Know?

It might not be entirely surprising that Mark's description of the route to knowing follows the priorities of the epistemological process found in the Tanakh. Mark's use of the Tanakh requires savvy to discern that there are two epistemological trajectories at work. Mark's Gospel begins by connecting the ministry of John the Baptist to Isaianic prophecy. As Mark implies John the Baptist to be Isaiah's "voice of one crying in the wilderness," so the reader might expect other connections of the same ilk to be identified by the evangelist.

Moving quickly from John the Baptist to Jesus' healing ministry in Galilee, a crowd amasses around Jesus as he calls his disciples and

6. Thanks to Kelly Iverson for pointing out this parallel to me.

Biblical Knowing

commissions the twelve as apostles (3:13–19). The narrative tempo is brisk, with Mark using the term "immediately" (εὐθύς) more densely than any other NT author.[7]

But the focus of the narrative takes a definitive shift when we arrive at Mark 4 and move onward to the Transfiguration. That shift is *from* Jesus' ministry in Galilee *to* an intentional concentration on the disciples themselves. At this point in chapter 4, we consider the two epistemological paths that Jesus sets out and the process by which he accomplishes those two trajectories. One path is Isaianic: epistemological deafening and blinding. The other is Deuteronomic: that which is hidden becomes revealed.

If we premise our reading of Mark upon an Isaianic path alone, then pessimism concerning the disciples' epistemological progress develops quite naturally. For instance, Mary Ann Tolbert and Werner Kelber take the view of an Isaianic background to both Mark 4:12 and 8:18, reflected in Tolbert's observation: "the disciples never seem to understand Jesus' miracles," and "the disciples cannot see who Jesus really is, hear what he teaches, or understand the way he must go."[8] Evidence of an Isaianic trajectory mounts as the story itself continues to beg the question as to whether or not the disciples are *getting it*. Surprisingly, outsiders exhibit trust in Jesus and they are commended for it (e.g., the Syrophonecian woman, 7:24–30). In contrast, the disciples appear to be lost, or worse, hard-hearted, seeming to confirm Tolbert's diagnosis. Adele Yarbro Collins, in her conclusion to Mark 8, offers that the disciples' incomprehensibility is itself incomprehensible:

> Despite their "being with him" (3:14), their "having the mystery of the kingdom" (4:11), their being given private instruction by Jesus (4:10–20; 7:17–23), their authority over unclean spirits (6:7, 13), their proclamation of the need for repentance (6:12), and their ability to heal the sick (6:13), the disciples do not yet understand who Jesus is or the significance of his mighty deeds.[9]

The problem created by two epistemological paths leaves the reader agnostic regarding the disciples. The disciples' trajectory is meant to end in knowledge of "the secret of the kingdom of God," but seemingly ends in intransigence. And yet, the outsiders for whom Jesus shows little concern appear *to get the gist* of his ministry, if not his identity. This duplicity in the flat reading of Mark is enough to cause Frank Kermode to question the

---

7. Εὐθύς occurs fifteen times in Mark 1–3 out of fifty-eight occurrences total in Mark.
8. Tolbert, *Sowing the Gospel*, 176, 206; Kelber, *The Kingdom in Mark*, 62.
9. Collins, *Mark*, 388.

provenance of the story itself: "All this is very odd. . . . It gives rise to suggestions that Mark did not understand the parable, that its original sense was already lost [to the Markan author]."[10] The narrative appears at cross purposes with itself, the disciples appear to the reader as seeing but not perceiving, hearing but not understanding—for most of Mark's Gospel, they are on the Isaianic path to confoundedness.

Generally, the scholarship has attempted to reconcile these two trajectories or has viewed them as evidence of source problems, sources ultimately foreign to the theology of Mark's Gospel.[11] Some believe that Mark 4 intentionally holds both goals in tension while focusing on a particular people group. For Rikki Watts, Mark's use of Isaiah 6 is aimed at the Jewish leadership, not the "Jewish people *en toto*."[12] Joel Marcus surmises that it is the disciples who are the primary audience of Mark 4.[13] He suggests that "look" and "hear" (4:12) have become a new term when used together, a hendiadys describing frustration where neither looking nor hearing yields understanding to outsiders. But for insiders like the disciples, discerning is needed in which brute *looking* and *hearing* alone cannot play a role. In short, looking and hearing must be guided by Jesus' prophetic voice.

Before continuing to build on Marcus' intuition, we suggest an important distinction. Marcus rightly notes the two epistemological trajectories, one revealed by God and the other obfuscated by Jesus' parables. However, we want to contend that Mark draws upon two sources in the Tanakh to show that these two paths to knowing are not mutually exclusive; one may actually entail the other. Isaiah is the first source to which most interpreters turn due to its direct, although abbreviated, citation in Mark 4:12.[14] But the second source, which has gone largely unexamined, is Deuteronomy 29. Without recognizing both sources paralleled throughout Mark, it is difficult to reconcile why the disciples do not understand what Jesus is showing them.

These two sources, Deuteronomy 29:4 (29:3 MT) and Isaiah 6:9–10 have exclusively similar material to each other in the Tanakh. Nowhere else

---

10. Kermode, *The Genesis of Secrecy*, 11.
11. Beavis, *Mark's Audience*, 87.
12. Watts, *Isaiah's New Exodus*, 210.
13. Marcus, "Mark 4:10–12 and Marcan Epistemology," 559–60.
14. Mark's use of Isa 6:9–10 is a loose quotation. The first two lines are reversed from Isaiah's order and the following lines are removed in their entirety, preserving only the final phrase: "lest they should turn and be forgiven."

Biblical Knowing

in the Tanakh do we find the lexical combination of heart, eyes/see, and ears/listen.[15] Despite this unique similarity, they differ greatly concerning the context in which they are stated. Deuteronomy 29 is part of the covenant renewal of Israel's young people, who are on the cusp of going into Canaan. YHWH has promised a circumcision of Israelite hearts, which will enable them to know his covenant promises: the ability to listen to YHWH and see a life of plenitude (Deut 30:1–6). In contrast, Isaiah 6:9–10 derives from the prophet's call, which focuses upon the frustration of speaking prophetically to a blind and deaf audience.[16] Indeed, Isaiah's prophecy itself might be the instrument of blinding and deafening the Israelites who hear him. These two sources have different epistemological goals which mirror the stated epistemological ends of Mark 4: one blinds and deafens while the other reveals. Mark's utilization of these parallel lines that mirror Deuteronomic and Isaianic routes to knowing rely upon metalepsis, where a citation/allusion is employed, but with the effect that characters in the story become part of the literature of the allusion.[17] For example, one might implicate their need to get attention by saying, "I need to be more of a squeaky wheel." This draws upon the saying "the squeaky wheel gets the oil (or grease)," but in a way in which the person speaking becomes part of the allusion employed. In Mark 4, the citation is clearly from Isaiah, but we must continue to ask if Deuteronomy is being simultaneously drawn upon as metalepsis or metonymy?[18]

We will argue that the disciples are on the Deuteronomic path, giving hope that they will indeed gain insight into the mysteries of the kingdom of God (4:11) by enacting Jesus' prophetic instruction. It metaleptically places the disciples in a similar position as the Israelites at the covenant renewal (Deut 29). Mark's use of Isaiah might mean to defer hope for the Israelites as a whole to immediately see the kingdom of God directly in Jesus' teaching and actions. Even though Israel as a whole is not excluded forever,

---

15. We only need to presume there are connections between the two passages without having to take a position on the primacy of one text's influence over the other. Grisanti, "Was Israel Unable to Respond to God?" 179, n. 10.

16. Beale has suggested that Isa 6:9–10 plays a larger role in the motif of idolatry. But even then, the blindness and deafness of idols are ridiculed because they do not have prophetic ability. Beale, *We Become What We Worship*, 36–63.

17. Hollander, *Figure*, 113–15 ; Hays, *Echoes*, 20–34.

18. "Metonymy" is the substitution of a word for the intended referent. For instance, "10 Downing Street" could metonymically refer to the governance of the Prime Minister of the United Kingdom.

avoiding error is the central concern for the disciples. The epistemological progress of outsiders impress the reader as being a secondhand matter. In order to convincingly demonstrate the necessity for understanding these two sources in Mark, we must look more closely at the use of Isaiah and Deuteronomy in Mark 4–9. Specifically, what goes wrong?

What Goes Wrong?

Notwithstanding the fact that Jesus intently focuses on bringing the disciples to a particular knowledge of the kingdom, the disciples cannot see what Jesus is showing them. Why not? According to the epistemological process in the Tanakh, we should expect that their error is of the first or second order, not listening to the accredited authority or not participating in their instruction to the degree require.

In the totality of the New Testament's historical books, it is difficult to believe that the disciples do not listen to Jesus, but that is exactly how Mark portrays the matter. The crucifixion appears to have an ultimate epistemological purpose for his disciples, part and parcel of their comprehension of the secret of the kingdom of God. But well before the crucifixion, we see the disciples showing signs of error in the epistemological process.

The fact that the disciples "have been given the mystery of the kingdom of God" is placed alongside the fact that others will be blind to this mystery. But the revelation of the secret and all that it explains is contingent on their prior ability to listen to Jesus as the prophet of Israel. Immediately after Jesus' explanation of the parable in Mark 4:13–20, he continues with the lamp under a basket illustration. The substance of the metaphor is that things hidden (κρυπτή) would some day be revealed (φανερόω, 4:22). Closing out this section, Jesus repeats, "If anyone has ears to listen, let him listen" (4:23). This is proceeded by the stern admonition, "Pay attention (βλέπω) to what you hear (ἀκούω)" (4:24). The passage taken as a whole leads Birger Gerhardsson to conclude, "It could not be more powerfully asserted that the material [4:1–24] is concerned with hearing and hearing in the right way."[19]

A negative response to Jesus features prominently in Mark and typifies people on the Isaianic path to obduracy.[20] Jesus' rejection at Nazareth im-

---

19. Gerhardsson, "The Parable of the Sower," 180.

20. We will not argue how the prophetic message either blinds or deafens, only that this call of Isaiah is negatively oriented in its epistemology. In favor of reading Isa 6 qua

Biblical Knowing

plies that some Nazarenes listened to him in amazement, but others rejected Jesus after hearing him (6:1–6). As well, his instruction to the apostles as he sent them out with authority presumes that there may be people who will not listen to them (6:7–12). Despite these negative reactions, Mark generally supports a positive reception of Jesus, specifically when people listened to him compliantly. Jesus calls his disciples to listen (4:23; 7:14; 8:18). And God himself commands the disciples *to listen*, not *see* in the Transfiguration account. Kee remarks of the call to listen at the Transfiguration:

> From it ["listen to him," 9:7] one can only conclude that Mark wants to present Jesus as the eschatological prophet whose coming Moses had announced. If Jesus is a second Moses for Mark, it is not as giver of the New Law but as fulfiller of the promise of the Prophet.[21]

Jesus' concern to be listened to, in and of itself, creates tension with the view that Isaiah 6:9–10 is the exclusive source of Markan epistemology. Isaiah 6:9–10 leaves us with no immediate hope that the epistemological process will lead to knowledge of the kingdom of God (4:11; 9:1). In Mark 4–9, Jesus expectantly calls the Jewish people to listen to him *and listen to his disciples* (e.g., Mark 6:11). If Jesus' teaching in Mark 4 only refers to Isaiah 6, then no recourse exists to explain accounts of outsiders who are not deaf and blind to the kingdom of God, but listen and therefore see. Even worse, we are left with disciples, the men who are meant to see the mystery of the kingdom of God, who do not enact Jesus' instruction and become hardhearted.

Of consequence, the disciples do not listen at very strategic points in the narrative. When Jesus quells the storm on the sea, the disciples pose an ironic question: "Who is this that even the wind and the sea listen to him" (4:41). When Jesus tells the disciples to feed the crowd of five thousand (6:30–44), they respond with questions instead of attempting to feed them.[22] When they later argue about lack of bread—immediately after witnessing a miraculous feeding of four thousand (8:1–10)—Jesus questions them in the

---

habitual sin as the means of blinding: Eichrodt, *Theology of the Old Testament*, vol. II, 432. In favor of YHWH as the agent of blinding: Von Rad, *The Message of the Prophet*, 122–26; For a summary of how Isa 6 is viewed in light of Isaiah's formation, see: Rendtorff, *Canon and Theology*, 171–80.

21. Kee, "The Transfiguration in Mark," 146.

22. Whatever a proper response would have looked like, and we can only speculatively imagine it, their bewilderment is not portrayed as positive here or in the next miraculous feeding episode either.

Knowing under the Prophet-Messiah: Mark, Luke, and John

Deuteronomic formulation: "Having eyes do you not see? Having ears do you not hear? And do you not remember? . . . Do you not yet understand?"[23] This last question indicates that Jesus envisions the disciples on an epistemological journey, which has yet to come to fruition. What then is the remedy to the disciples' blindness, their inability to *get it*? Which epistemological organ takes priority in order for them to know the mystery of the kingdom? Is it the eyes, ears, or heart?

What Resolves the Problem?

First, Mark emphasizes the need for the disciples to listen to Jesus, above all else, as their authoritative prophet. Despite the plain Christological and covenantal tropes that persist in these narratives, Jesus' role as a prophet takes priority in establishing his other roles.[24] In short, Jesus needs the cultural-political capital as prophet to guide his disciples to see him as the Messiah. Although obduracy also persists to the prophetic teaching of Jesus, the disciples are called to listen first, so that they can see. The larger question as to whether or not Jesus should even be viewed as a prophet resolves by surveying how Jesus portrays himself.[25] Jesus saw himself as a dejected prophet (6:4); justifies his authority on the basis of John the Baptist's status as prophet (11:27–33); considers his own teaching as final (13:5, 22); and calls Israel to listen (7:14–23). Whatever else we can say about Jesus' ministry, he identifies himself as a true prophet of Israel and he justifies his call to listen upon his prophetic authority.[26]

---

23. For a full lexical and conceptual argument as to why this should be seen as a primarily Deuteronomic echo and not Isaianic, see Johnson, "Error and Epistemological Process," 149–56.

24. This is exactly what N. T. Wright has convincingly demonstrated in Part II of *Jesus and the Victory of God*: "the best initial model for understanding this praxis is that of a prophet; more specifically, that of a prophet bearing an urgent eschatological and indeed apocalyptic, message for Israel." And, "All the evidence so far displayed suggests that he was perceived as a *prophet*." 150, 196.

25. Goppelt answers definitively in the affirmative. *Typos*, 61–77.

26. "It is true that from the historian's point of view the working concept which guided Jesus in the task of his ministry was that of prophet." Hill, *New Testament Prophecy,* 48–68.; "On balance the Jesus of Mark's Gospel appears as one who in his teaching supersedes and transcends Scripture more than as one who makes the Scripture point to himself as its fulfillment." Re Jesus' lack of Scripture citation, "This may well have contributed to the impression of authority which distinguished his preaching from that of the scribes." Anderson, "The Old Testament in Mark's Gospel," 304.

Biblical Knowing

This continued use of "listen" (ακουω) when Jesus instructs the people as their prophetic voice does not stop in Mark 4. He continues on in this discourse about what the kingdom of God is like and the writer comments that Jesus spoke "as they were able to *hear* it" (4:33). In the very next passage, Jesus calms the storm, and the perplexed disciples inquire about this man's identity, "that even wind and sea *listen to* (ὑπακούω) him" (4:41).

In chapter 6, Mark directly links Jesus' rejection in Nazareth to his self-ascribed role as a prophet. The Nazarenes reject Jesus after they *hear* (ἀκούω) his teaching (6:2). Listening to Jesus is equated with listening to a prophet. And immediate to this instance, when he sends out the apostles, his instructions specifically home in on whether or not the recipients of their ministry "listen" (ἀκούω) to them (6:11). In the excursus about Herod and John the Baptist, the gospel writer plays off the fact that Herod "heard" (ἀκούω) about Jesus (6:14, 16, 29) and feared because it might be John the Baptist reincarnate. Herod's fear of John particularizes in Mark's note that Herod used to "listen" (ἀκούω) to John the Baptist gladly (6:20).

When confronted by the Pharisees about the practices of his own disciples, Jesus calls for a public audience: "Listen to (ἀκούω) me, all of you, and understand" (7:14).[27] As noted before, in Jesus' final chastisement of his disciples for failing to follow the epistemological process, he pleads, "Having ears do you not hear?" (8:18). But the zenith of this hearing motif is in the Transfiguration itself.

Mark 9 pictures for the reader a scene of YHWH's descent in the Septuagint's language of Deuteronomy, not Exodus (cf. LXX Deut 4:36–37 and Mark 9:7). While one generally imagines the Transfiguration experience to be visual, it is markedly targeted at hearing, not seeing. A voice which they could not see commands them: "This is my beloved Son; listen (ἀκούω) to him." In all, Mark uses the verb "listen" (ἀκούω) forty times and over half of those instances are found here in 4:1–9:17.[28]

As well, Mark's quotation from Deuteronomy 18 has deeper implications for Jesus' accreditation as the prophet of Israel. The context of that passage in Deuteronomy is the crisis of Moses' impending death and the

---

27. We should point out that Jesus begins with "Hear me . . . and understand" (7:14), but continues on to say that they cannot "understand" by questioning, "Do you not see . . . ?" (7:18). Once again, the priority is placed upon hearing in order to see.

28. Several instances come across as mere report, but still fit the epistemological process offered here. In the cases of the hemorrhaging woman (5:27), the haranguing crowds (6:55), and the Syrophonecian woman (7:25), their positive response to Jesus is precipitated by their prior "hearing" (ἀκούω) regarding his ministry.

fear of lacking prophets.[29] The promise of a future prophet is being fulfilled in Jesus. Why does YHWH not cite messianic prophecies at the Transfiguration? Presumably, if the disciples were not listening to the voice of Jesus as Israel's prophet, then they would never be able to discern that he is Israel's messiah. Peculiarly, Jesus acts as his own prophet, bringing the disciples to know the mysterious kingdom through himself. So Joel Marcus concludes in his commentary:

> On the one hand, this divine acclamation implies Jesus' continuity with Moses and Elijah, since "listen to him" echoes Moses' own words about the arising of a prophet like himself (Deut 18:15, 18), an oracle that by the first century was being read eschatologically. ... On the other hand, however, the voice designates only one of the three personages, Jesus, as God's Son, and this is a title that hints at an identity greater than that of Moses or Elijah.[30]

Second, trumping competing voices appears to be necessary for proper knowing. Jesus' immediate reaction to Peter's rebuke seems harsh in Mark 8:31–33. Peter vaingloriously states that Jesus is the Christ (8:29). Yet, when Jesus begins to teach the lived reality of that statement, Peter assumes the role of primary interpreter like the serpent in the Garden. In essence, Peter assumes the authoritative voice on the matter of the Messiah and tells Jesus that he has misinterpreted the messianic role. There are two competing voices in this brief scene and it is clear to the reader that Peter's authority cannot be given credence. For readers of the canon who understand the precarious nature of authoritative voices that compete with God's authoritative direction (Gen 3), Jesus's rebuke "Get behind me Satan" is actually quite polite. But the rebuke evinces Jesus' sensitivity to misinterpretation gaining status as authoritative. Peter is not yet accredited as an authority and not yet ready to be accredited.[31]

As was the case in the Pentateuch, the epistemological goal is not always clearly defined, nor is the content of knowledge clearly articulated. But for Mark's Gospel, avoiding erroneous knowing is defined by whether or not one acknowledges Jesus as prophet and then performs according to

---

29. Olson, *Deuteronomy and the Death of Moses*, 1–5.

30. Marcus, *Mark 8–16*, 640; Calvin takes this view as well: *Matthew, Mark, and Luke*, vol. 2, 191.

31. Peter will be definitively accredited later to the readers of Acts and the diaspora in Acts 2.

Biblical Knowing

his direction. Again, we have described these two layers in epistemological process as errors of the first and second order, respectively.

Summary

Mark's Gospel has been aptly described as an "interwoven tapestry," and there is much more that we could say concerning the intricacies of epistemological themes woven throughout Mark.[32] But we have chosen these few uses of Deuteronomy and Isaiah to show that Mark's narrator is concerned to demonstrate proper knowing under the authoritative direction of Israel's prophet-Messiah.

THE RHETORICAL PURPOSES OF LUKE AND JOHN

Having looked at the narratives internal to a gospel, we now turn our attention to the rhetorical intentions of the narrator. Normally, this would be a very precarious maneuver, as pretending to understand the mind of the author can easily lapse into a study of unsupportable presumptions. However, we will restrict ourselves to the plainly stated rhetorical intentions of the narrators of Luke and John. By using the term "rhetorical," we do not mean to connote the pejorative and flat sense in which it is often bandied about today (e.g., "Now you're just speaking in *rhetoric*!"). We simply mean to convey that authors use texts to persuade readers, to see something they could not see otherwise, to effect a change in the reader, and so on. Since both Luke and John have a brief and open discussion of their rhetorical purposes (Luke 1:1–4; John 20:30–31), we feel that we are on safe grounds to explore them epistemologically.

The Epistemological Role of the Narrator

It is uncontroversial to claim that the Tanakh and New Testament intentionally recount history through story. Together, they tell the story of Israel. So while the genres of poetry, wisdom, and epistle are clearly not telling story, these non-narratival parts of Scripture are contingent upon the totalizing story of Israel in order to make any sense. For instance, the reason as to why Israel would sing a song of praise is framed in narratival terms:

---

32. Dewey, "Mark as Interwoven Tapestry."

Knowing under the Prophet-Messiah: Mark, Luke, and John

"I will sing to YHWH, *for he has triumphed gloriously. The horse and his rider He has thrown into the sea*" (Exod 15:1). Moses sings, a non-narratival genre, but his song is grounded exclusively in the victory at the Red Sea. The embodied actions prescribed in the Bible—singing, sacrificing, writing, feasting, fasting, meditating, camping, releasing debts, and more—all presume the story of Israel. Even one of the greatest commandments is predicated upon the story. Although it has been reductively moralized in the West, the justification of the Golden Rule is contextualized to Israel's story: "for you all were strangers in the land of Egypt" (cf. Lev 19:18, 34).[33]

In the New Testament, the gospel accounts of Luke and John are self-reflective about their special role in telling the story of Jesus (John 21:30–31; Luke 1:1–4). The fact that these writers chose story and not sutra, for example, is significant. This was not necessarily the case with pseudepigrapha like the Gospel of Thomas or even later texts such as the Nestorian gospels that were translated for the T'ang dynasty emperor in seventh-century China.[34] Those authors preferred aphorism and sutra-like sayings over narrative structure.[35] This is to say that story was not a necessary form for relating the content of the gospel, but it is the chosen form preserved in our canon. The epistles, like the psalms and wisdom literature that preceded them, presume the narrative of Israel in order to be basically coherent.

That Scripture should be conceived of primarily as narrative gives it a particular role to play in shaping us as knowers. Scripture, when seen as story, emulates the epistemological process described within because in narratives, the narrator leads the reader by the narrative's logic.

Narratives have a logic internal to them that restricts the range of exposition. Settings, characters, conflicts, plot tensions, climaxes, resolutions, and continuing actions all work together logically. This means that if we can accurately identify a conflict, then the resolution must necessarily follow, even if it does so in an unanticipated manner.[36] The telling of a story is a process and in order to know what the storyteller is trying to show you, then you must participate in the process. Hearing, seeing, or reading

---

33. This storied grounding makes the ethic remarkably different from Buddha's semblance of the Golden Rule or Kant's categorical imperative.

34. Moffet, *A History of Christianity in Asia*.

35. See Legge, *The Nestorian Monument*; Tang, *Nestorian Christianity in China*; Takakusu, "The Name of 'Messiah' Found in a Buddhist Book"; Saeki, *The Nestorian Monument in China*; Foster, *Church of the T'ang Dynasty*.

36. For a superb and gruesome example of an unexpected resolution, cf. 1 Kgs 21:17–19; 22:35–38.

Biblical Knowing

a story all require imaginative participation which means that we embody a process to see where it goes. But it's not an open-ended or indeterminate process.

Stories are constrained by the narrative's logic. When Jesus picks up the first loaf of bread in Mark 6:30–44, we might not have guessed exactly what he was going to do, but Jesus could not have done just anything. For instance, he could not have pulled out a laser pointer and used it to play with the local cats.

The narrators of the Gospels ensure that Jesus of Nazareth, the roundest character in the New Testament, surprises us often.[37] While we cannot always see through the plot twists, nothing in the plots of Scripture violates the narrative logic. Unlike syllogisms, narratives can retain an internal logical structure without telegraphing the exact conclusions to the reader.

Recalling that the biblical epistemology places an absolute priority on identifying and apprenticing under an authority accredited to Israel, narratives then model the epistemology that Scripture describes. The narrator acts as the authoritative voice guiding the reader to see what the narrator is showing them. The narrator could choose to focus the logic of the narrative on only one or two aspects of the events where dozens might be available. Indeed, John's Gospel is overt about the narrator's discretion (John 20:30–31). That narratorial discretion makes the epistemology of narrative especially sensitive to the role of authority in knowing.

For instance, in the attempted sacrifice of Isaac (Gen 22), the narrator is clearly not interested in bringing the reader to answer questions such as: What kind of a god would ask a man to kill his only son? While this is the pressing question foremost in many readers' minds, the narrator chooses instead to direct our attention to the fact that YHWH is testing Abraham and Abraham then interprets the whole scene as an act of YHWH's provision.[38] Even the editorial comment at the end of the attempted sacrifice highlights YHWH's provision, not His request to kill a boy (Gen 22:14b).

Narratives, then, have a logic and authoritative voice that resist attempts to theologically bend them beyond what the narrator is trying to accomplish by means of the story. The epistemological process described in the content of Scripture and the fact that its mode of shaping us is in the

---

37. E.g., Jesus' response to the Syrophonecian woman (Mark 7:24–30), the Samaritan leper who returned (Luke 17:11–19), and the Samaritan woman at the well (John 4).

38. Gen 22:14. Depending on how one interprets the term *yireh* (יראה), as either seeing or providing, the narrator is either highlighting vision or provision.

form of narrative means that there are better and worse uses of Scripture in theological discourse—ways which reflect the type of epistemological shaping that Scripture is trying to accomplish and ways in which we can bend the Scripture beyond its ability to shape knowers. The narrators of Luke and John consciously adopt their authoritative role and weave it into the rhetoric of their gospels.

Lukan Epistemology

The rhetoric of epistemology could not be stated more clearly than Luke's prologue.[39] The purpose of the gospel is so that Theophilus "may have confidence (ἀσφάλεια) concerning the things that you have been taught" (Luke 1:4). In his study of knowing in Luke-Acts, Thomas Stegman focuses on a question of coherence from the author's perspective: How does the writer of Luke then go on to "instill a sense of psychological assurance in his readers"?[40] Stegman then explores Luke's depictions of the gospel—one gospel among "many" (cf. Luke 1:1)—at the micro and macro layers of the combined story of Luke-Acts. He finds that Luke's Gospel succeeds in that "Luke offers 'the big picture' of God's working among both Jews and Gentiles by telling the story 'in order.'"[41]

Building upon Stegman's work, I would like to suggest three matters that make a difference in reading Luke as a text that wants the reader to know with confidence: 1) Luke's understanding of authority in the epistemological process, 2) the interpretation of *asphaleia* as "certainty," and 3) Luke's depiction of the disciples at the conclusion (Luke 24) as a portrait of confident knowers.

First, Luke's Gospel posits that in order to know well, the narrator must be the authority. Luke presumes his accreditation with Theophilus and the rhetoric of the prologue could not address authority more plainly. Luke 1:3 could be paraphrased: There are many accounts, but mine is authoritative *for you* [Theophilus]. In other words, there are competing voices trying to help the reader cohere a pattern among the historical particularities of the Jesus narrative. Luke's narrator advocates his own voice as particularly authoritative to Theophilus for reasons unknown to the reader and only with the slightest tug of authority due to its sources being eyewitnesses and

---

39. Stegman, "Epistemology in Luke-Acts."
40. Ibid., 91.
41. Ibid., 90.

Biblical Knowing

its *orderliness* (Luke 1:2–3). As well, the narrator's authority—and perhaps his authentication—derives from his ability to discern a pattern from the chaotic history of Jesus' life. The narrator's authority is telling because we have already seen that the disciples themselves had trouble discerning basic patterns, even when they were present with Jesus. Luke's author conveys a sense of discernment where he claims to have "followed all things closely for some time past" (Luke 1:3). Luke claims to be attentive to historical fidelity in order to compile an "orderly account." This statement of Luke implicitly claims to properly know that which is being described well enough to instill confidence of that skilled discernment in the reader. In short, Luke is our authoritative guide.

Second, the common choice to translate *asphaleia* as "certainty" is unfortunate.[42] After Descartes' seventeenth-century *Meditations*, the term "certainty" took on the connotative force of a belief that is indubitable or without any doubt, which is not the connotation of the term employed by Luke. The two most prominent uses of the term in the Septuagint and New Testament are: 1) to indicate physical safety in the context of covenant promises (e.g., Lev 26:5; Deut 12:10; Phil 3:1, etc.) and 2) to reassure someone because of wavering confidence in testimony (e.g., Luke 1:4, Acts 2:36; Heb 6:19, etc.). Of all the other connotations outside of these two uses, what *asphaleia* cannot mean for Luke's contemporary readers is "knowing without a doubt" in the juridical sense in which we understand it today. The firmness of Luke's assurance is best captured in the letter to the Hebrews' use of *asphaleia*: "We have as this confident (ἀσφαλῆ) and confirmed (βεβαίαν) anchor of the soul, a hope that enters into the inner place behind the curtain" (Heb 6:19). The metaphor is wonderfully pictured. Our confidence is not based in our rational ability to find no fault in the argument. Rather our *asphaleia* is anchored, a nautical scene that requires us to envision something in which our anchor is set. Certainty, for us, connotes an unswayable belief because of what we have seen or from what we have reasoned. Confidence breaks out of individually reasoned belief into the

---

42. The following translate ἀσφάλεια (Luke 1:4) as "certainty": *New International Version, American Standard Version, English Standard Version, King James Version*, and *New King James Version*.. The *Common English Bible* translates ἀσφάλεια as "confidence." The *New American Standard Version* chooses to render ἀσφάλεια as "the exact truth." The *New Revised Standard Version* translates ἀσφάλεια as "the truth." Interestingly, *The Message Bible* choose the Enlightenment phrase "that you may know beyond a shadow of a doubt."

realm of trust, which makes us reflect on the source of our trust. It is a subtle, but detectable, difference in the connotative force of the terms.

While the choice to use "certainty" is understandable, it might conjure up the wrong connotations in our minds, where we imagine that Luke is attempting to argue and argue well for his version of the Jesus narrative. But what we find is that Luke wants to instill confidence in the eyewitnesses and the historical account as he interprets them. When hearing the word "confidence" in this use, the question then becomes, "Confidence in whom?" The answer is that the narrator wants us to put our confidence in his authoritative voice so that we can see the Jesus narrative coherently, able to discern a pattern that extends from the Abrahamic covenant (Luke 1:55, 73), through Israel (Luke 1:54), Israel's past prophecies (cf. Mal 3:1; 4:6 and Luke 1:16–17) to the present realities in the days of Theophilus. Again, Stegman's summary of how we should understand Luke's use of *asphaleia* is most helpful: "Undoubtedly, Luke seeks to instill a sense of psychological assurance in his readers."[43]

Finally, the strategic use of *asphaleia* in the combined work of Luke-Acts has its own rhetorical force.[44] However, Both Luke and Acts can be read independently as coherent narratives. If so, Luke's Gospel paints a peculiar portrait of confidence from its depiction of the disciples. While none of the four Gospels characterize the disciples favorably, Luke does give us some details about their very last moments with Jesus. What we see in the end is a mixture of elation and confoundedness, but confidence in that which they know. The episodes at Emmaus and Jesus' ascension are worth our examination.

On the road to Emmaus, this Balaam-like blindness to Jesus' identity is shared by the two disciples. Seeing him, they did not perceive: "But their eyes were kept from recognizing him" (Luke 24:16).[45] Hearing him, they did not understand: "And beginning with Moses and all the Prophets, he interpreted to them in all the Scriptures the things concerning himself" (Luke 24:27). However, like the man in the Garden who discovered his wife, the

---

43. Stegman, "Epistemology in Luke-Acts," 91.

44. Stegman helpfully notices that what is promised in Luke 1:4 is finally delivered in the speeches of Acts where Peter says to the gathered people of Pentecost, "Let all of Israel know with confidence (ἀσφάλεια) that God has made him both Lord and Christ, this Jesus whom you crucified" (Acts 2:36). This is only the second time we encounter this word in Luke-Acts and here it is used with reference to their knowledge. Ibid., 90–91.

45. I am thankful to Esther Meek for pointing out this epistemologically rich episode to me.

disciples have an embodied *eureka* of Jesus' identity. Luke focuses in on the embodied act that they saw, which enabled them to see and perceive. For the man in the Garden, it was the flesh and bone similarities that enabled him to know that woman was his fit mate (Gen 2:23). For the disciples, the breaking of bread enabled them to know that it was Jesus, a skilled seeing and discerning of all the particularities of the past events. They themselves articulated this tacit sense that they were aware of coming to know, even when they could not name the particularities that would enable them to know: "Did not our hearts burn within us while he talked to us on the road, while he opened to us the Scriptures?" (Luke 24:32).

For the reader and hearer of Scripture, more direct evidence of the Garden narrative is present. In what can only be considered a reversal of the improper knowing of good and evil, Luke quotes the Septuagint (Gen 3:7) "and their eyes were opened and they knew" when the disciples finally saw who Jesus was.[46] In both scenarios, knowledge comes in the context of food, through embodiment, and by means of an interpretive authority. We could ask these disciples: Are you *certain* that this is Jesus of Nazareth? We would expect a well reasoned answer. But we certainly would *not* expect an indubitable answer from reason itself. We would expect an appeal to their personal history and the ability to discern Jesus' teaching, oral and embodied. Answering purely by means of reason—

> Premise 1: Jesus foretold his resurrection
>
> Premise 2: This living man breaks bread like Jesus
>
> Therefore: This living man is the resurrected Jesus.[47]

—may cause us to suspect unreasonable thinking on those disciples' part. In this instance, Jesus as the embodiment of the Pentateuch's authoritative teaching (Luke 24:27) leads these two disciples to the waters of discovery, but the actual *eureka* moment was all theirs.[48]

---

46. Cf. Gen 3:7 . . . διηνοίχθησαν οἱ ὀφθαλμοὶ τῶν δύο, καὶ ἔγνωσαν . . . and Luke 24:31 . . . διηνοίχθησαν οἱ ὀφθαλμοὶ καὶ ἐπέγνωσαν. . . .

47. I am aware that this is not a functional syllogism. The point is that even if the two disciples could produce dozens of functional syllogisms as evidence that they know Jesus' resurrected identity, they would not be reasonable grounds for claiming that they know that "this man is Jesus."

48. We are not discussing the ambiguity of how "their eyes were opened," either by God Himself or as an independent act of the disciples as epistemic agents. We are merely following the report of Luke's Gospel.

Knowing under the Prophet-Messiah: Mark, Luke, and John

Leaving Emmaus, Jesus appears to the twelve with a startle. Although it seems queer to the reader, the disciples think they are seeing an apparitional form of Jesus. Why are they surprised and why are they not able to discern that Jesus' resurrection fits the pattern taught to them so clearly? Luke does not address that question directly. Nevertheless, the disciples' pattern of befuddlement repeats often enough for the attentive readers not to be surprised by it. In order to demonstrate that he is no ghost, Jesus eats some "broiled fish" (Luke 24:42). This action in and of itself requires a whole apparitional anthropology in order to make sense, but it suffices us to say that the resurrected body acts like the normal body—or at least enough for us to comprehend a resurrected person eating fish. Contrary to the later development of Docetism, Jesus is not an appearance, but a regularly embodied person.[49] Unlike the episode on the way to Emmaus, the reason for their fright is that they immediately recognize Jesus, whom they know to be dead. They can only reasonably conclude that Jesus is a ghost. Again, food resolves the matter of faulty theology. Eating, which is pictured to us in the unusual detail of "broiled fish" (ἰχθύος ὀπτοῦ), is the embodied act which rectifies their misunderstanding of who Jesus is—or, at least, that Jesus is not a ghost.

Again, what shocks the reader is that Jesus highlights their inability to place his teaching and life into a coherent pattern. They cannot make sense of the particularities, especially the largest particularity: Jesus' death and resurrection. "These are my words that I spoke to you while I was still with you, that everything written about me in the Law of Moses and the Prophets and the Psalms must be fulfilled" (Luke 24:45). The epistemological pattern should be regulative to the reader of the canon by this point, and so it comes as no surprise that Jesus again acted as their authenticated authority so that they would know how creation and covenant now come to fullness in himself (Luke 24:45).

At the close of Luke's Gospel, we see Jesus surrounded by disciples who are confident and confounded. The end of Luke couples together with the opening of Acts where we still see confusion on their part and other authoritative voices feeding into their understanding of the Messiah and the restoration of the kingdom (Acts 1:6–7). In what or who is their confidence? Of what are they certain? If anything, their confidence in what they know is meager, and they are still the same confused lot that we encounter

---

49. We are setting aside notions of glorified body here and merely following the report of Luke's Gospel.

Biblical Knowing

in all the Gospels. But they do know one thing confidently which they exclaim, like the man's *eureka* in the Garden, and upon which the rest of their discernment hinges: "The Lord has risen indeed!" (Luke 24:34).

The rhetoric of Luke as a gospel works when the reader heeds the narrator's authority and participates in the story by considering what confident knowing looks like in the story of the disciples. It is not a picture of indubitable factitive knowledge, but of tenuous-yet-confident points of discernment, which hint at promises of future discernment.

John 20

For many who have studied John's Gospel, it is the most conspicuously epistemological of the Gospels—using the key lexical terms "know" (γινώσκω) and "believe" (πιστεύω) drastically more than the others.[50] Although there is much that could be fleshed out from John,[51] we will restrain our comments to what has already been noticed by scholars reading the text with the author's frame of mind in view. Similar to Luke, John's narrator is aware of the importance of authoritative interpretation. This is especially acute in the coupling of Thomas' glaring incredulity and the narrator's exhortation to the reader in John 20.

Thomas' unbelief is put on display for the reader, which is then followed by an editorial comment maintaining the rhetoric of Jesus' words to Thomas:

> Jesus said to him, "Have you *trusted* because you have seen me? Blessed are those who have not seen and yet have *trusted*." Now Jesus did many other signs in the presence of the disciples, which are not written in this book; but these are written so that you may *trust* that Jesus is the Christ, the Son of God, and that by *trusting* you may have life in his name. (John 20:29–31)

The term most commonly interpreted as "believe" (*pisteuō*; Greek: πιστεύω) appears four times in the above section. However, the English

---

50. As minimal evidence for this claim, John's Gospel uses different forms of "to know" (γινώσκω) approximately fifty times. The same root term is used approximately sixty-five times in Matthew, Mark, and Luke combined. That same goes for "believe" (πιστεύω) used in John approximately eighty-five times and approximately thirty times in Matthew, Mark, and Luke combined.

51. For work on epistemology in John's Gospel, see Bennema, "Christ, the Spirit and the Knowledge of God."

word "belief" creates unnecessary epistemological duress for the modern reader. I have chosen, then, to translate the Greek term *pisteuō* as "trust" here for three reasons. First, "trust" is an equally viable interpretation of the Greek *pisteuō*. Second, the English "believe" carries with it the connotation of opinion or mere belief. Third, "trust" means that we must maintain a focus on whom we are trusting.

I believe that the primary question broached by this episode with Thomas is: Who do you trust and who should you trust? The simple answer is presumably: Thomas should trust Jesus. However, that does not follow the logic of the story. Recalling Jesus' first appearance to the disciples, the narrator tells us that Jesus appears and reveals "his hands and his side" to the gathered disciples, sans Thomas (John 20:20). The implication is that their trusting belief is based, at least in part, on seeing and possibly touching Jesus' wounds. The next story is conjoined with the phrase "Now Thomas ... was not with them when Jesus came. So the other disciples told him ..." (John 20:24). In the end, Thomas demands the same evidence the other disciples witnessed, otherwise he would "never trust" (οὐ μὴ πιστεύσω; John 20:25). The operative question being begged here is: Trust who?

It appears that the authentication of *the disciples' authority* is in question, and for the reader of the gospel this is no small defamation. Thomas' incredulity toward the disciples' authority on Jesus' resurrection defames the very authority of the text that we are reading. Remarkably, Jesus then appears and offers himself as accreditation of the disciples' prior authority. Jesus' mild chastisement of Thomas homes in on the fact that he did not trust *the disciples'* testimony: "Do not be un-trusting (ἄπιστος), but trusting (πιστος)" (John 20:27). His words could be restated, "Do not mistrust your fellow disciples, but trust."

This then makes sense of the editorial comment that demands that the ancient hearer and modern reader has substantive reasons to trust the authority of the author. Like Thomas, the reader has no access to see or touch Jesus' wounds. Then, in one fell swoop, John's author establishes his own authority to the reader as constitutive of the disciples' authority itself while showing how and why the narrative functions to make us trust them both.

> Now Jesus did many other signs in the presence of the disciples, which are not written in this book; but these are written so that you may *trust* (πιστεύητε) that Jesus is the Christ, the Son of God,

and that by *trusting* (πιστεύοντες) you may have life in his name. (John 20:30–31)

Again, John's rhetoric queries the ancient hearer and modern reader: Whom should I trust? It is a rhetorically brilliant maneuver. The implicit message seems to be that we readers are like Thomas and the veracity of the text we are reading should be as plain to us as the veracity of the disciples' testimony should have been to Thomas. Who do we trust? The testimony that we deem to be authoritative as it has been authenticated to us gains our trust, and hence, becomes our authority. The author even acknowledges the epistemological aspects of the narrative structure itself being used to evoke our trust. Many things could have been written by this narrator, but because the author is the authority—the skilled discerner of this reality—he chose these stories in this order that we would know.

CONCLUSIONS

In this chapter, we have looked at the content of the disciples' epistemological process as portrayed in Mark. We found that Mark picks up the Deuteronomic pattern of a heart to know, eyes to see, and ears to hear. Deuteronomy 29 is employed in order to evince the process by which the disciples came to know the "secret of the kingdom of God"—that the Messiah must suffer and die. To know this, the disciples must first listen to Jesus as the prophet of Israel, who can guide them to discern a kingdom-of-God-pattern in all the chaotic particularities of the Jesus' life. Jesus' death appears to be the most stultifying particularity of the pattern for the disciples. They did not seem to be capable of incorporating the public execution of Jesus into their framework of the kingdom of God. Jesus expects them to listen to him and do what he says (e.g., "You give them something to eat"; Mark 6:37). But their reticence to act ends in hardened hearts (Mark 6:51–52; 8:17–18). Hence, the descent of YHWH's voice from the heavens at the Transfiguration focuses on their cardinal failure: the disciples do not accredit Jesus as the promised prophet of Israel (Mark 9:7).

In looking at what the authors of Luke and John are attempting to do through the text—the narratorial rhetoric, if you will—it became clear that they both have a sense of their own authority by which they must guide the ancient hearer and modern reader to know a specific pattern in Jesus' life. This pattern, which the narrator is already expert at discerning, collates the chaotic particularities of all the fragments and whole stories about Jesus that wandered throughout ancient Judea and Galilee. Both narrators viewed themselves as authorities who were accredited to lead us to know Jesus himself, not merely things about Jesus. If we submit ourselves to their authority and participate in the narratives that they present, then we can see what they are showing us. Otherwise, what we have is merely an amalgam of narratives.

These writers and collators not only follow the epistemological process that we have seen described in the Pentateuch and beyond; they undisguisedly call the reader to indwell the process as well, in order to know and know well.

6

Scientific Epistemology, Wisdom, and the Epistles

IN THE NEXT TWO chapters, we will take a dramatic turn toward recent scholarship in epistemology. We have examined both the historical books of the Tanakh and the Gospel accounts in which an epistemological process is present, relevant, and persistent. Early on, we made the claim that this view should not be reduced to a religious epistemology, but that it covers knowing writ large. In this chapter, we want to argue that there is an extant view of scientific epistemology that provides us with an overlapping model of what we see in the Christian Scriptures. How scientists know, as an enterprise of discovery, mimics normal human knowing, and normal human knowing is exactly what we find in the biblical texts. If these basic aspects of knowing are commensurable between science and Scripture, then that has implications for how we view the epistemologically sensitive texts of the Tanakh and New Testament—that they might be describing much more than *religious* knowing.

We begin with a discussion of Michael Polanyi's scientific epistemology and its relevance to what we have found already in the prior chapters. Then, we will consider how his view of maxims and maximic language in the epistemological process are consistent with some of what we find in the wisdom literature and the New Testament epistles. Finally, we will need to clarify the difference between scientific and biblical knowing.

Scientific Epistemology, Wisdom, and the Epistles

MICHAEL POLANYI'S SCIENTIFIC EPISTEMOLOGY

Why engage Polanyi? Many have found that contemporary accounts of epistemology significantly lack the necessary concepts to describe what is observed in Scripture. Polanyi provides a rigorously-argued view of knowing that grew from his participation within the scientific community and accredited aspects of knowledge that were often disregarded as un-analyzable by epistemologists.[1] Polanyi is descriptive in his approach, attempting to relate what scientists actually do in order to know.[2]

Directly pertinent to what we have seen operative in the Scriptures, Polanyi develops the sociological fabric of science as a community of skilled knowers, which is the requisite structure to all scientific knowledge:

> Science will appear then as a vast system of beliefs, deeply rooted in our history and cultivated today by a specially organized part of our society. We shall see that science is not established by the acceptance of a formula, but is part of our mental life, shared out for cultivation among many thousands of specialized scientists throughout the world, and shared receptively, at second hand, by many millions.[3]

Testimony between scientists, which is built upon skilled observation and trust, then creates a community of knowers who can confidently move toward what we call scientific knowledge.[4]

---

1. As an example, Polanyi takes the *focused human effort* and *appropriation of skill* to be fundamental to all acts of knowing, propositional or otherwise. Skilled knowing makes epistemology an act which can be coached from experts to novices. Esther Meek, an interpreter of Polanyi, echoes his disquiet that rationality is not best explained reduced to deductive inferences: "An inferential structure is not impoverished by the addition of [Polanyi's] unspecifiable features of our knowing. Rather, the inferential structure, if thought to express the act exhaustively, is the thing that impoverishes our knowing." She goes on to pose the dilemma: "If a key kind of knowing doesn't fit our model, it's not right to discredit the knowing; it's right to discredit the model." Meek, *Longing to Know*, 63. Similarly suggestive moves have also been made within analytic philosophy itself. See Stump, "The Problem of Evil," 253; Goldman, *Pathways to Knowledge*, 139; Kvanvig, *The Intellectual Virtues*, 181–82; Zagzebski, *Virtues of the Mind*, 45, 66.

2. Hence, there is a notable absence of abstract entities in Polanyi's thought, as they cannot be argued for descriptively.

3. Polanyi, *Personal Knowledge*.

4. Inspired by Polanyi, Thomas Kuhn would go on to describe what happens when communities of scientist strike upon an epistemological conflict: their skilled observations are not explained by the scientific theories *du jour*. However, this historical retelling

Biblical Knowing

In the Scriptures, we find an account of communal discovery (i.e., epistemology) guided by skilled seers, sometimes labeled prophets, who attempt to bring Israel toward skilled knowledge, sometimes labeled discernment or wisdom.[5] Merely considering some of the Scripture's suppositions for proper knowing requires a robust epistemological model; one that can account for the role of the human body, the community, and analogical reasoning, which Scripture presumes at many places.[6]

Specifically, we will focus our attention on Polanyi's discussion of scientific epistemology in terms of scientists' 1) skill/connoisseurship, 2) reliance upon testimony, 3) interaction with scientific controversy, and 4) use of maximic language in epistemology. Further, we will address why socio-epistemological constructs, such as Thomas Kuhn's paradigm shift,[7] do not sufficiently grasp a biblical way of describing the community's knowledge and epistemological controversy when deciding between two competing interpretations.

In appealing to examples from the Pentateuch, wisdom literature, and New Testament epistles, we hope to demonstrate that the biblical process of knowing requires accreditation similar to that which Polanyi focuses his work in *Personal Knowledge* (1958). As a physician, then chemist, turned philosopher, Polanyi could not reconcile the mechanistic views of Scientific Positivism with the actual logic of discovery that he observed as a member of the scientific guild. In preparing for the Gifford Lectures (1951–52), he struggled to make sense of the often ineffable sense in which propositional claims actually garnered meaning for the scientist. Polanyi wrestled with describing the logic of discovery in science, so much so that he had to defer his Gifford Lectures for several years, which ultimately resulted in his tome: *Personal Knowledge.*[8]

---

of *how* scientific theory has been revolutionized does not actually go far enough to explain the requisite epistemological structures required for that revolution to take place. Polanyi actually describes the structures and the revolutionary process several years before Kuhn worked it out in *The Structure of Scientific Revolution.* Cf. Polanyi, *Personal Knowledge*, 150–60.

5. Of the difference between "wisdom" and "knowledge," Fox says, "A variety of words are used for wisdom and knowledge—two concepts that are virtually identical in Proverbs." "The Epistemology of the Book of Proverbs," 669, n. 1.

6. E.g., The role of trust in testimony, accreditation of authoritative guides, the role of language in guidance, and the necessity for a definitive point of illumination beyond brute observation.

7. See Kuhn, *The Structures of Scientific Revolution.*

8. See further: Moleski and Scott, *Michael Polanyi.*

Scientific Epistemology, Wisdom, and the Epistles

Regarding Polanyi's structure of scientific epistemology, we will first examine the skilled aspect of scientific knowing that requires apprenticeship under a skilled knower. Second, we will consider the role of testimony in the scientific community and constituent factors for relying upon it. Third, we will explore the competition between proffered explanations and the revolutionary force of the interpretation to overthrow less precise explanations. We will address fundamental differences between scientific knowing and the epistemology of Scripture. Finally, in order to demonstrate the use of language as a tool in knowing, what Polanyi terms a maxim, we will consider the role of aphorism in the wisdom literature and New Testament epistles.[9] This *maximic* language guides the knower in a particular way, but the plain meaning is obscured outside of the embodied effort to know.[10]

Polanyi's scientific epistemology is ideal for our task because his is a unifying epistemology that can accommodate:

1. the sense of knowing through one's body,

2. epistemological confidence maintained through trusted testimony in a community,

3. the employment of inference that is not limited to a deductive view of rationality, and

4. language without precise propositional content that is necessary to express what one knows.[11]

---

9. E.g., "The wise of heart will receive commandments, but a babbling fool will come to ruin" Prov 10:8.

10. Maxim is used here by Polanyi in the least Kantian sense of the word possible. A maxim is a statement that helps to guide, but only in the action being embodied and pursued. For instance, a biology professor might encourage a student to "extend their gaze" down the microscope to see some cellular phenomenon. The *maximic* language, for Polanyi, is "extend your gaze." It's not a truism, but a guide that aides the one who is intentionally trying to see biological features at the cellular granularity.

11. Rather, this more robust version of inference is what Esther Meek calls *transrational*. "An inferential structure is not impoverished by the addition of unspecifiable features of our knowing. Rather, the inferential structure, if thought to express the act exhaustively, is the thing that impoverishes our knowing. Integration is not irrationality; it is transformed rationality." *Longing to Know*, 76–77.

Biblical Knowing

Knowing as a Skill

> Science is operated by the skill of the scientist and it is through the exercise of his skill that he shapes his scientific knowledge.[12]

> I shall take as my clue for this investigation the well-known fact *that the aim of a skilful performance is achieved by the observance of a set of rules which are not known as such to the person following them.*[13]

Polanyi's intent to re-orient us from *knowledge as an object* to *knowing through a skillful performance* highlights a cardinal feature of his epistemology with manifest implications. First, Polanyi believes that we know by a mental performance, a sentiment with which most would agree. After all, most believe that reasoning through a set of premises is something like a process that occurs mentally.[14] But second, he removes our reliance upon specifiable and discrete premises as grounds for this performance. In other words, knowing is an act by which the exact logical arguments that brought us to know cannot necessarily be specified.

Polanyi suggests that honing a skill, what he terms connoisseurship, requires apprenticeship—a time in which the scientist submits to the authority of the senior scientist who guides her to sift through an indiscernible grouping of particularities, to notice what is significant, to cohere a pattern within a seemingly chaotic field of instances, and so on. The honing of expertise develops *discernment in observation*—being able to see what one could not previously see because of such training. For instance, Spanish and Portuguese might sound as if they were near dialects of the same language to the unknowing ear. Nevertheless, if we actually learn either Spanish or Portuguese as a language, it would be immediately obvious that they are not dialects, but both are distinct languages. We cannot answer the question "What makes Spanish a different language from Portuguese?" while we are initially learning Portuguese. The ability to discern only comes through apprenticeship. Then discernment can be individually performed, but only after it is known. To this end, Polanyi notes that while we are coming to know, we are trusting the instruction of our teacher, the rules of

---

12. Italics original, Polanyi, *Personal Knowledge*, 49.
13. Italics original, ibid.
14. For the sake of this argument, we must shelve reductive physicalist accounts.

which we cannot state but must follow in order to know the very thing being shown to us.

In the realm of biology, we could observe in a microscope that a blood cell shrinks when we place it in salt water. However, brute observation does not bring us to know what we have seen. In Norwood Hanson's terms, we have seen, but not "seen that."[15] What could bridge the logical gap between seeing a cell shrink and *see that* a cell shrunk due to salinity in water? We would need to understand the biological construct of tonicity: the osmotic pressure of a cell that causes fluid to come and go through a membrane due to the salinity of the water. Tonicity is a construct in that it gathers particular observations and concepts, which are organized into a dynamic understanding of complex relationships.

In order to understand tonicity, why a cell shrinks in salt water, we must understand the relationship between cell construction, solutions and salinity, cellular osmosis, fluid pressure, and so on. In the nexus of all these constructs, we can make sense of what we see when we place a red blood cell in salt water. But according to Polanyi, we cannot come to know this on our own. Importantly, as we listen to the voice of instructors who guide us to know the complex features of tonicity, we cannot restate all the rules we employ to understand what we see in the microscope. When we come to know tonicity, we know why the cell shrinks because we can discern its pattern—as a construct which generalizes—and can now view a particular instance of *tonicity in action* in light of that construct. Whereas we previously saw a red blood cell shrinking, we now see tonicity, we now have a sense of osmotic pressure, and we now *see that* there is a nexus of actions that results in a cell shrinking.

Key for Polanyi is that while we are developing the skill of *seeing that*—coming to know tonicity or anything else at all—we are in a submitted and fiduciary relationship with our guide, where we cannot articulate the reasons by which we come to know. "To learn by example is to submit to authority. You follow your master because you trust his manner of doing things even when you cannot analyse and account in detail for its effectiveness."[16] Only after we have come to know, or know of, the reality before us can we begin to name the clues that led us to understand.

---

15. As Norwood Hanson suggested, Tycho and Kepler could both recognize the sun rising if they were to watch it together, but within wholly different cognitive frameworks. "Observation," 146.

16. Polanyi, *Personal Knowledge*, 53.

Biblical Knowing

So it is for Israel. While the Israelites are enslaved in Egypt, they must rely upon Moses' authoritative directions to know YHWH and the Abrahamic promises on the distant horizon of the exodus, an authority they could not yet fully justify. Knowing YHWH as "your God" is one of the explicit motivations of the exodus account (cf. Exod 6:7; 7:17; 10:2).[17] However, it should be noticed that smearing blood on a doorpost, leaving Egypt, or even walking through an open sea does not have a direct correlation to knowing God in the way intended by the distinct use of the possessive pronominal suffix: *your* God (אלהיכם). From the narrator's position, if Israel was to know YHWH as *her* God, then they would have to pay attention to the instructions of Moses in order to cohere YHWH as *her* God. While they embody those instructions, they cannot vet nor verify how this process is going to lead them to that knowledge. According to Polanyi, it is the same for scientists as well.

This should not be reduced to a plea for blind religious trust, or that antagonistic misnomer in the West: faith. Rather, in the scientist's training and the exodus of Israel, there are discrete reasons given for trusting the guidance of an authority and a definitive goal in knowing: so that others could know.[18] The goal of knowing is to become a skillful knower, discerning enough to direct others toward the same skill. Even more, the level of sophistication required to discern particulars in light of the whole is elevated significantly by the time of Deuteronomy, where Israelites are not only required to distinguish true from false prophets, but to even distinguish orthodox from presumptive prophecy out of the mouth of an accredited prophet. Even when Jesus is being accredited to Israel through signs and wonders, he must still pass Moses' test guarding against presumptive prophecy (Deut 18:15–22). We will maintain that we are not discussing blind or even naïve trust in the Scriptures, but the stated ideal of skilled knowing.

---

17. I.e., וידעתם כי אני יהוה אלהיכם ("You *all* shall know that I am YHWH your God." Exod 6:7).

18. The Abrahamic covenant of Genesis 12 and Deuteronomy as a whole could be framed under that heading: knowing YHWH so that others might know Him. After all, this is the ultimate epistemic *telos* of the Jeremiah's new covenant (i.e., Jer 31:34).

Scientific Epistemology, Wisdom, and the Epistles

Reliance upon Testimony

> Any attempt to define the body of science more closely comes up against the fact that the knowledge comprised by science is not known to any single person. Indeed, nobody knows more than a tiny fragment of science well enough to judge its validity and value at first hand. For the rest he has to rely on views accepted at second hand on the authority of a community of people accredited as scientists. But this accrediting depends in its turn on a complex organization. For each member of the community can judge at first hand only a small number of his fellow members, and yet eventually each is accredited by all.[19]

Polanyi's statement about the social distribution of scientific knowledge is focused onto two matters: authority and authentication (i.e., accreditation).[20] In order for the social fabric of science to be operative, it requires that scientists know and trust each other, for the disjunctive work done in the field or labs cannot be verified by any one person or entity. The whole enterprise rests in a web of trusts and so it should be careful about who is accredited. Accreditation is not a badge to be worn, but the confidence that a scientist has been trained, developing her skills as a scientist, under the supervision of other trusted scientists.

The implications of this description are weighty in that they imply that the experimental facts do not speak for themselves. The scientist *herself* stands immediately behind *her* results and *her* accreditation is what allows those results to authoritatively enter the arena of scientific discourse.[21] We will address controversy more below, but a central claim of Polanyi's description of science is that it fundamentally (necessarily) requires impressive amounts of reliance upon the testimony of others, which cannot be personally verified by any one scientist.[22]

---

19. Polanyi, *Personal Knowledge*, 163.

20. These must be viewed separately because the scientific controversy will often be contingent on accreditation, not authority.

21. Polanyi argues that this confusion between information and testimony can be described in the supposed belief that there are bare propositions (e.g., p = "mammals have hair"). In reality, all propositions are claims that find their legitimacy in who is asserting them. He suggests, along with Frege's symbology, that all propositions have ⊢ implicitly proceeding them where the signpost indicates "I assert that" (i.e., ⊢p). Polanyi, *Personal Knowledge*, 27–28; Frege, *Grundgesetze der Arithmetik*, vol. 1, §5.

22. We could imagine that for Logical Positivism, the logical structure of knowledge was meant to safeguard against a mere reliance upon other peoples' observations. After

Biblical Knowing

Polanyi bypasses the possibility that science as a whole could ever be accredited by vetting each individual part (i.e., the lab, the scientists, the experiments, etc.). He claims that working scientists cannot vet the whole by the parts, and even if they did, it would not affirm the enterprise. By the nature of human epistemology, science mimics normative human knowing, though scientific communities have much more systematic requirements for methodology and accreditation. Even today, most will point to the scientific method itself as the center of scientific confidence, citing rigor or repeatability as the reason to trust the facts of science. Yet Polanyi points us back to the scientists in community instead of an idealized methodology. Thus, tradition and community standards of accreditation take priority in any scientist's epistemological confidence.

The Scriptures we have surveyed place a clear emphasis on authenticating Israel's authoritative voices. For instance, when Moses is made the Prophet of Israel, his jurisdiction to speak on behalf of YHWH and circumscribe all future prophets is almost absolute. The picture of Moses' accreditation begins almost as a reversal of the serpent's. Moses has no inherent authority, but is systematically authenticated as the voice through whom YHWH speaks. What is compelling is the historical phases of that accreditation. First, Moses himself must be convinced through signs (Exod 3:1–4:17); then Aaron is convinced to be his mouthpiece (Exod 4:27–28); then the Israelite leaders are convinced (Exod 4:29–31); then Pharaoh is convinced metonymically for Egypt (Exod 7–12); and finally Israel is convinced as a whole (cf. Exod 14:13–14; 14:30–31). This process of a phased and historical accreditation of Moses to all is immoderate, involving both lowly slaves and geo-political engagement at the highest layers of the ancient world.

In short: Polanyi's insistence on accreditation as a central hub of the scientific endeavor is minimally commensurate with the Scripture's maximal concern for the authoritative guide to be clearly accredited to Israel. Further, Israel's prophets guide her to know, which means having the skill of discerning.

---

the fall of Logical Positivism, we imagined that if we wanted to, we could vet the whole enterprise of science by vetting each individual part.

The Role of Scientific Controversy

> To the extent to which a discoverer has committed himself to a new vision of reality, he has separated himself from others who still think on the old lines. His persuasive passion spurs him now to cross this gap by converting everybody to his way of seeing things.[23]

In a section titled "Scientific Controversy" Polanyi briefly sketches out what happens when competing interpretive frameworks must be adjudicated within the scientific community. "The two conflicting systems of thought are separated by a logical gap, in the same sense as a problem is separated from the discovery which solves the problem."[24] He then goes on to describe how advocates of each system begin trying to persuade others in their community to appropriate their system for looking at the evidence. "Those who listen sympathetically will discover for themselves what they would otherwise never have understood. Such an acceptance is a heuristic process, a self-modifying act, and to this extent a conversion."[25]

Here, the matter is not of accreditation, something that would have easily disqualified a competing view. Rather, the matter turns on how we discern between two incommensurate views, both from accredited scientists. Again, Polanyi describes how scientific communities arbitrate conflicting paradigms apart from naïve and popular accounts that insist the evidence always wins.

You will be forgiven if you thought that we were describing Thomas Kuhn's 1962 work *The Structure of Scientific Revolutions*, published ten years after Polanyi's Gifford Lectures. We cannot discuss here the ongoing debate about Kuhn's reliance upon Polanyi in developing the seminal ideas in *Scientific Revolutions*,[26] but the ubiquitous attention that Kuhn has received in comparison to Polanyi has made Kuhn's thinner version of paradigms more renown. Polanyi differs from Kuhn on this point in that Polanyi more roundly situates controversy within an extensive epistemological description of discovery. Struan Jacobs summarizes the differences in Polanyi's and Kuhn's approaches to scientific discovery this way:

---

23. Polanyi, *Personal Knowledge*, 150.
24. Ibid., 151.
25. Ibid.
26. See further: Jacobs, "Michael Polanyi and Thomas Kuhn."

> Kuhn sees most scientific research ("normal science") as assuming, and extending, currently received knowledge which exists in the form of a "paradigm." Kuhn's paradigms in effect *present* normal scientists with "puzzles," whereas Polanyian scientists draw from personal knowledge in order to *choose* problems. "In choosing a problem," Polanyi argues, "the investigator takes a decision fraught with risks." . . . Polanyian problem-solving discovery looks to be a less structured affair, calling for acumen and audacity on the part of the individual scientist.[27]

Fortuitously, the popular reception of Kuhn's work (and Hans Georg Gadamer among others) has caused the naïve view of brute evidence to abate, even among accredited scientists. It had to be acknowledged that the paradigm—what Polanyi calls heuristic passion—controls the scientist's view of the evidence. The result of which is that scientific controversy is not resolved by a mere return to the facts, but occurs at the same socio-epistemological layers in which Polanyi has always described science itself: "deeply rooted in our history and cultivated today by a specially organized part of our society."[28]

In other words, there are schools of interpretation, even within scientific communities, and merely revisiting the facts will not change the interpretation. We will give a fuller illustration of interpretive frameworks in science in the next chapter.

Regarding Scripture's controversies over interpretive frameworks, there are many places where we could evince a similar history of theological controversy. Ultimately, Israel's theology is contingent upon listening to the accredited voice of a prophet and then following the prophetic instructions to the degree required.

However, many are wary of Polanyi's suggestions about scientific discovery and controversy because it appears to leave truth, or objective reality, merely floating in the minds of interpretive communities accredited as scientists.[29] Seemingly, there is no ultimate ground for truth in reality itself. Both Polanyi and the Scriptures directly address the problem of grounding our interpretive frameworks in an objective reality.

Polanyi posits a world where reality intrudes upon and reforms our knowing. As well, the goal of Polanyi's description of knowing is to "make

27. Jacobs, "Michael Polanyi and Thomas Kuhn," 25.
28. Polanyi, *Personal Knowledge*, 171.
29. Similar suggestions have been made by Stanley Fish's work on hermeneutical communities. See Fish, *Is There a Text in This Class?*

Scientific Epistemology, Wisdom, and the Epistles

contact" with reality, not to attain knowledge for which we have to seek epistemic guarantors or foundations.[30] From the Preface of *Personal Knowledge* he contends:

> Such knowing is indeed *objective* in the sense of establishing contact with a hidden reality; a contact that is defined as the condition for anticipating an indeterminate range of yet unknown (and perhaps yet inconceivable) true implications. It seems reasonable to describe this fusion of the personal and the objective as Personal Knowledge.[31]

The Scriptures argue relentlessly for a knowledge of God through accredited authorities and resolves the question of theological controversy by bringing Israel into contact with objective historical actions as well. The Hebrew Bible is exceptional in that theological controversy is clarified through drastic historic means. For instance, a scene in Numbers 16 calls our attention to two notably conflicting paradigms about holiness: Korah with his band of men and YHWH with his prophet Moses. Korah claims that all are holy and YHWH is among all. This claim questions the paradigm that only the Levites are holy and can serve in the Tabernacle. But the equally substantial claim is found in the literary symmetry in the story. Korah begins his revolutionary theology with the charge that Moses has gone "too far" (Num 16:3; רב-לכם). Moses' rejoinder to Korah and his Levite cohort states, "*You* have gone too far sons of Levi" (Num 16:7: רב-לכם בני לוי). YHWH's instruction then emphasizes the separation of Korah's band and their offerings of lit incense. The narrator offers a visible, spacial, and objectively real resolution to this controversy by which Israel comes to know.

The ensuing scene shows that the paradigm offered by Korah is not only at conflict and incommensurate with YHWH's paradigm, but that YHWH clearly distinguishes the appropriate view of holiness by a definitive act, an objectively real and physical removal of the wrong framework. Importantly here, the narrator frames the entire scene of Korah's rebellion in epistemological terms. The purpose of the objective and brutal judgment of Korah, et al., is stated clearly within the narrative, "... then you shall know that these men have despised YHWH." Similar comments could be made about Miriam and Aaron (Num 12), Elijah and the prophets of Ba'al (1 Kgs 18), and the challenges to Jesus' theology of healing (Mark 2:1–12).

---

30. Meek, "'Recalled to Life,'" 72–83. See also: Meek, "Contact with Reality."
31. Italics original. Polanyi, *Personal Knowledge*, vii–viii.

Biblical Knowing

Two factors then help us to see the connections between Polanyi and the Scriptures concerning epistemological controversy. First, conflicting paradigms are definitively resolved by objective actions in the real world. These actions are meant to give sufficient epistemological justification to the correct paradigm. In the above cases, the normal theology of Israel must begin within a framework that clearly identifies Moses as YHWH's unique prophet (Num 12), the priesthood as the uniquely holy mediators of Israel (Num 16), YHWH as a unique god of Israel who answers by name (1 Kgs 18), and Jesus as the prophet-Messiah (Mark 8–9).

Second, these are not brute nor bare theological points. They require discrete actions by YHWH who frames these controversies (e.g., Num 12, 16; 1 Kgs 18; Mark 8, etc.) so as to highlight the incommensurability between the normative and faulty paradigms. But the Christian canon, as a work of literature, has prepared the reader for these controversies. What is clear to the reader of the canon, with the aid of the narrator, is that any claim or action that is *not* rooted in the instruction of Moses will be framed as leading Israel to false or erroneous knowledge of her covenant with YHWH. The point remains, that each party looks at the same data, the same events, and the same words spoken. Each advocate in the theological controversy interprets the evidence differently. Korah interpreted Moses' commands about holiness as hoarding. Mariam interpreted Moses' intimacy with YHWH as unfair. Peter interpreted Jesus' understanding of the messianic figure as horribly misguided. Remarkably, YHWH acts within these narratives right at the point where the epistemological interest of the community is at stake. They all need to know which paradigm will allow them to know, and YHWH acts "so that [they] will know."

Polanyi's Maximic Language and Wisdom

Finally, when thinking about epistemology in Scripture, most of us immediately rush to the wisdom literature. We might even think of the oft-supposed hierarchy of knowledge and wisdom, wisdom being the greater and mere knowledge being the lesser. We hope to show below that an epistemology developed from the foundational texts of the Pentateuch and Gospels helps us to understand how wisdom literature and the epistles function within the epistemological process. Of course, the epistemology of wisdom literature is an entire study on its own,[32] but we have sufficient

---

32. For sources explicitly on the study of wisdom as epistemology, see: Von Rad,

reasons to suspect that we are deficient in our understanding of wisdom's functionality without a developed picture of the epistemology that undergirds it (note that we are including epistles along with wisdom literature here). Let us first consider Polanyi's discussion of maxims.

Polanyi's general philosophy of language is minimalist. For him, knowing is ineffable. It is because we already know that we can then articulate what we know with language, but our speech only approximates and grasps at what we know. However, language never approaches nor exhausts our knowledge.

> These observations show that strictly speaking nothing that we know can be said precisely; and so what I call "ineffable" may simply mean something that I know and can describe even less precisely than usual, or even only very vaguely.... Although the expert diagnostician, taxonomist and cotton-classer can indicate their clues and formulate their maxims, they know many more things than they can tell, knowing them only in practice, as instrumental particulars, and not explicitly, as objects. The knowledge of such particulars is therefore ineffable, and the pondering of a judgment in terms of such particulars is an ineffable process of thought. This applies equally to connoisseurship as the art of knowing and to skills as the art of doing, wherefore both can be taught only by aid of practical example and never solely by precept.[33]

If we know more than we can say, then we are left with the problem of transferring knowledge.[34] How do we bring others to know that which we know if we cannot articulate what we know? Polanyi proposes one specific way in which language is employed to aid in knowing. He terms this pedagogical use of language a maxim. Maxims are peculiar statements that have no substantive meaning unless contextualized within a performance, doing the thing prescribed by the accredited authority. If we have ever played tennis, cricket, baseball, golf, or shinty, we can imagine that a coach might

---

Wisdom in Israel; O'Dowd, *The Wisdom of Torah*; Fox, "Ideas of Wisdom in Proverbs 1–9," 620; "The Epistemology of the Book of Proverbs."

33. To his detractors, Polanyi warns: "It is not difficult to recall such ineffable experiences, and philosophic objections to doing so invoke quixotic standards of valid meaning which, if rigorously practised, would reduce us all to voluntary imbecility." *Personal Knowledge*, 87–88.

34. "To speak ... is therefore a performance based on knowledge, and it is indeed only one of an indefinite range of conceivable performances by which such knowledge can be manifested. We grope for words to tell what we know and our words hang together by these roots." Polanyi, *Personal Knowledge*, 102.

advise us: "Tighten up your swing."³⁵ The maxim is a speech-act that comes to the foreground in the epistemological process of scientific discovery:

> Maxims are rules, the correct application of which is part of the art which they govern.... Maxims cannot be understood, still less applied by anyone not already possessing a good practical knowledge of the art."³⁶

The maximic sentence as direction, "Tighten up your swing," is incomprehensible in and of itself. The only way in which that sentence becomes meaningful is if we have a bat or club in our hands and are actively swinging it. In the context of listening to our coach and performing the act that they are prescribing, the maxim guides us to know not just the brute category "what it is like to hit a ball," but "what it is like to hit a ball *well*." Polanyi wants us to understand that this is not only true of sports, but of the scientist's ability to know well too:

> The true maxims of golfing or of poetry increase our insight into golfing or poetry and may even give valuable guidance to golfers and poets; but these maxims would instantly condemn themselves to absurdity if they tried to replace the golfer's skill or the poet's art. Maxims cannot be understood, still less applied by anyone not already possessing a good practical knowledge of the art. They derive their interest from our appreciation of the art and cannot themselves either replace or establish that appreciation. Another person may use my scientific maxims for the guidance of his inductive inference and yet come to quite different conclusions. It is owing to this manifest ambiguity that maxims can function only—as I have said—within a framework of personal judgment. Once we have accepted our commitment to personal knowledge, we can also face up to the fact that there exist rules which are useful only within the operation of our personal knowing, and can realize also how useful they can be as part of such acts.³⁷

Israel's wisdom literature resembles Polanyi's maxim in some specific ways. In order to see this, we will have to ignore other prevalent features of wisdom literature. For instance, we must set aside the poetic nature of wisdom, although it could be argued that the poetic and parallel literary

---

35. In order to proceed, we must set aside the analogical use of "tighten" as well.
36. Polanyi, *Personal Knowledge*, 31.
37. Ibid.

forms of wisdom sayings contribute significantly to knowing. We do not have the space for that argument here.

Instead, we must focus on a single aspect of meaning found most readily in the book of Proverbs and also later in the epistles. That single axis of our study must elucidate how aphorism, metaphor, and analogy is meant to act maximally on knowers. To do this, we must first show that the lexicography of wisdom reveals an affinity most closely to a developed skill. Second, the book of Proverbs frames its wisdom teaching in light of accredited authorities. Third, aphoristic wisdom then acts like Polanyi's maxim, shaping the knowledge of the one who is performing the prescribed covenantal actions.

First, the range of Hebrew terms used to connote wisdom in the Tanakh is exceptionally broad, especially considering how commonly the disparate terms for "wisdom" are employed outside of Proverbs. The semantic range of overlapping terms includes:

> discern (בין),
> wisdom/skill (חכמה),
> particularly true wisdom (תושיה),
> instruction (מוסר),
> knowledge (דעת),
> understanding (תבונה),
> discretion (מזמה),
> clever (ערום), and
> the antonyms of wisdom: folly (אולת) and fool (כסיל).[38]

The most common term for "wisdom," *hochmah* (חכמה), also appears in unexpected contexts. In Exodus, the requisite qualifications for the tabernacle craftsmen is given by YHWH to Bezalel.[39] Wisdom (חכמה), understanding (תבונה), and knowledge (דעת) are pictured as the skills of a craftsman for making the Tabernacle of YHWH. Within Proverbs, wisdom is not only attainable (e.g., Prov 3:13), but attained by apprenticeship (e.g., Prov 4:10–16; 9:9–10; 13:1). Accordingly, in the English speaking world, wisdom should be conceived of as *skill* above its more sagacious and mystical connotations developed in the West. Von Rad describes wisdom's connotations from the Tanakh:

---

38. The dizzying field of semantically overlapping terms causes Gerhard von Rad to comment (re: Prov 1:1–5): "How can an exegesis which takes words seriously deal adequately with this series of statements?" *Wisdom in Israel*, 13.

39. Cf. Exod 31:3; 36:31; 36:1.

Biblical Knowing

[הכמה] describes men who, in some sense and in some sphere, are "competent," "skilled." It can be used even of manual workers or sailors.... [I]t describes a man who is an expert in the shady tricks and dodges.... Even an embryo which cannot find the way out of the womb can be described as "unwise" (Hosea 13:13).[40]

Second, the epistemological process retains the priority of accredited authority in the book of Proverbs. Wisdom is not a commodity that can be attained. Rather, to whom one listens is a primary concern of Proverbs 1–9. One cannot miss the conversational tone of the opening chapters, where a father and the female personification of wisdom are all coaching the sons of Israel. This entire conversation is premised upon the call to listen to the appropriate authority, one of several competing authorities at that (e.g., Prov 7–8). Twenty-five individual summons to "listen" are given in the Proverbs, fourteen of which occur in the first nine chapters.

"Let the wise listen ..." (Prov 1:5)
"Listen, my son, to your father's instruction ..." (Prov 1:8)
"whoever listens to me will dwell secure." (Prov 1:33)
"My son, if you receive my words ... making your ear attentive ..." (Prov 2:1–2)
"My son, do not forget my teaching ..." (Prov 3:1)
"Listen, O sons, to a father's instructions ..." (Prov 4:1)
"Listen, my son, and accept my word ..." (Prov 4:10)
"And now, O sons, listen to me ..." (Prov 5:7)
"I did not listen to the voice of my teachers or incline my ear to my instructors." (Prov 5:13)
"And now, O sons, listen to me and be attentive ..." (Prov 7:24)
"Listen, for I will speak noble things ..." (Prov 8:6)
"And now, O sons, listen to me ..." (Prov 8:32)
"Listen to instruction and be wise ..." (Prov 8:33)
"Blessed is the one who listens to me ..." (Prov 8:34)[41]

In Proverbs 1–9, YHWH, the father, the mother, and Wisdom herself are lauded to us as the rightful possessors of skilled discernment and the sons are cautioned against salacious seduction under Folly's sway. Hence,

---

40. "In the majority of instances, the wise man is not the representative of a position, but simply the wise man who is contrasted as a type, with the fool." Von Rad, *Wisdom in Israel*, 20.

41. Eleven more similar instances of "listen" act as the bases for wisdom in Proverbs 10–31: Prov. 12:15; 13:1; 15:31–2; 19:20; 19:27; 21:28; 22:17; 23:19; 23:22; 25:12; and 28:9.

Scientific Epistemology, Wisdom, and the Epistles

the only viable route to wisdom is portrayed as submitting to instruction under a skilled knower.

Third, Polanyi's understanding of maxims participate in this epistemological process at the point of apprenticeship and human action. Again, we are not considering wisdom as knowledge content which can then be practically applied. Rather, the aphoristic language of wisdom instructs us while we are performing the coached actions. We come to know as we listen, act, and thus see how the proverb is true in ways we could not have anticipated apart from the performance.

The didactic poem was valued for its role in fostering Israelite wisdom, not in building up content-knowledge which can be transferred from one generation to the next, as if the knowledge existed within the literature. Strictly speaking, wisdom is honed when we do while we listen. Von Rad views this didactic expression as particularly precious:

> Indeed, it requires an art to see objectively things which have always been there and to give them expression. . . . [F]or every sentence and every didactic poem is pregnant with meaning and is unmistakably self-contained, so that, notwithstanding the many features common to them all, they strike us as being peculiarly inflexible.[42]

That is, the ability to discern is embedded in the act.

Consider the adage, "Youth is wasted on the young." Although my great uncle regularly rehearsed this expressive poem to me while I was in my twenties, it is not until I now approach my forties that the sentence begins to make sense to me, even if only barely so. This is not necessarily a didactic poem, but the truth of this statement gains meaning as we perform life and our bodies begin to underperform life.

For a more direct version of a maxim in the Polanyian sense, consider the pair of aphorisms in Proverbs 13:2–3, which are introduced by: "A wise son listens to his father's instruction, but a scoffer does not listen to rebuke":

> From the fruits of a man's mouth, he relishes good.
> But the desire of the treacherous is violence.
> The one who guards his mouth keeps his life.
> The one who opens wide his lips, ruin is his. (Prov 13:1)

Those who have reared children, mentored youths, or been mentored themselves recognize the truth in this pair of sayings because we have

---

42. Von Rad, *Wisdom in Israel*, 5–6.

experienced it in action. But as maxims, they function differently for those who are coming to know the fidelity of these statements. Von Rad notices, "In Ecclesiastes the effectiveness of the wise men's words is compared to that of ox-goads" (Eccl 12:10).[43] The aphorism whips us, correcting and guiding us *as we go*.

If Polanyi's notion of maxim is commensurable here, then we should be able to see that the sentences do not convey any sense of propositional content in and of itself, for lack of a better term. Fruits do not bear out of the mouths of men, nor can we "guard" or keep watch over our own mouth. As metaphor, the proverb advocates something that we know to be physically impossible. But we are not arguing against the deep and rich metaphors of "relishing," "wide lips," or the analogical use of "ruin."[44] And we certainly should not neglect the fact that Hebrew wisdom found its expression in rich metaphors such as "the fruits of a man's mouth." Rather, we need to show that this metaphoric language only attains meaning in praxis.

Let me attempt to describe a way in which these maxims play a role in the epistemological process. The gap in knowing addressed in this proverb appears to be the idea that "what we say burgeons from within us and can bring good or ill," or something to that effect. Hence, we ought to attend to those things which we say. But this proverb does not seem to instruct us about the mere act of speech, but speech in the context of relationship to others. It presumes a covenantal good (טוב), not individualistic good, which can only be known in the social/covenantal sphere. In other words, the fidelity of this proverb cannot be fully known as an isolated individual. Its ability to coach us only occurs in relationship to a community.

The lesson many of us young men learned the hard way was that our speech often betrayed more than the content that we presumed we were delivering to others. Our statements conveyed arrogance, carelessness, or insecurities of which we were not even aware. According to this aphorism,

---

43. Von Rad, *Wisdom in Israel*, 21.

44. As a reminder, in analogical reasoning one rationalizes from within a construct they could only gain through an embodied experience. For example, the only reason we can understand the meaning of a phrase like "career path" is because we have physically vectored our bodies down a path from Point A to Point B. The physical experience becomes our way of understanding the relatedness between events. For more on analogical reasoning, see: Johnson,"Some Constraints on Embodied Analogical Understanding," 28–33; Lakoff and Johnson, *Metaphors We Live By*; Also, Polanyi deems the awareness to be "tacit awareness" where the awareness process is inherently embodied. Polanyi, *Personal Knowledge*, 69–124 passim.

there is some correlation between the content (what we say) and the performance (how we say it) and we need to focus on that correlation. When we attend to those dimensions of our speech, while we are performing the act of speaking, these proverbs then act like a coach, or goads, highlighting to us aspects of how others perceive us or how we want to be perceived, which were previously unknown to us. Or as Michael V. Fox tells us: "a proverb must meet a particular need, and this imbues it with ever fresh 'performance-meaning.' A proverb receives its full meaning only in application, when it is spoken to a particular end."[45]

This didactic aspect of the wisdom literature, of which we have only scraped the surface here, shows signs of following the same epistemological priorities spoken of in previous chapters. It begins with an intent focus on listening to accredited authorities. Even more, knowing is not merely listening, but rather doing and seeing. The proverbs extend the epistemological process into the embodying of the authority's instruction and their maximic coaching along the way. We are not handed instructions and left to our own, like some horrendous piece of Swedish furniture meant to miraculously erect from a flat box. But with an allen wrench and effort, we can be guided by those who are accredited to us by use of maximic language: in this illustration, maxims are like the little pictorials found in the furniture's assembly instructions. We find these maxims meaningful only to the extent in which we submit, listen, and adjust according to them while we perform what they are prescribing. Consequently, we will always be logically separated from the meaning of "tighten up your swing" until we actually perform the swing.

THE DIFFERENCE BETWEEN KNOWING IN SCRIPTURE AND IN SCIENCE

Although we have made a big show of the similarities between a working scientific epistemology and the biblical epistemology proposed in this book, several obvious questions linger: What about miracles? Do not people know by supernatural revelation? Is not the Bible revelation, which excludes it from reason?

Again, addressing these questions could consume the space of several books. However, we want to point out one key difference between scientific/normal human knowing and the miraculous epistemic episodes in the

---

45. Fox, *Proverbs 10–31*, 484.

Bible (e.g., Elijah and the prophets of Ba'al; 1 Kgs 18). The so-called miraculous or supernatural acts, for lack of better terms, function to authenticate. Knowledge is not generally represented as divinely implanted, but revealed through normative human knowing with extraordinary authentication.

Two matters must be considered in order to make this case. First, we have already shown that even the most extraordinary acts of YHWH did not act as brute or bare evidence for the Israelites. The staff-snake sign, the opened Red Sea, the manna, the descent of flames onto Elijah's waterlogged sacrifice, and even Jesus' healings required an authoritative voice to guide knowers to cohere these acts as evidence toward knowing. Brute evidence always requires interpretation, making the very notion of brute evidence a misnomer.

Second, YHWH acts extraordinarily to authenticate his prophet to Israel (e.g., Moses' staff-snake, the coming of rain with Elijah, Jesus' feeding of the 5,000, etc.). All authorities must be accredited, both in science and with YHWH's people. Where we see the most brute and extraordinary actions ascribed to YHWH by the authors of Scripture, there is an ongoing accreditation process involved. Moses pre-interpreted the opening Red Sea (Exod 14:13–14) and that act resulted specifically in the people's trust "in YHWH and in His servant Moses" (Exod 14:31). Jesus also views his own miracles as sufficient accreditation to his disciples. In exasperation due to the disciples' failure to recognize his authority, Jesus explicitly connects his miraculous feedings with an expected epistemic response:

> Do you not yet perceive or understand? Are your hearts hardened? Having eyes do you not see, and having ears do you not hear? And do you not remember? When I broke the five loaves for the five thousand, how many baskets full of broken pieces did you take up?" They said to him, "Twelve." "And the seven for the four thousand, how many baskets full of broken pieces did you take up?" And they said to him, "Seven." And he said to them, "Do you not yet understand?" (Mark 8:17b–21)

The author of Acts ensures the reader that the authenticating signs and wonders of Moses were parallel to Jesus' authenticating "signs and wonders" (cf. σημείοις οἷς ἐποίησεν, Acts 2:22; 7:36). The writer of Acts steadily notes the same miraculous "signs and wonders" as authenticating the apostles too (Acts 2:43; 4:30; 5:12; 6:8; 14:3; 15:12).

All authorities—prophets, pilots, and biologists—must be accredited to knowers. Because novices need the discernible skill of knowing that only

Scientific Epistemology, Wisdom, and the Epistles

those authorities can guide them toward, accreditation plays a primary role in knowing well. Knowledge is not supernaturally induced in Scripture, but personally guided, just as in science. By "personal" we mean that a person who already has the skill to know well must guide those who do not. With airline pilots, their knowledge is imbued in rigorous training, apprenticing under senior pilots. Those training organizations, such as the military or flight schools, guide the pilot to an authoritative knowledge of flying, but in the United States, the Federal Aviation Administration authenticates them as legitimate pilots. In some sense, we are all folk psychologists, folk dentists, folk runners, folk biologists, and more. But the biologist who has trained under the discerning knowledge of recognized experts in her field is the one who will be accredited to speak in formal scientific discourse.

Likewise, the prophets of Israel required authentication and their authentication follows the epistemological process in science as well. The unmissable difference pertains to the means of authentication, but not the mode. The means are extraordinary, unconceivable outside of a special relation to creation. Signs and wonders are pregnant with other meaning, as we discussed with Mark's rhetorical use of the blind healing narratives, but they are at least meaningful to authenticate the prophet so that Israel will listen, follow their guidance, and know the reality being shown to them.

EPISTLES AS WISDOM LITERATURE

If the above is correct, then maximic language becomes a rubric for thinking about wisdom teaching writ large. In the New Testament, there are many places in the Gospels where we find maximic language. However, this kind of injunctive speech is most thick in the epistles. In a brief space, it is necessary to demonstrate this with Paul's epistle to the Ephesians with the hope that the implications for reading other epistles manifests similarly.

Before discussing Ephesians, we must notice some distinct ways in which Hebrew wisdom literature and the NT epistles differ. First, for the most part, the wisdom literature is anonymous. Even though Ecclesiastes and Proverbs present a provenance that seemingly points to King Solomon, no appeal to his authority as king is made within those texts. In the NT epistles, the whole letter rests on the authority of the apostle.[46] Second, although there is much scholarly debate about it, the Proverbs appear to be

---

46. With the glaring exception of Hebrews, but even there, the greetings (Heb 13:22–25) suggest a very intimate context within which the letter is meant to be heeded.

Biblical Knowing

more universal in scope where the epistles are written to specific contexts. Though many would argue that Proverbs is universal wisdom *for Israel alone*, its aphoristic teaching certainly speaks wisdom beyond Israel herself.[47] How universal is the scope of wisdom found in the epistles? Even the Petrine epistles, which state no exact locale, certainly have a first century Southwest Asian and Christian audience in mind.

For our purposes, we can set aside these differences in order to focus on how Paul intends for the Ephesian audience to know in a way that parrots maximic language found in Proverbs. First, we must ask if Paul is actually attempting to bring his readers to know something? We must now demonstrate that epistemological themes are present, relevant, and persistent in the epistle.

Is an epistemological concern *present* in Ephesians? Consider the following instances of "know" in the letter:

> "Blessed be the God and Father of our Lord Jesus Christ, who ... making *known* (γνωρίζω) to us the mystery of his will." (1:3a, 9)

> "that you may *know* (εἰδέναι) what is the hope to which he has called you" (1:18)

> "how the mystery was made *known* (γνωρίζω) to me by revelation" (3:3)

> "so that through the church the manifold wisdom of God might now be made *known* (γνωρίζω)" (3:10)

> "and to *know* (γινώσκω) the love of Christ that surpasses *knowledge* (γνῶσις)" (3:19)

> "until we all attain to the unity of the faith and of the *knowledge* (ἐπίγνωσις) of the Son of God" (4:13)

> "They are darkened in their understanding, alienated from the life of God because of the *ignorance* (ἄγνοια) that is in them, due to their hardness of heart." (4:18)

These merely represent the instances of "know" (γνοσις) in Ephesians and could be expanded to include "perceive" (e.g., 3:4), "wisdom" (e.g., 1:8, 17; 3:10), "wise" (e.g., 5:15), and "understand" (e.g., 5:17). An emphasis on coming to know is clearly present in the language and concepts of Ephesians. Looking closer at these passages in context reveals that an attentiveness to

---

47. For a discussion of the universal and particular scopes of wisdom, see Bartholomew and O'Dowd, *Old Testament Wisdom Literature*.

Scientific Epistemology, Wisdom, and the Epistles

knowing is also *relevant*, detectable to any reader of the letter. As well, this theme is *persistently* developed by the writer throughout the letter.[48]

Now that we have made a minimalist case for an epistemological bent to Ephesians, we can consider in what way it parallels proverbial aphorisms. Let us look at one series of maximic sayings in Ephesians and attempt to understand how they fit the epistemological pattern proposed thus far. Paul states in Ephesians:

> And you were dead in the trespasses and sins in which you once walked, following the course of this world, following the prince of the power of the air, the spirit that is now at work in the sons of disobedience—among whom we all once lived in the passions of our flesh, carrying out the desires of the body and the mind, and were by nature children of wrath, like the rest of mankind. But God, being rich in mercy, because of the great love with which he loved us, even when we were dead in our trespasses, made us alive together with Christ—by grace you have been saved—and raised us up with him and seated us with him in the heavenly places in Christ Jesus, so that in the coming ages he might show the immeasurable riches of his grace in kindness toward us in Christ Jesus. For by grace you have been saved through faith. And this is not your own doing; it is the gift of God, not a result of works, so that no one may boast. For we are his workmanship, created in Christ Jesus for good works, which God prepared beforehand, that we should walk in them. (Eph 2:1–10)

In order to consider how deeply analogical this instruction to the Ephesians is, it might help if we pretend that we are a robot (or a three year old) attempting to understand the meaning of the above passage.[49] We would have to ask basic questions, such as:

> How can we be dead in our trespasses?
> How do we walk in sin? Is sin a substance to be stepped in?
> How does flesh have passion?

---

48. The use of "walk" as metonymy for "conduct one's life in such a manner" is telling where it appears to follow a ethical line of reasoning, but then becomes epistemological. Early in the letter, the writer notes that the Ephesians formerly "once walked" in their trespasses (2:1), but now they "walk in" good works prepared by God (2:10). Paul urges them "to walk in a manner worthy of the calling" (4:1), which then turns explicitly epistemological: "no longer walk as the Gentiles do, in the futility of their minds" (5:8) and "Look carefully then how you walk, not as unwise but as wise" (5:15).

49. Paul presumes a spiritual transformation that backlights his theological metaphors with meaning.

> How do "rich" and "mercy" correlate?
> From what have we been saved?

These statements found in Ephesians make little if no sense in and of themselves. There is not a logical way to build a bridge from the grammar, syntax, meaning of the words, and then to the presumed intention of the communication. In the same way that we cannot understand the sentence "choke up on the bat" unless we understand 1) the physical act of choking someone or something with two hands, 2) that the bat stands in for the neck of the thing that we are choking, and 3) what direction "up" refers to in reference to the hand-hold we have on the bat. Although the sentence necessarily requires imaginative participation in order to make sense, when we are physically participating (i.e., maneuvering our grip on the bat), the sentence can be fully coherent to us. Our ability to combine our analogical reasoning with our current embodied situation makes the instructions like wisdom to us—maximic language that guides us in the act of doing.

Similarly, the writer of Ephesians employs a string of cryptic phrases with the intention of bringing the reader to know something. If the epistle contains this maximic language, then there is no way to understand the meaning—or at least, understand it well—apart from embodied participation. The description "by grace you have been saved through faith" can only make sense to us if we have had prior experiences that can be aptly represented by concepts like "trust" ("faith") and "salvation," both very embodied constructs.

Paul's rhetorical employment of "walking" throughout Ephesians could become slippery here, so let us clarify. If the summarized version of the letter's teaching is something akin to "since we have been saved, walk like we have been saved," walking in wisdom refers to discernment between the foolishness of the world (cf. 2:1b; 5:17a) and the will of God (cf. 2:10b; 5:17b). The epistemological implications of maximic language become acute at this very point: If we have not been saved, whatever that might mean, then we cannot walk as if we have been saved. This type of "walking in wisdom" is a skilled discernment that requires certain experiences and actions based on what Paul is teaching. As an analogical metaphor, "walking" must be imaginatively employed in order to make any sense *because Paul is not referring to actual walking.*

We cannot understand the analogical reasoning behind maxims such as "polish up your finish" without actually swinging a golf club. The meaning is not only logically separated from us, it has another meaning entirely (i.e., polishing silver to a shiny finish). Similarly, much of what Ephesians advocates can miss us without a prior knowledge by experience in the world of something analogically like physical salvation. Being saved is a physical concept referring to a time when we were in physical peril, but were saved from it. If we know Paul's salvation, and then live (or "walk") according to what Paul is instructing us, then we should come to know well the veracity of his other claims *as we participate*. This does not mean that we must have a near-death experience in order to understand salvation, but that the Scriptures tug on the analogical concept of physical salvation from death in order to relate to us the broader concept. The point is that the physical experience precedes the concept.

I do not play golf, but I can imaginatively consider what the maxim "polish up your finish" could mean through my other experiences in baseball or tennis. But my only access to even imagine what that might mean is because of my embodied participation with bats and rackets. To swing a golf club well, the maxim becomes wisdom only when I submit to the coach's authority and enact the maxim with which they are directing me. It is genuinely difficult to conceive of a way in which Paul's rich analogical language (e.g., "walk as children of the light" 5:8–10) can be reasonable outside of human participation as the ingrafted people of Israel in order to know that which he is showing us.

CONCLUSION

Although much more could be said about the connections between Polanyi and Scripture, I have offered these four central points as tropes to consider in developing views about Scripture's epistemology. Knowledge, for Polanyi and the Tanakh, share primary concerns regarding:

1. coming to skilled knowledge,
2. the knower's reliance upon testimony that demands accreditation,
3. the role of controversy in knowing, and
4. use of maximic language in order to guide knowers.

In discussing the overlap in scientific knowing and Israel's knowledge of the kingdom of God, we proposed that there is no need for *special* knowing as a separate way of knowing God or the world. Instead, we know the kingdom of God and God Himself the way we know everything else, through personal guidance. The chief difference, which should not be understated, is that our authority in biblical knowing must be extraordinarily authenticated to us.

Finally, the epistles follow in suit with wisdom instructions where maximic instruction is concerned. The sayings are richly analogical and require embodiment of the life prescribed in order for this apostolic coaching to be significantly meaningful.

7

Broad Reality and Contemporary Epistemology

HAVING PROFFERED EVIDENCE FOR a particular epistemological process which the Scriptures are keen to develop, our attention must now turn to engaging the various conversations about epistemology today. Most of these epistemologies can be championed by atheist and theist philosophers alike. But the controlling question for the next two chapters is: What view of epistemology best serves the theological enterprise concerned to reflect these biblical texts?

INTRODUCTION

Thus far, we have argued that the epistemological process found in the Scriptures appears to have monolithic features that span across Scripture: authority, authentication, embodiment, participation, and maximic direction in order to know. Of the aspects of knowing proffered, the matter of prophetic authentication and the enactment of the prophetic instructions arose repeatedly as determinative for knowing and avoiding error.[1] In order to know what God is showing his people, God must authenticate an authority to them, and they must both acknowledge that authority and participate in the process specified. We have seen that rejection of the authenticated prophet and failure to enact the prophetic injunctions ended in errors of the first and second orders.

---

1. In the case of Genesis, it was not a "prophetic guide," but an authoritative guide in the garden. However, the epistemological process appears commensurate between Genesis and the Pentateuch and Mark whether it's an authority or formal prophet in that role of guide.

Of particular interest is the fact that errors were often accompanied by propositional statements affirmed by the characters of Scripture. These statements were often vacuous or ill-conceived when contrasted with how those assertions were manifested in their actions. For instance, the propositional affirmation by the serpent that humans would "be like God" was ill-conceived by the woman when she took the fruit.

Regarding Israel's belief that Moses was her prophet, "And the people believed..." (Exod 4:31).[2] Calvin argues *against* Israel's propositional belief as conclusive evidence of her knowledge. For Calvin, actions must accompany the belief as an embodied participation in the prophet's instruction. He associates Exodus 4 with the parable of the sower (Mark 4):

> But we shall presently see how fickle and infirm was their belief [Exod 4:31]. It is plain, from its levity and inconstancy, that it was without any living root. But it is not unusual that the word belief should be improperly applied to a mere assent and disposition to believe, which speedily passes away.[3]

Likewise, Peter's confession in the Gospels follows the same current, an affirmation that reveals something about what Peter understands (Mark 8:29). But the proposition "Jesus is the Christ" is clearly not the final epistemological goal to which Jesus was guiding the disciples. *Peter's confession is not knowledge of the kind or quality that Jesus means to induce, nor does it reveal final insight.* The proposition "Jesus is the Christ" could have just as easily masked Peter's ignorance if not prodded further by Jesus' teaching. It was not wedded to the embodied participation required to understand what "Christ" means, which is exactly what Jesus intended to demonstrate among his disciples (Mark 8:31–38). In short, believing a proposition akin to "Jesus is the Christ" does not help Peter to fathom the crucifixion as one gruesome particularity on the route to the epistemological goal of seeing the "secret of the kingdom of God." We want to suggest that perhaps the proposition is formally true, but materially vacuous. However, the disciples are not called by Jesus in order to believe correct formal propositions; rather they are known by living a particular kind of life. By enacting this life (Mark 8:31–38), the disciples will see what is being shown to them.

With these emphases in view, we are now in a position to assess current epistemological theories for their commensurability with the

---

2. The New Jewish Publication Society (NJPS) offers a better translation: "And the people were convinced..."

3. Calvin, *Four Last Books of Moses*, vol. 1, 68.

epistemological process discovered thus far in the biblical texts. Below, we begin by reckoning the breadth of objective reality to be known and the embodied skills required to know even the most simple statements of fact, the so-called propositions.

Because analytic philosophy, as opposed to Continental philosophy, is the primary type of philosophy taught and practiced in the English-speaking world we will have to pay special attention to its epistemological claims. As will be illustrated later in the chapter, analytic philosophy focuses on being clear and precise in arguing for and attempting to understand reality. It generally seeks clarity rather than context and history, which gives it some unique strengths in arguing for particular views, but also some possible failings if practiced without a wider view of the methodology.

On the other hand, Continental philosophy has traditionally been understood as being less methodologically rigorous for the sake of capturing existence as it is experienced. While Continental philosophers are notably concerned for history and context, the equal and opposite errors of a naïve analytic method are prevalent. Some Continental philosophers have been so local and contextual as to be incapable of meaningfully writing to a wide audience. This has been why we have tried to navigate the path between (or apart from) a reduction of either analytic or Continental philosophy and have advocated for Michael Polanyi's epistemology. Polanyi is a methodologically rigorous scientist who understands that the phenomenology of scientific discovery has as much to do with the lived life of the scientist as it does with the clarity and rigor employed in the scientific process.

While there will be debate about which is most influential in Christian theology, analytic or Continental philosophy, no one would dispute that most English-speaking philosophers who are Christian and writing on theological topics are analytically trained. Hence, we will examine the four most prominent views of analytic epistemology to discern the best fit with what is chronicled in Scripture. The criteria will be the two centralizing features established above: authenticating the guide and participation in that guidance.

THE PROBLEM OF KNOWING BROAD REALITY

> This is a timely warning against the danger, to which analytic theology is not immune, of lapsing into scholasticism in the

pejorative sense of the term, allowing metaphysics to become separated from spirituality (love of God) and ethics (love of neighbor).[4]

Westphal's warning to theologians tempted by the analytic tradition in philosophy homes in on the concerns we have with the majority of epistemological conversation. The analytic tradition of philosophy narrows its focus on propositional forms and individual knowers in isolated instances of knowledge.[5] The discipline values individual agency, logical inference, which reveals the bent of most Anglo-American philosophy. Most in the tradition are aware of the liability associated with such a methodology.[6]

What typically surprises newcomers to philosophy is how narrow analytic epistemologies tend to be in contrast to the breadth of human experience. In fact, Eleonore Stump (a well-respected analytic philosopher herself) goes even further to say that it is not a matter of narrowness, but *hemianopia* (a blind spot to a fuller reality not discernible through propositional knowledge):

> It is therefore misleadingly imprecise, I think, to diagnose the weakness of analytic philosophy as its narrowness. Its cognitive hemianopia is its problem. Its intellectual vision is occluded or obscured for the right half of the cognitive field, especially for the part of reality that includes the complex, nuanced thought, behavior, and relations of persons.[7]
>
> Theories of knowledge that ignore or fail to account for whole varieties of knowledge are correspondingly incomplete.[8]

Most analytic philosophers will admit that non-propositional knowledge exists, but they do not attempt to account for it within their epistemological frameworks. Even more troublesome, attempts are rarely made

---

4. Westphal, "Hermeneutics and Holiness," 279.

5. Although Rea has made the case that analytic modes are not necessarily wedded to propositions, he then goes on to argue as if "analytic theology" will be methodologically propositional. *Analytic Theology*, 1–25, especially 6–12.

6. Goldman glibly descries his own field of analytic epistemology: "[E]pistemic agents are often examined who have unlimited logical competence and no significant limits on their investigational resources." Goldman, *Pathways to Knowledge*, 139.

7. Stump, *Wandering in Darkness*, 25.

8. Ibid., 59. Stump's solution is to offer a complementary approach where the analytic rigor and precision (the Dominican mode of analysis) is brought together with a person and narrative sensitive approach (the Franciscan mode of analysis).

to clarify the explicit relationship between propositional and non-propositional knowledge. For instance, an oft unanswered, yet fundamental problem in epistemology would be: Is non-propositional knowledge founded in or funded by propositional knowledge, or vice versa?

"Epistemology," as a term, generally means something like: a theory of knowledge that explains the circumstances under which we can affirm that "Subject knows Proposition," most often abbreviated "S knows P." This immediately conjures concerns about rationality, justification, confidence, beliefs, and the ability to use knowledge. But equally important: Why do we not also focus on social relationships, trust, reliability, authority, and more as essential to knowing anything at all?

We have argued that the biblical texts are centrally interested in the epistemological process and specifically, the prophetically guided aspects of knowledge. These two facets, process and prophetic guidance, are rarely addressed or only peripherally acknowledged in current analytic epistemology.

There appears to be a vital disparity between current theories of knowledge and what Peter Hicks deems the broadness of reality. In critiquing the narrowness of evangelical notions of truth, Hicks says:

> Despite this trend to reduce truth to something very narrow indeed, as human beings we do in fact find ourselves operating with a broad concept of truth. Each one of us regularly encounters and copes with many different types of truth: mathematical ("2 + 2 = 4"); logical ("If A then not non-A"); truth about the world around us ("There is a tree in the garden"); historical truth ("There used to be a tree in the garden, but we cut it down last year"); future truth ("This tree won't last forever"); truth about values ("Every person should be free to exercise his or her human rights"); moral truth ("Destroying the planet through pollution is wrong"); relational truth ("My wife loves me"); religious truth ("The universe was created by God"); and so on. If our epistemology, then, is going to be adequate for human experience in the real world, it will need to be broad in its interests and application, covering as fully as possible the whole range of the epistemological data.[9]

While we could quibble with the use of "truth" in the above quote, the point remains that reality (i.e., Hicks' "truth") and our apprehension of it is broad. Epistemologies should explain how we know this broad reality. The

---

9. Hicks, *Evangelicals & Truth*, 144. See also: Torrance, *Theological Science*, 141–202.

extent to which an epistemology captures the breadth of reality should also act as the measure of the most satisfactory theory of knowledge. Conversely, an unsatisfactory theory is indicated by the extent to which it narrows in upon only one aspect of reality without relating it to the broad reality within which it finds itself. Or, if we practice this type of epistemology, then we must concede that we have sacrificed the ability to explain precisely and broadly for the sake of logical clarity.

This is commonly done in the sciences. However, that narrow explanation has no guarantee of better explanatory power in the narrow sense unless it can be substantively related to knowing in broader terms. As an analogy, studying cellular biology of skin tissue in order to explain the social-psychology of family systems behavior guarantees no explanatory power in either domain, cellular biology or family systems, unless one can relate the two in a substantive way. The very notion of precision to mean logical, clear, and rigorous knowledge might be a misapplication of the term. After all, why is precision not equally descriptive of a nuanced understanding of a particularity in its context?

Nietzsche acerbically details how philosophers attempting to study a complex reality of *becoming* have instead killed and mummified the object of study for the sake of conceptual precision. When philosophers study epistemology in a narrow sense without adequate justification to do so, they are subject to Nietzsche's voracious critique of *philosophical mummification*. Ironically for Nietzsche, while their object of study is actually *in mortem*, they falsely believe that they are studying the living and complex reality *in vivem*:

> You ask me what is idiosyncratic about philosophers? ... There is, for instance their lack of a sense of history, their hatred for the very notion of becoming, their Egyptianism. They think they are honoring a thing if they de-historicize it, see it sub specie aeterni—if they make a mummy out of it. Everything that philosophers have handled, for thousands of years now, has been a conceptual mummy; nothing real escaped their hands alive. They kill and stuff whatever they worship, these gentlemen who idolize concepts; they endanger the life of whatever they worship.[10]

The matter of theoretical narrowness and broadness is a meta-epistemological matter concerning how we conceive of our examination. The explanatory power of an epistemology is analogous to the relationship

---

10. Nietzsche, *Twilight of the Idols*, 464–565.

between sample size and generalization in experimental methodology. Generally speaking, the explanatory power of an experiment's results is constrained by how well the sample represents the population about which it hopes to draw inductive conclusions. For instance, the broad reality of British children with head lice will not be explained by a narrow study of two tribal elders in Indonesia.[11] To have strong explanatory power, a study must take as broad a sample as is feasible to be its object of study. In order to generalize, these must also bear as much similitude to the target population as possible. The broad reality of British children with head lice might be better explained by the narrow study of 2,000 British children from different socio-economic backgrounds and in disparate schooling systems.

So too, the broadness of epistemological reality, biblical or otherwise, cannot be explained by a narrow study of propositions in predicate relationships as if they represent and can generalize to the entanglement of broad realities, as cited by Hicks. As seen above, reductions of skilled knowing ("knowing how") to propositional knowledge ("knowing that") will not sufficiently cover the realities being described.[12] The question remains as to whether traditional, naturalized, virtue, or Reformed epistemologies will be able to account for this broadness.[13] What is needed is an epistemological theory that takes into account the breadth of reality, but also reconciles the multifarious epistemic relationships that constitute knowing.

As an extended example of reality's breadth in seemingly narrow instances, we can examine the epistemological process that lays behind a believing a simple fact (i.e., a proposition) represented by the sentence, "The sky is blue." Yet even presuming that there are simple facts might have already looked beyond the breadth of the reality. For we must ask whether or not we mean to discuss the proposition "The sky is blue" or the epistemological claim: "I assert that 'The sky is blue.'" Polanyi picks up Frege's point that personal affirmation is inherent in all such propositions as there are no such things as bare sentences.[14] So we cannot speak about a

11. Neither is it the case that head lice in Indonesian elders has *nothing* to do with head lice in British children.

12. Stanley and Williamson, "Knowing How," 411–44.

13. These will all be examined below.

14. Polanyi argues that this confusion between information and testimony can be described in the belief that there are bare propositions (e.g., p = "mammals have hair"), where in reality, all propositions find their legitimacy in who is asserting them. He suggests, along with Frege's symbology, that all propositions have ⊢ implicitly proceeding them where the signpost indicates "I assert that" (i.e., ⊢p). Polanyi, *Personal Knowledge*, 27–28; Frege, *Grundgesetze der Arithmetik*, vol. 1, §5.

brute fact, but only our personal belief of the fact. The narrow fact is always situated in a more complex reality: our systems of beliefs. For the question is immediately begged: From where did we arrive at such a proposition, "The sky is blue"? The answer can only propose the parts that make the whole and put them in proper relations. So, the sky is blue iff[15] we look at the referent "sky" and see something like blueness, allowing for variations on the hue of blue.[16] Again, the question comes as to how we know the referents: "sky" and "blue." For that, we can refer to our childhood where some caregiver showed us the *genus* and *differentia* (what is and is not) of the sky and the color blue.

So the terms and their referents (i.e., "sky" and "blue") are conventions that are only attained through an embodied experience with an external reality of both the actual sky and actual blueness as taught to us by an authoritative guide. Notice that we did not say that we had a sensory experience. The reduction of knowledge to sensory input also takes a very narrow approach to epistemology. Nevertheless, a person must be situated in time and space, history and location, in order to refer to the sky which is a place in reference to spacial location on earth. There must also be a guide, pointing out what is and is not the sky. It is not merely a sensory experience, as Empiricists may have once claimed (and some neuro-scientists currently claim), but a historically and socially-situated experience: a participatory process.[17]

History and embodied knowing in a place are fundamental, even in knowing basic facts. This whole undertaking of coming to know "what is sky" and "what is blue" happens within the context of a more experienced knower who differentiates those external realities of *sky* and *blueness* to a less experienced knower.[18] The assertion cannot be a so-called fact, a brute statement about the world external to us. For there are more obvious problems, such that at any given time or place the sky is not blue. For instance, the sky is not blue when it is gray with clouds or in the middle of the night. Many inhabitants in the west of Scotland are left to wonder whether or not the sky is really blue at all. So when we say "The sky is blue," we really mean

---

15. "Iff" here means: "If and only if . . ."

16. Hume, *A Treatise of Human Nature*, Book I, section I.

17. Craig Bartholomew offers an excellent biblical and historical treatment of the reduction of history and place to time and space. *Where Mortals Dwell*.

18. For the problems inherent to delimiting so-called "brute facts," see: Anscombe, "On Brute Facts," 69–72.

Broad Reality and Contemporary Epistemology

to say something like: "I assert that 'The sky is blue' in certain places, times, and conditions *mutatis mutandis*."

Epistemologies that attempt to reduce knowing merely to knowledge of propositions often trust that the resulting sentence expresses the proposition. Because the proposition "The sky is blue" is a true and known fact, then the sentence is said to gain meaning upon that fact of the matter (the actual material blueness of the sky!).[19] Regardless, we are arguing here that "The sky is blue" can only have meaning if it is couched in terms of personal affirmation ("I assert that . . .") and further couched in the understanding that the sky and its blueness are constructs derived non-propositionally through interaction with an external reality and trust in an authoritative knower who guides us to know the referents and their relations in the statement. Or to state it chronologically:

> Because I have an embodied (i.e., non-propositional) encounter with visible light waves
>
> 1. with a wavelength of 475 nanometers,
> 2. which is then interpreted to me by an authoritative knower as "blue,"
> 3. "blue" being the English-speaking social convention for the mental "sensation" generated by exposure to that particular light frequency (the "what-it's-like-ness" of seeing blue),
> 4. and I also trust that authority because of prior authentication,
> 5. I can then begin to associate other things external to me that exhibit the feature of blueness.

When that association is agreed upon in some way, we often call it knowledge. If several English-speaking persons were observing the sky and believed it to be some hue of blue, then we would say that they have confirmed the statement "The sky is blue" *mutatis mutandis*.[20]

We must notice that the statement "The sky is blue" comes at the end of the epistemological process and only has significance in a social structure of knowers who have previously come to know the referents "sky" and "blue" through their prior submission to an authority, presumably their parents who taught them. *But, there is nothing bare, brute, nor individual*

---

19. Or at least, this is one way of dealing with the problem per the correspondence theory of truth.

20. Ignoring for now the problem of inductive logic that observing a blue sky *supposedly* confirms "The sky is blue" as much as does observing brown dirt confirms "The sky is blue." See Hempel, "Studies in the Logic of Confirmation (I.)."

about the affirmation "The sky is blue." It is thoroughly enmeshed in an embodied experience with reality external to the knower and interpreted through a hierarchical social structure that imbues experience with linguistic convention. There is nothing simple about this fact. If what we have suggested is true of "The sky is blue," it may be equally and more impenetrably true for any facts that require conventional language to be related to the real world by an authoritative knower (e.g., "The earth's atmosphere contains nitrogen").

The difficulty with propositionally dependent epistemologies, which we will explore below, is that they have trouble accounting for knowledge outside of individual epistemic feats wedded to statements which correspond to propositions. This bumps up against the conspicuous and persistent problem of the broadness of reality described above. Knowing does not only occur at the individual level. In fact, as we have already discussed, scientific knowledge by definition cannot be learned individualistically. Even more crippling, the presumption that propositions are somehow the end goal of epistemology is made difficult by the investigation into the reasons we could ever affirm any proposition, scientific or otherwise. "The sky is blue" requires significant embodied discernment in order to how it reflects reality meaningfully and how it can be believed even when it does not reflect reality (e.g., at night, during a storm, etc.).

Polanyi argued against Logical Positivism, a propositional epistemology *du jour* not yet defeated in his day. Specifically, he argues that knowledge is inarticulable because fundamentally, knowledge is not propositional. But this does not mean that we cannot speak about our knowledge. It only argues against the notion that articulation can exhaust our knowledge; that articulation bears a direct relationship to our knowledge in the sense that sentences bear a direct relationship to the facts they represent. "To assert that I have knowledge which is ineffable is not to deny that I can speak of it, but only that I can speak of it adequately."[21] Theologian Thomas F. Torrance, following Polanyi, challenges biblical scholars and theologians with the claim that language itself, propositional or otherwise, cannot be equated with knowledge. Words and statements are tools, instrumental means to guide others to knowledge of the referent to which they point:

> Hence if words or signs are to do their job properly, they must have some measure of detachment or incompleteness or even discrepancy to allow them to point away from themselves to the

---

21. Polanyi, *Personal Knowledge*, 91.

realities intended, in the light of which their truth or falsity will be judged.[22]

PROPOSITIONAL AND NON-PROPOSITIONAL KNOWLEDGE

So far, we have been utilizing the common terms for propositional and non-propositional knowledge to refer to knowledge of facts and knowledge without language, respectively. But this dichotomy masks what we have been describing: knowledge cannot be propositional, because language appears propositional by convention or as a heuristic. For some propositional accounts of knowledge—if not most propositional accounts—when I agree with you that "the sky is blue," I am agreeing that there is an abstract entity called a proposition which can be linguistically stated as "the sky is blue." Further, that proposition attains truth because the sky's color corresponds to the color in the proposition "the sky is blue." We suggest that because I have the skill of discerning the sky's color apart from particular contexts (e.g., rain, night time, etc.) and I have the skill of using language, I can therefore affirm that your statement grips onto my experience of reality in a meaningful yet conventional manner. The basic question that we can propose is: *Do we need the propositional/non-propositional dichotomy in order to describe knowing most accurately?*

The Propositional Turn

In philosophical discourse, a proposition refers to a fact that can be expressed by a sentence, thus, an abstract entity. Importantly, the proposition and the sentence are not the same thing. For instance, there is one proposition (e.g., "The sky is blue.") that can be expressed many ways with the use of the Romance languages:

1. O céu é azul.
2. Le ciel est bleu.
3. El cielo es azul.

However, we will argue below that propositional knowledge (that is, thinking about affairs as abstract facts of the matter) is heuristic, a

22. Torrance, *Reality and Evangelical Theology*, 65.

Biblical Knowing

conceptual tool that is employed in order to affirm significance. Because a proposition does not exist apart from knowers, it acts like a tool that can have fidelity in the act of coming to know a particular external reality. Traditionally, "the sky is blue" is a proposition in that the sentence is meant to represent an actual fact of matter. Without ejecting the notion that there is something we are trying to convey, we can assert that the sentence is a tool to affirm the knower's experience and the circumstantial reality of a sky that is blue has a positive correspondence, or more accurately, a *real contact* with reality through personal history from an embodied place on the earth.[23] What we must challenge is the popular notion that facts (i.e., propositions) have inherent truth value apart from the epistemological process, that there is such a thing as a brute proposition or a fact that *just is*.

In his cutting critique of analytically reductive attempts at epistemology, Charles Taylor details the problem with propositional/representational epistemologies:

> What you get underlying our representations of the world—the kinds of things we formulate, for instance, in declarative sentences—is not further representation but rather a certain grasp of the world that we have as agents in it. This shows the whole epistemological construal of knowledge to be mistaken. It doesn't just consist of inner pictures of outer reality, but grounds in something quite other. . . . We can draw a neat line between my picture of an object and that object, but not between my dealing with the object and that object.[24]

How does this notion of propositions as a true or false representation of reality service the discussion of epistemological process? We will claim that there is no informational content to a proposition, and that claim must now be defended.

Words in sentences are ways of drawing on conventions of language, rich metaphors, and paths of analogical reasoning through embodied experience in order to align knowers to see the same things, confirming and disconfirming similar experiences.[25] To say "I *know that* the couch is brown" is

23. Meek, *Longing to Know*, ch. 17.
24. Taylor, *Philosophical Arguments*, 12.
25. I am borrowing a bit from W. V. O. Quine's concept of the *observation sentence*, but only to the extent to which it refers to confirmation, not propositions themselves. Observation sentences are, "precisely the ones that we can correlate with observable circumstances of the occasion of utterance of assent, independently of variations in the past histories individual informants." Quine, *Ontological Relativity*, 87–89.

Broad Reality and Contemporary Epistemology

to say I have a knack for spotting objects and their qualities and verbalizing them in my own enculturated language. We are contending that the sentence "The couch is brown" is an observation—a claim to understanding reality in a particular way, and as Frege argued, a personal affirmation. The difficulty with construing "the couch is brown" as a true proposition is that it puts the claim in a slightly different realm of meaning, hence the propositional turn. Again, traditionally supposed, a proposition can be queried as to its veridicality—it is either true or false that the couch in question is actually brown. When the *brownness* of the couch corresponds to an actual state of affairs, the proposition is deemed to be true. But we will argue that it is not either true or false, because the sentence represents my skilled discernment of an embodied reality. In some way, the couch might be brown, but I could mean many things by that statement and so the propositional statement can be as much a help in knowing as a hindrance. Take, for example, Peter's statement in Mark to Jesus that "You are the Christ" (8:29). It is clear to the reader that this simple proposition is true, but certainly not in the way that Peter believes it to be true (Mark 8:30–33). What mitigates the truth of "you are the Christ" is not its propositional facticity, being true in and of itself. Rather, that Peter as an embodied and historical person cannot discern the real messianic pattern from what he has seen and heard thus far.

Statements such as "the couch is brown" or "you are the Christ," can be sufficiently qualified to get down to what we *really* mean, but the qualifications will necessarily pursue our affirmation in relation to reality, not necessarily the brownness of the couch. Even after qualifications, the question we must push is whether we need to affirm anything about the color of the couch outside of our affirmation of the color. If we say yes, then we must demand justification as to why we need to talk about the couch outside of our experience of it—or Jesus' messiahship outside of any experience of it. If "The couch is brown" is an observation, then just as Frege argued, it is an affirmation. It is genuinely challenging to endorse it as a proposition (a fact apart from any affirmation of it).

When viewed this way, all propositions can be viewed equally as affirmations and become tools on the way to our confidence in knowing. We are attempting to avoid propositions as *things*. The sentence, "The couch is brown," does not gain meaning because it transcends to a proposition. Rather its significance is only between human knowers and the role it plays as a transparent tool in epistemological process. If we believe that propositions can be true in the biblical sense of "truth" (i.e., *aman/aletheia* [אמן/

161

Biblical Knowing

αλήθεια] most often connote "accurate to reality") despite anyone knowing the fidelity of the proposition to reality it describes, then it is unclear how this is not some form of Platonism.[26]

To help illustrate the complications of affirming facts as true or false things, imagine that propositions (i.e., facts of the matter) are like binary data on a computer's hard-drive. Is there any informational content on a hard-drive? While a hard-drive carries loads of encoded language within it, the informational content cannot be located *in* or *on* the hard-drive itself. It is the human activity of code translation, expressed in the computers functions, that enables the communication.

If we examine the content of the hard-drive, we will find disks with millions of positively and negatively charge places on them. We should be generally hesitant to use computers as examples of human activity, but this instance is effective without cross-projecting too many traits between the two analogs: humans and computers alike. The only way in which you can understand anything about what is being communicated via a hard-drive is to translate those binary magnetic polarities through multiple layers of language translations which will eventually end in something meaningful to someone, but not from the hard-drive itself. Each of these translations (binary to hex, hex to unicode, machine languages, application languages, etc.) are transparent to the next, *but they are precisely not transparent to each other* in the order in which they present translations to each other.[27]

---

26. This is not an indictment of Platonic thought, but an acknowledgement that if true propositions exist apart from knowing, then we have to have a metaphysical reality that explains where or what they are. Some theist philosophers simply affirm that all true propositions exist in the mind of God. This is one such explanation.

27. As a simplified example of how code translations work in computing platforms, imagine that we had the following people in a room and gave them Dostoyevsky's *The Brothers Karamazov* in Russian: 1) an English-speaker who also speaks Greek, 2) a Greek-speaker who also speaks Russian, 3) a Japanese-speaker who also speaks English, and 4) a Russian-speaker who also speaks Japanese. There is a way in which they could all come to know that story, or at least enough of it to pass along to someone else? More precisely, there is exactly one way in which they could pass the basics of the story to everyone in the room:

1. The Russian-speaker could translate to the to the Japanese.
2. The Japanese-speaker could translate to the English.
3. The English-speaker could then translate to the Greek.

At each translation, the two people in translating and receiving understand the language common to them and so what is being communicated is transparent to both of them. However, what is being said between the Japanese, English, and Greek persons are precisely not transparent to the Russian, for instance. And yet, the story is told to all the people in the room despite the lack of transparency to all in the room.

In other words, each of these translations must be placed in a rigid architecture and the language translations and architectures themselves all have their own parlance, culture, and structure *at each layer*.

If we write "Earth has a moon" in a document and save it on the hard-drive, is there a fact about the earth on that hard-drive? In order for that sentence to mean anything at all, it has to go through layers of cultural translation in order to be presented on the computer monitor. Each layer of translation requires a community of language speakers who are proficient and enforce linguistic and material norms (data encoding and the media with which to encode). In short: the only way in which a hard-drive can be accused of containing meaningful content is when it is connected to the larger computing platform for which it is very precisely designed.

When it is nestled into its correct cultural context (i.e., a physical computer and the various code translations), then its binary content in magnetic form can be rendered into something meaningful on a monitor. Further, the hard-drive is merely a transparent, yet necessary, tool in that task. So it is with the proposition, *or more precisely: the clear use of language*. It is a tool that can render experience meaningful when placed in the right cultural context (i.e., between human knowers).

If this is correct, then the common charge of atomistic methodology stems from much of analytic philosophy performing the equivalent of staring at hard-drives and attempting to assess whether or not things on the hard-drive itself are true or false.

Propositional Language: Nestled in History, Culture, and Place

Continuing the hard-drive example, imagine that we set a laptop computer to record from its camera until the hard-drive is full. We set the computer's camera facing down Fifth Avenue in Manhattan, hit record, and then we give the hard-drive to a third party once it is full. The third party is then tasked to verify if the camera did indeed record video and specified this question: Did the computer's camera record a crime? How could they possibly answer such a question other than to watch the video? They cannot. All they have is a piece of well-crafted digital medium, which cannot possibly reveal the significance of its material contents by looking at it or touching it. The only way you could answer such a question is to nestle the hard-drive within a similarly enculturated device, put it through the requisite strings of code and language translations and render the video onto a monitor.

Biblical Knowing

We should point out the absurdity of claiming that the hard-drive itself contained the record of a crime when it is merely the physical device for conveying the video from one location to the next. The analogy will break down rapidly, but this part holds: like the binary on a hard-drive, so-called proposition language is the tool that conveys meaning when nestled within the appropriately enculturated context. And once language is nestled in that context, by necessity the computer language within which the video data are encoded becomes transparent to the epistemological process for which it is being used. When we nestle the hard-drive into a computer, a device that employs dozens of languages and cultures, it would be absurd to continue to stare at the hard-drive itself while the video is being displayed on the monitor. The pertinent information regarding criminal activity is between the monitor and the person watching it. Everything that aids in the task of viewing the video becomes transparent to the task. The hard-drive, the video card, the motherboard, the logical and physical code translations, and even the voltage differentials going to the input on the monitor are all completely transparent to the task of viewing the video.

If this analogy is correct, that propositions are linguistic tools like magnetic bits on a hard-drive, then how we derive meaning from a hard-drive should be the corrective model for how propositional language aids in confirmation and knowing, but is not itself "the object to be known." If we cannot assess the truth value of a hard-drive's contents without nestling it (embodying it) within an appropriately enculturated computer (i.e., Mac, Linux, Unix, Microsoft, and then the physical connections and firmware, drivers, etc.), then we cannot assess propositions without nestling them within human knowers with similar experiences. Once we have admitted the necessity of nestling a proposition in layers of culture in order to be known, it stretches us to think of propositions as abstract entities apart from whether someone knows them or not.

So then, asking whether or not a certain proposition is true is akin to asking whether or not a certain spot on a hard-drive is true. It is an absurd question. For instance, "Is it true or false that Bob was at home all evening?" The sentence (or proposition represented by the sentence) "Bob was at home all evening" cannot be true or false if it just a tool to affirm our belief in the real experience of Bob's location. When a sentence is culturally translated, the sentence becomes a tool re-nestled and embodied in the knower in order for the knower to understand the reality of Bob's location. The proposition "Bob was at home all evening" cannot be any more true

Broad Reality and Contemporary Epistemology

or false than a pointing finger. Stated otherwise, can a pointed index finger indicating the "thatness" of Bob's location be true or false? It appears to apply the quality of truth too strongly, or perhaps veers to widely from the biblical notion of truth. So-called propositions, pointing fingers, tone of voice, body language, etc., are all tools that make claims in order to point us toward reality. Again, seeing the proposition or its expressive sentence as the thing to be known is akin to staring at the fingertip which is pointing toward the moon. As the popular dialogue in Asian philosophy says:

> Words are (just) a means to get the meaning. But the meaning is not the words themselves. For example when a person points to the moon with his finger in order to enable the confused to see the moon, if the latter would see only the finger, the person would ask: "While I point to the moon with my finger in order to enable you to see it, how is it that you see only the finger and miss the moon?" The case is the same even here. Words are pointers to, indicators of, meaning; words are not themselves the meaning. It is therefore that one should not take one's stand simply on words.[28]

The proposition is a tool, a certain grasp of the world, to help understand an affirmation of a knower's sense of what they know. Bob really was at home and there is no propositional analysis needed to establish that. Either Bob and his wife experienced his presence at home and can affirm it with their language or they cannot. But the so-called proposition *in se* cannot be true or false any more than my body language can be true or false or a point on a hard-drive can be true or false. The actual referents set in relationship to each other via the tool of language can be a more accurate or less accurate description of an experience. But the accuracy can only be assessed by those linguistic affirmations being shared through cultural translation and compared in order to see if the *experiences* jive, *not if the propositions jive with each other apart from knowers.*

Finally, an illustration of a similar reasoning in Scripture might be helpful. Though not a proposition per se, Jesus means for us to understand that the command to "not kill" points beyond mortality and toward interior human dispositions (Matt 5:21–26). In Jesus' discourse, murder moves from the act of physical killing to the heart, a disposition towards humanity and its Creator. This leads Strecker to claim: "The sharpening of the Torah leads us to the edge of our existence as human existence. Through the message of Jesus [i.e., Sermon on the Mount], the annihilating power of the law

---

28. Ramanan, *Nagarjuna's Philosophy*, 130.

is experienced."²⁹ Once Jesus makes this rhetorical move, from parochial meaning of a statement to transcendent meaning, he has taken the propositional directive and re-nestled it within its appropriately enculturated context to then use as a lens (an instrument) with which to view the larger reality of human/divine communications and relations. Stated otherwise, the proposition becomes transparent to the epistemic act, a tool to point to the grander reality to which it was always meant to refer, per Jesus.

In the Gospels, Jesus regularly employs this type of hermeneutical reorientation using the same proposition statements from Israel's prophets and re-nestling them in order to point beyond their superficial meaning toward a grander reality.³⁰ But Jesus' disposition is important because he is chiding and rebuking as he reorients the gaze of those who follow him beyond the propositional particularities of the Pentateuch. More clearly, Jesus appears to act as if the Jewish authorities have blundered *because* they looked at the propositions of the prophets as the actual objects of knowledge.³¹ Jesus appears saddened by this propositional reading of the prophets that fails to use these articulations as tools to see beyond the surface of the law (e.g., Luke 18; Mark 10). This failure generally regards propositions as the content of God's knowledge to man. But with Jesus, the propositions become transparent to the task of revealing what was hidden (Mark 4:22–23). Westphal cautions Christian philosophers against the temptation to *propositionalize* Christian belief without practice, "[O]ur own God talk should not primarily consist in asserting true 'propositions' **about** God but in speaking **to** God in prayer, in praise, in confession, in gratitude, and so forth."³²

CONTEMPORARY EPISTEMOLOGICAL APPROACHES

Below, we will look at four major movements in analytic epistemology that have found their way into theological starting points (i.e., prolegomena),

---

29. Strecker, "The Law in the Sermon on the Mount," 37.

30. See Jesus' frustration with his disciples who are stuck on the superficial particularities of Jesus' actions rather than the "kingdom of god" reality they are meant to reveal (Mark 4–9). Similarly, the "young ruler" narratives: Matt 19:16–22; Mark 10:17–22; Luke 18:18–23.

31. This parallels Westphal's concern of the theological danger regarding the domesticating of God's truth when "we claim to be in possession of true propositions." Westphal, "Taking Plantinga Seriously," 177.

32. (Emphasis original) ibid., 178.

Broad Reality and Contemporary Epistemology

both formally and informally in the past few decades.³³ This is not meant to be a comprehensive review, but to identify the main characteristics that drive and distinguish each initiative. These summaries are meant to act as types in their respective fields of epistemology. If the type can stand in here for variations of the same kinds, then we can make judgments about their general commensurability with what we have found in the biblical texts. But we want to be clear in our critique that we are evaluating these epistemologies only upon their ability to describe reality. We are not necessarily critiquing their efficacy, coherency, or structure other than to look at their scopes of explanation and the sufficiency of each to correspond with the epistemological process found in the biblical texts. That said, we will give the basic claims of Reformed Epistemology special attention because of its conspicuous employment of Christian Scripture and theology.

Traditional Analysis of Knowledge

The *Traditional Analysis of Knowledge* (TAK) simply proposes: Knowledge is *justified true belief*. A person knows a proposition (e.g., "The world is round") when they have a belief about it, the belief is justifiable, and the belief is true. Richard Feldman begins his primer on epistemology by distinguishing the different types of knowledge and gives his reason for an exclusive focus on propositional epistemology:

> The most reasonable conclusion seems to be that there are (at least) three basic kinds of knowledge: (1) propositional knowledge, (2) acquaintance knowledge or familiarity, and (3) ability knowledge (or procedural knowledge). . . . Furthermore, many of the most intriguing questions about knowledge turn out to be questions about propositional knowledge.³⁴

Different versions of the TAK exhibit varying dependence upon principles of justification, theories of truth, and/or the grounds for believing a particular proposition.³⁵ But they all take for granted the basic construct of

---

33. For a recent attempt at wedding analytic philosophy with theology, see Crisp and Rea, eds., *Analytic Theology*.

34. Feldman, *Epistemology*, 12.

35. Some analytic philosophers are trying to bridge the gap between these perceived "types" of knowing. One attempt by a non-epistemologist is Eleonore Stump's text *Wandering in the Darkness*. She develops the idea that there are two modes of epistemology operative, Franciscan and Dominican, which are narrative-based and propositionally analytic respectively. *Wandering in the Darkness*, especially chapters 3–4.

167

Biblical Knowing

knowledge as a *justified true belief*.[36] This epistemological framework has weathered severe critiques. But our only critique is to controvert the claim that a propositional view of epistemology is the only one in which "the most intriguing questions about knowledge turn."

This view of knowledge as justified true beliefs has suffered from two main critiques: the Gettier problem and the "myth of the given." First, Edmund Gettier eloquently posed a scenario where someone holds a justified true belief that is an error in point of fact. The problem is specifically that the proposition believed does not correspond to the actual circumstance.[37] Briefly, Gettier imagined the following situation:

- Smith and Jones applied for the same job in their company.
- Smith saw Jones count ten coins and put them in his pocket.
- Smith overheard his boss mistakenly report that Jones would get the job.
- Smith is unaware that he also has ten coins in his own pocket.
- Smith forms the *justified true belief* that "The man with ten coins in his pocket will get the job."

Gettier simply poses the question: Is Smith's belief real knowledge? Essentially, what can count as knowledge if it is universally the case that:

1. Someone can generate many situations where they believe a proposition,
2. Someone has justifiable reasons to believe the proposition,
3. the proposition is true, *but*
4. the proposition does not correspond to the state of affairs in the way construed by the knower.[38]

This calls into question the idea of a proposition's truth value corresponding to one's belief. But more importantly for this thesis, error appears to lay outside of TAK's ability to account for it, or at least the original version of TAK.

---

36. Reliabilism, coherentism, truth-tracking, modified foundationalism, and different flavors of each type will rise and fall upon justification for "S's belief in P" where S is the believing subject and P is the corresponding proposition.

37. Gettier, "Is Justified True Belief Knowledge?"

38. Ibid.

Second, and more broadly damaging to the variations of the TAK, Wilfrid Sellars argues that TAK's view of *justified true beliefs* presumes that we can have unconceptualized access to sensory concepts. Stated otherwise, the TAK presumes that we have epistemic access to a state of affairs as an uninterpreted "given" (e.g., I can just have plain and unconceptualized beliefs about the number of coins in my pocket). Sellars argues that what we take to be given actually has conceptual girth to it and therefore each individual aspect of belief regarding justified true beliefs must be justified as well.[39] The TAK and its kindred epistemological variants assume that beliefs can be given, basically accessible without conceptualization or interpretation, and therefore do not need justification. In short: the Traditional Analysis of Knowledge suffers the death of a thousand justifications if individual beliefs are not given to the knower in the way the TAK presumes them to be given in brute form.

The TAK and its various forms attempt to adjust and accommodate for Gettier's and Sellars' defeaters. However, those adapted forms of the TAK do not alleviate our specific hesitancy with this analysis of knowledge. Like other epistemological models, the TAK vests itself in the notion that knowledge is fundamentally analyzable through propositional examination. Because of that vesting in propositional analysis, the TAK has little flexibility to engage the breadth of reality to be known. This problem of propositional narrowness will become more pointed as we progress through the next epistemological offerings.

Naturalized Epistemology

On the other side of recent epistemologies, W. V. O. Quine, et al.,[40] naturalizes epistemology by reducing it to psychology. For Quine, knowing becomes ultimately pragmatic, knowing is what works. In the post-Logical Positivist despair, Quine wants to reduce epistemology to scientific pursuits precisely because the "doctrinal" search for justifying our knowledge (e.g., TAK) is forever plagued by the "Humean predicament."[41] Hume's predica-

---

39. Sellars, *Science, Perception and Reality*.

40. Quine might hold the most extreme form of Naturalized Epistemology, ultimately usurping epistemology with psychology. But other offerings to naturalize epistemology suffer similarly from our critique here: Kornblith, "What is Naturalized Epistemology?"; Kim, "Naturalized Epistemology"; Kitcher, "The Naturalists Return"; Dretske, "Précis of Knowledge"; Goldman, "What is Justified Belief?"

41. Hume, *A Treatise*, 1.3.6.7.

ment centers around the logical problem that most knowledge is actually some form of inductive hope that past instances will resemble future instances or local observations will generalize to distant events. Science can probabilistically rely on inductive inferences; after all, inductions are the wheelhouse of the scientific enterprise. However, induction has no internal rationality, per Hume, and hence leaves human knowledge largely afloat in the "Humean predicament." Therefore, knowledge cannot be funded by inductive inferences, but neither can it take root in deductive inferences, even those with mathematical certainty. Deductive-mathematic systems cannot be internally complete, they must be justified by premises external to the system itself. Employing Gödel's theorem of incompleteness,[42] Quine argues that justification of knowledge cannot solely rest upon deductions because deductive inferences have no guarantor either.

Quine's *Naturalized Epistemology* (NE) posits that in light of the problems of induction and deduction, we can only justify our knowledge via scientific pay off.[43] We cannot justify what we know by founding our knowledge in reality, rationality, or even the scientific process itself, because those justifications would involve making logically tenuous claims based on induction. If science is our best case scenario of epistemology, as Quine argues, then epistemology should be focused on assessing how well our science works. We can clarify instances of knowledge when science is successful, when theories explain and calculations are predictive.[44]

To some extent, we can endorse Quine's argument as refreshingly honest about the problematic ground floor of deduction, induction, and the eschatological hope that we could confirm any truth on the basis of either logic alone. Quine's case, built upon the deep problems of rationality raised by Hume,[45] Gödel,[46] Hempel,[47] and Goodman,[48] needs to be weighed with considerable attention.[49] Due to these problems, Quine ends up in despair

42. Gödel, "On Formally Undecided Propositions," 592–616.

43. "Epistemology is concerned with the *foundations of science*." Italics mine. Quine, "Epistemology Naturalized," 15–31.

44. Thus Reno's perceptive observation that Quine was a realist. Reno, "Theology's Continental Captivity," 30–31.

45. Hume, *Treatise*, 1.3.6.7.

46. Kurt Gödel, "On Formally Undecided Propositions," 592–616; Parsons, "Platonism and Mathematical Intuition."

47. Hempel, "Logic of Confirmation," 1–26.

48. Goodman, "Reply to an Adverse Ally."

49. Quine, "Natural Kinds," 114–38.

about justification and opts for bare pragmatism. Yet, his turn to science as a best-case-scenario of knowing is not necessarily unfortunate. We have also sought in this book to use Polanyi's scientific epistemology as a model for knowing in Scripture and in general. The question for us is whether or not Quine and others have correctly captured the epistemology of science itself. In other words, is pragmatic pay-off the center hub of scientific epistemology? Naturalized Epistemology must hear Marjorie Grene's warning: "Fruitfulness [i.e., pragmatic payoff] is a test of truth; positivists make it not a test, but the essential nature, not of truth only, but of meaning as well."[50] We cannot follow Quine in his despaired reliance upon pragmatism, even if we can appreciate his critique of the TAK.

Between the poles of justifying true beliefs (i.e., TAK) and abandoning justification for scientific pragmatism (i.e., NE) there is a range of epistemologies that find their justification in tracking truth, proving the reliability of propositional beliefs, showing the coherency of belief systems, and flat skepticism that we can know an external reality at all.

Virtue Epistemology

A recent return to the ancient Greek concept of virtue has engendered a discussion concerning its noticeable absence in current epistemological treatments.[51] Linda Zagzebski has provided a critique of propositional epistemology and offers epistemological virtue as the answer to problems of justifying knowledge:[52]

> The thrust of most contemporary epistemology is to make us like the fox. If the object of knowledge is a proposition, the person who is greatest in knowledge is the one who has amassed in his mind

---

50. Grene, *The Knower and the Known*, 220.

51. Sosa's essay is taken to be the first significant move towards "virtue" in English speaking analytic epistemology. In it, Sosa rejects foundationalism (the pyramid) on the grounds for what he proposes to be a "fatal dilemma," but sketches a promising new path in reliabilism (the raft): "The important move for our purpose is the stratification of justification. . . . Here primary justification would apply to *intellectual* virtues, to stable dispositions for belief acquisition, through their greater contribution toward getting us to the truth." Sosa, "The Raft and the Pyramid."

52. Other significant works in Virtue Epistemology: Greco," Virtues and Rules"; Kvanvig, *Intellectual Virtues*; Sosa, "Raft and Pyramid"; Axtell, *Readings in Virtue Epistemology*, "Recent Work".

the highest number of true propositions that pass whatever test for warrant the theory has proposed.[53]

Zagzebski's proposal of *Virtue Epistemology* (VE) is the most promising yet in connection to what we see described in Scripture. Virtue Epistemology focuses on knowing as a process rather than a static event like "Subject knows proposition." Instead, knowing is habituated, historical, and skilled beyond natural talents.

Citing Jonathan Kvanvig's critique concerning analytic epistemology's narrow focus on propositions, Zagzebski sees atomism as the problem of analytic epistemology.[54] Her answer is to reject belief-based epistemologies because they focus too narrowly on singular instances of a single person knowing a discrete proposition at a particular time and under very unrealistic conditions. Zagzebski proposes knowledge as coming from a non-nascent virtue that is honed toward excellence, thus requiring her to reject act-based and rule-based ethical theories as a foundation for epistemology as well.[55] The problem with contemporary epistemologies is their "neglect of understanding and wisdom," which can only be arrived at through virtuous epistemic acts.[56]

On this account, Zagzebski defines knowledge: "Knowledge is a state of true belief arising out of acts of intellectual virtue."[57]

> It requires the knower to have an intellectually virtuous motivation in the disposition to desire truth, and this disposition must give rise to conscious and voluntary acts in the process leading up to the acquisition of true belief (or cognitive contact with reality),

---

53. Zagzebski, *Virtues of the Mind*, 45.

54. Kvanvig, *The Intellectual Virtues*, 44; Zagzebski, *Virtues of the Mind*, 181–82; 274.

55. Rule based (deontological) ethical theories are those such as Kant's categorical imperative or Bentham's utilitarianism. See Kant, *Metaphysics of Morals*; Nussbaum, "Mill between Aristotle and Bentham," 60–68.

56. "Virtue" is defined as an uncontroversial concept with some degree of univocity with its philosophically historical roots in the ancient Greek concept of ἀρετή: "Virtue is an excellence; virtue is a deep trait of a person; those qualities that have appeared on the greatest number of lists of the virtues in different places and at different times in history are, in fact, virtues. These qualities would probably include such traits as wisdom, courage, benevolence, justice, honesty, loyalty, integrity, and generosity. Some virtues are intellectual, others are moral, and some may be neither intellectual nor moral." Zagzebski, *Virtues of the Mind*, 89.

57. Ibid., 271.

and the knower must successfully reach the truth through the operation of this motivation and those acts.[58]

Even though Virtue Epistemology is the most promising of the epistemologies surveyed thus far, Zagzebski does not pursue three avenues that would bring her proposal more in line with what we have encountered in Scripture. First, while she acknowledges a social aspect to the development of intellectual virtue, she leaves it unexplored. Individualistic virtue appears to be the goal of her discussion. Second, this epistemology of virtue has little or no somatic features to it. There is no discussion of how this is a distinctively human and embodied epistemology. Third, while she critiques the tendency of analytic epistemology to focus singularly on individuals and propositions, she appears to land in the same mode of analysis. In the end, she is still exploring intellectual virtue as an individually acquired and maintained feature of knowing. But in the end, for Virtue Epistemology, knowledge is still a *true belief*.

Reformed Epistemology

In stark contrast to the above epistemologies, which are proposed by both atheists and theists, *Reformed Epistemology* (RE) gives us recourse to compare the findings of this study for commensurability with a theologically-minded and analytic epistemology.[59] Alvin Plantinga's Reformed Epistemology is the most robust and well-defended of several analytic epistemologies and therefore requires a closer inspection in this brief treatment.[60] Unlike most epistemologies, Plantinga puts *unjustifiable* beliefs at the center of knowing. His notion of *properly basic beliefs* contains within it beliefs that we cannot justify but which we must hold in order to navigate the world epistemically. Because our most fundamental beliefs (i.e., properly basic beliefs) cannot be justified, we must decide if our beliefs are warranted. Do I have logical justification for believing that there are other minds in the world apart from my own mind? This turns out to be a very difficult belief to justify in a rigorously logical way.[61] The goal, then, is to

58. Ibid., 273.

59. Moser's recent work would be the notable exception to this statement. Although he is still utilizing the vernacular of analytic epistemology, he often comes close to espousing a kindred epistemology to the present study. See Moser, *The Elusive God*.

60. E.g., Wolterstorff, *Reason within the Bounds of Religion*; Alston, *Perceiving God*.

61. For example, is it justifiable to believe in other minds external to ourselves? Plantinga would say, "No, but it is warranted." Plantinga, *Warranted Christian Belief*.

argue for what about human knowers and the situations they seek to know provides warrant to hold beliefs.

Plantinga et al.[62] are also describing something uniquely different from current epistemologies in that his theory of knowing includes belief about God and also requires a theological conviction about sin. In *Warranted Christian Belief*, Plantinga goes further to posit that his *properly basic beliefs* can correspond to theologically necessary concepts. Sin and sinfulness have now been incorporated by Plantinga as modes that corrupt proper epistemic faculties.[63] As well, Plantinga takes Calvin's "sense of the divine" (*sensus divinitatis*) as a theological tenet of RE. This *sense of the divine* has been implanted in all humans and is offered by Plantinga as a *properly basic belief* from which other beliefs about the world must be funded. Beyond sin, Plantinga also provides a provisional case for error in epistemology. Most basically, if our cognitive processes functioned properly, then error can largely be avoided.[64] This forms an eloquent panacea to the problem of error: if our epistemic faculties functioned correctly (e.g., before the Fall of humanity), then we would not err. But Plantinga's analysis of error and knowing appears too narrow to comport fully with what we have discovered in the biblical texts.

Even within analytic epistemology, Plantinga's work may be too narrow. Jonathan Kvanvig, a virtue epistemologist, critiques Plantinga and others of the analytic tradition exactly because of their myopic "focus on a single belief of a single person at a single time and also to the fact that the object of a belief is presumed to be a discrete proposition."[65] Or as Alvin Goldman puts it, "[Epistemology] typically consider[s] the prospects for knowledge acquisition in 'ideal' situations."[66]

For Kvanvig, propositionally-reduced epistemologies reverse the actual order of knowing by experiencing reality: "[E]xperience conveys information only en masse, and the individuation into propositional form often imposes structure rather than conforming to it."[67] Kvanvig does not

62. See also: Alston, *Perceiving God*; Wolterstorff, *Reason within the Bounds of Religion*.

63. Plantinga, *Warranted Christian Belief*, 199.

64. Ibid., 146.

65. This pithy quote from Zagzebski is a summary of Kvanvig's position. *Virtues of the Mind*, 44; Kvanvig, *The Intellectual* Virtues, 181–82.

66. For this and other reasons, Goldman actually believes that testimony "departs from traditional epistemology and philosophy of science." *Pathways*, 139.

67. We do not adhere to the totality of Kvanvig's argument for information as "chunks." This quote is Zagzebski's summary of Kvanvig's critique. Kvanvig, *Virtues*, 182.

want to argue that propositions have no use in epistemology, rather that they may atomize epistemic content that is actually meant to be understood as a whole and is only interpretable as a whole because that is the way our minds are structured.[68]

This general critique digs most incisively at Plantinga in the examples he uses to illustrate his epistemology. For instance, Plantinga poses the problem of mistaking one twin brother for another or the happenstance of a broken clock being correct once a day. Such examples of error exemplify Kvanvig's singularity critique against the narrow epistemological approach of Plantinga and others.[69] They are all problems due to ignorance of a wider context and historical setting.[70] These Gettier-type errors are uninteresting examples because they turn on synchronic happenstance: "a single belief of a single person at a single time." How would one ever be able to rectify that Peter (Paul's twin) was mistaken for Paul without appealing to the broader context of the situation?[71] Errors of interest occur diachronically in a process, not synchronically in one time slice of life. The errors we have examined in this book are remedied by social interaction, not singular reasoning upon singular propositional beliefs within a singular knower's mind at a single moment in time.

Having given a terse description and critique of RE, two questions emerge: How does Reformed Epistemology account for the social epistemic role of authority? And, is RE commensurable to what we have found in Scripture?

First, to the matter of authority, problems persist most acutely where Plantinga neglects the communal nature of epistemology as a core function of all knowing. In his section titled "How Does Faith Work?", Plantinga sidelines testimony or authentication of testimony as a sub-par and non-normative route to knowledge.[72] Van der Kooi comments:

> Plantinga too characterizes testimony as a *de iure* [sic] second-class citizen in the republic of epistemology.... We must keep well

---

68. Ibid., 183.
69. Plantinga, *Warranted Christian Belief*, 157–58.
70. See "Contextualism and Communitarianism" in Kusch, *Knowledge by Agreement*, 131–68.
71. Plantinga, *Warranted Christian Belief*, 155–58; Anscombe and Morgenbesser are exposing these problematic aspects of "mistakes" as lack of broader historical context in their 1963 essay "The Two Kinds of Error in Action."
72. Plantinga, *Warranted Christian Belief*, 249–52.

> in mind that there is a difference between uncertainty with regard to a specific item of testimony, and a skepticism which in principle finds little to go on in the witness of others in general. . . . He does certainly suggest that knowledge which is obtained through one's own perception is superior to knowledge which people have based on the testimony of others.[73]

In other words, Plantinga elevates the testimony of Scripture as authoritative while simultaneously devaluing testimony today and he does this without making adequate distinction between testimony offered by Scripture and non-Scripture based testimony.[74]

Second, to the epistemological role of sin, Plantinga's account of sin and sinfulness have been found wanting as well. This aspect of his work is important for our analysis because of the central significance of the first error in Genesis 2–3 (more below). Early in Plantinga's career, Merold Westphal found fault with Plantinga for inadequate treatment of sin in his earlier work, especially for an epistemology claiming the Reformed banner.[75] Plantinga remedies this lacuna regarding sin in *Warranted Christian Belief*, although many of his critics remain unsatisfied.[76]

---

73. Van der Kooi, "The Assurance of Faith," 102–3.

74. This suspicion of testimony prompts Helm to criticize Plantinga regarding his "quick" move from Scripture (i.e., testimony) to inferred belief: "What decides what inferences are elementary or obvious or quick? To illustrate, Plantinga says that 'what I know in faith, is the main lines of specifically Christian teaching—together, we might say with its universal instantiation with respect to me. Christ died for my sins' (pp. 248–49). But the proposition that Christ died for my sins is certainly a momentous inference from the Scriptures, not a good candidate for an inference which is quick and easy and obvious." In Helm's mind, this move seems too rash. Helm, "Review: *Warranted Christian Belief*."

75. We are referring here to Westphal's critique of Plantinga: "Sin as an epistemological category cannot be, as Fichte and Plantinga, Marx and Freud seem to want it to be, merely a device for discrediting one's opponents. To take Paul [the apostle] seriously is to take seriously the universality of sin. . . . Isn't this in fact Calvin's own conclusion, his critique of natural theology being but a subordinate moment in a larger argument denying that we can have any trustworthy knowledge of God, direct or inferential, apart from the divine gift of the Word and the Spirit?" Westphal, "Taking St. Paul Seriously," 216–17. See also Helm, "John Calvin."

76. We cannot actually settle the matter here of the "Reformed" value of Plantinga's Reformed Epistemology other than to say it is not entirely clear that Plantinga is using Calvin in a way that expresses Calvin's Humanistic tendencies toward the biblical texts. Or perhaps this simply raises the question as to whether Plantinga is appropriating the Neo-Calvinian Protestant scholasticism rather than Calvin himself. The *Institutes* are exclusively cited in Plantinga without much reflection upon the biblical texts to

Broad Reality and Contemporary Epistemology

Despite the synchronic epistemologies of Plantinga et al., there looms an more problematic silence in their scholarship that may hinder theological work: the nature of trust and the prophetic voice.[77] We have suggested that the epistemological process demonstrated in Scripture centers upon two facets: 1) knowing whom to trust based on external authentication and 2) participating in a process prescribed by the prophetic voice in order to know what is being shown.[78]

To the former, Plantinga's discussion of sin is most revealing of his view of the significance of trust. Sin, per Plantinga, not only makes one imperceptive, dull, or stupid, but also keeps one from loving one's neighbor as oneself (i.e., participating in the prophetic injunctions of Scripture).[79] But absent from his discussion is why one would ever assent to the belief that they ought to love their neighbor in the first place. Because Plantinga sets aside the authentication of the prophetic authority of Scripture, the question is: Why should one trust the witness of Scripture at all? Further, sin keeps us from trusting God, per Plantinga, which he roots in the primeval

---

which those sections reflect. But Plantinga has not necessarily attempted to be faithful to historical theology and biblical scholarship as his central task. And we also have acknowledged in our introductory chapter that there can be theological accounts that comport with biblical epistemology, yet do not make specifically exegetical arguments (e.g., Kierkegaard's epistemology).

77. Although we have not explored it here, there is an emerging subsection of epistemology concerned with the problem of trust and social epistemology. While these wrestle with some of the pertinent questions raised in the biblical texts, they do so within the narrower analytic modes. Trust is a "problem" for these analyses because they mostly view trust as if it is beyond deductive inferences, as something ultimately foreign to normative epistemology. Trust as a topic "departs from traditional epistemology." Goldman, *Pathways*, 139. See major works: Hardin, *Trust*, especially ch. 5; Brandom, *Making It Explicit*, 213–21; Lackey, *Learning from Words*; Foley, *Intellectual Trust*, especially ch. 4; "Egoism in Epistemology"; Coady, *Testimony*; Goldman, *Pathways*, especially Part III. Also significant and helpful are Anscombe, "Believe Someone"; McMyler, "Second Hand." Kusch has an interesting attempt at bringing together a communitarian "play" of language (think early Wittgenstein) with a contextually determinate and relativist notion of truth. *Knowledge by Agreement*.

78. Plantinga has inexplicably chosen to pick up Calvin's argument for the *sensus divinitatis* in Book I chapter 3 of the *Institutes*, while largely ignoring Calvin's foundation for proper epistemology in I, 2. In this move, Plantinga appears to shift Calvin's epistemology from fundamentally social to semi-autonomous. Calvin begins with the knower in a subjected relationship to his Creator who cannot think of such a being without realizing his own utter dependence upon and service due to that Creator (I, 2). Calvin, *Institutes of the Christian Religion*.

79. Plantinga, *Warranted Christian Belief*, 208.

Biblical Knowing

story of Adam and Eve.[80] At this point, Plantinga is exploring the roots of sin and epistemology in the middle of a story that features the two key aspects we have observed in Scripture: why should we trust the prophetic voice of Scripture and how sin keeps us from enacting the prophetic directives. These two could be reconciled in a discussion of Genesis 2–3 (as has been attempted in this book), but Plantinga chooses another route.

To the latter issue of the authoritative voice, Plantinga comes very close to exploring the serpent's voice as it relates to the error in the garden. But he ends his discussion of the Fall by simply concluding that the error lay in man's self-deception because he believed he could be both autonomous and like God. In other words, Plantinga believes the error to be autonomy, achieved solely through the epistemic faculty of the man without any necessarily socio-epistemic roots. The failure to enact God's commands ensues as a consequence of man's rebellion. For Plantinga's version of error, the man is "self-deceived" and "contemptuous of truth." And so, on the cusp of addressing the role of the serpent's prophetic voice, Plantinga instead identifies the mystery of free will and the man's envy as the ultimate error in the Fall:

> Of course the final mystery remains: where does this sneaking desire to be equal with God come from in the first place? How could the very idea so much as enter Adam's soul? . . . I can take pleasure in my [the man's] condition, which is wonderfully good, or I can give in to envy.[81]

Like Kierkegaard, there is no larger discussion of how exactly humanity went from being in truth to being in error. If the centerpiece of Plantinga's epistemology is proper functioning, then a deeper analysis of how the first properly functioning humans, the most properly functioning, fell into error is needed.

Plantinga has provided what no other contemporary philosopher has done: a comprehensive analytic epistemology that attempts to represent the Christian tradition in epistemology. Notwithstanding the merits of his work, what is our critique of propositionally reductionistic epistemologies of which Plantinga is another type?

The focus of Plantinga's Reformed Epistemology appears to be disjunctive with the aims of theology because of its synchronic and singular

---

80. Ibid., 212.
81. Ibid., 212.

analysis. Reformed Epistemology's precision still suffers from what Eleonore Stump calls *hemianopia*, having blind spots to reality large enough to render RE unsuitable for addressing the epistemological process found in the biblical texts explored here.[82] Plantinga et al. do not seek to clarify the social-prophetic role in epistemology because it does not factor into RE's emphases. His choice to make the Eden error a matter of self-deception shelves the problem as diagnosed by YHWH himself: "Because you listened to the voice of your wife . . ." (Gen 3:17a). While a scriptural epistemology need not be properly Reformed, it must correctly diagnose the error that it takes to be the type of error ubiquitous to humanity. While we might want to affirm the broad contours of Plantinga's RE (i.e., broken epistemic faculties, proper function, properly basic beliefs, etc.), due to the deficiencies noted above, Plantinga's RE can only function as a theological tool with great difficulty.

CONCLUSIONS

Above, we have briefly surveyed four views of epistemology in the analytic tradition: the Traditional Analysis of Knowledge, Naturalized Epistemology, Virtue Epistemology, and Reformed Epistemology. In considering their fit with a biblical epistemology, all four take for granted the basic construct of knowledge being related to our ability to cohere or justify a propositional belief with an external reality. In these four models, knowledge is primarily concerned with reconciling our rationality by propositional analysis, and so we find them fundamentally wanting.

Quine and other epistemologists have looked to science as the best-case-scenario of knowing and we would agree, in part. Polanyi's scientific epistemology reflects much of human knowing at its best. Good knowing, according to the Scriptures that we have investigated, like science seeks authenticated guides and submits to them, enacting the process meant to engender knowing as a skill that transcends individual epistemic feats.[83] It is doubtful that any of the contemporary epistemologists surveyed above would deny these aspects of science. But for whatever reasons, it is not their interest to pursue this diachronic view of epistemology. They have

---

82. Van der Kooi, "Assurance of Faith," 100.

83. Attempts in analytic philosophy at reducing "know how" to "know that" remain unpersuasive given the nature of knowledge in these texts as explored here. See Stanley and Williamson, "Knowing How."

narrowed their focus largely upon synchronic instances of knowing that are supposedly propositional in nature and can be argued for in deductively logical relationships. This propositional narrowness for the sake of precision runs the risk of being a study of knowing that is artificial to the point of losing contact with reality and biblical epistemology. But even if propositional epistemologies can escape Nietzsche's philosophical mummification critique, epistemology *in mortem,* they still do not reflect the intense interest of Scripture in depicting epistemology as a process.

COMPATIBILITY

It should be pointed out that we can still affirm aspects of each epistemology. First, there is little doubt that all epistemological frameworks require some kind of justification. We must be able to defend our account of how we know reality, but not necessarily articulate it in propositionally-argued logic. However, in asking the question "How do you know X to be the case?," we must not presume that the answer either originates or terminates in a proposition. For instance, how do we know the proper mixture of cement, sand, and rock in a batch of concrete? We can fail to provide a formula or proposition, yet we know it when we stir it. So here, one's knowledge is inarticulable, but real nonetheless, and articulation may actually interfere with what we know. Plainly, our justification of any knowledge, scientific or common, bears no necessary relationship to propositions. Epistemologies that require knowledge to be propositional can, at best, only coincide with the epistemological process we have examined in Scripture.

Ultimately, it seems that Reformed Epistemology, along with all the epistemologies surveyed here, asks fundamentally different questions than those which theology seeks to answer. Their synchronic and propositional scopes appear to be outside of our observations from the Christian Scriptures. Therefore, our critique of them is limited to comparison. In short, they are doing something distinctly different from what we see in Scripture. We cannot contend that they wrongly approach epistemology, only that they narrowly approach epistemology—or, *hemianopically* approach it. The question then becomes whether or not Reformed Epistemology (or another analytic method) represents the best approach to what we find in the Scriptures and how we practice theology. We have answered that question negatively, preferring Polanyi's scientific epistemology as one that is most commensurable to what Scripture is describing.

8

Analytic Theology and Biblical Scholarship

IN THE PRIOR CHAPTER, we were hesitant about appropriating any of the analytic epistemologies surveyed because they appeared incapable of addressing the broad sense of knowing required to do theology. However, there is a burgeoning group of philosophers and theologians who are advocating that theology might benefit from being more like analytic philosophy, at least, more like the analytic method. This most recent effort to encourage Christian theologians toward the analytic method was captured by the anthology *Analytic Theology*. Yet the question seemingly absent in the philosophy of religion and among analytic theologians has been: What do the sacred texts of these religious traditions have to say about the philosophical premises underpinning analytic theology? Hence, we might need to be more specific about our commitments to the relationship between the authority of the Scriptures and their prescriptive obligations upon scholarship. Despite the lack of an answer to the former question, analytic theology's central question is actually epistemological: How can we confidently know the philosophical content of Scripture, even in its systematic form of theology? Hence, this chapter will focus on the epistemological functions of theology.

We offer here a few ground-clearing questions, the answers to which determine whether we should proceed, and then how. First, does the Scripture itself present a systematic view of philosophical matters? Certainly, we hope to have shown that the Scriptures minimally present a view (or views) of knowledge.[1] If the answer to the first question is yes, then second, by what

---

1. Carasik argues that there are more than one in the Tanakh, hence the "Theologies" in the title of his work. *Theologies of the Mind*.

method do we investigate epistemological concerns in the sacred texts? We will survey several scholarly attempts below, but it is fair to say that the answer to this question has not been universally obvious. And third, if we are able to discern an epistemology from these disparate texts, how is it to be prescriptively applied back into our own epistemological presumptions? Presuming that Scripture is authoritative in its understanding of epistemology and therefore prescriptive for theology, does the epistemology we find in Scripture then become a feedback loop that is prescriptive for our own reading of the Bible itself. We have spent the entirety of this book on the first and second questions. Now, the remainder of this chapter will seek to answer the third.

Regarding the methodology proposed by Analytic Theology,[2] we are addressing a specific movement in current Anglo-American philosophy and theology. Due to the relative youth of this movement, appropriately titled "Analytic Theology," a precise description of it is difficult. The book *Analytic Theology*, as an anthology, collects essays representative of different ideas about the nature of this project. Within this spectrum, there is a palpable tendency toward reliance on a particular belief about propositions: that they could be epistemological ends in and of themselves.[3] However, there exists a reasonable fear that when theology ventures upon this premise, it becomes disembodied, de-historicized, and incarcerated by predicate logic, even if this end is neither desired nor intended. Indeed, Michael Rea wrestles with this exact fear in his astute introduction to the volume.

WHAT IS ANALYTIC THEOLOGY?

If there exists a propositional fascination within analytic philosophy, what then is the proposal of *Analytic Theology*? In brief, Analytic Theology is proposed in this volume as the precision and clarity of analytic philosophy more rigorously applied to theology. The exact nature and extent of that application varies among its practitioners, but the basic thrust persists.

---

2. I will capitalize "Analytic Theology" when referring to the general proposal captured by the collection of essay in the text *Analytic Theology*.

3. Rea anticipates this objection by claiming that Analytic Theology must not be "committed to belief in propositions." However, every essay in the volume then goes on to suppose that propositions are real and essential to doing Analytic Theology. "Introduction," 6.

"[C]larity and precision" with "attention to possible objections" creates the centerpiece of the Analytic Theology proposal.[4]

Analytic Theology is then conceived as an investigation of the topics of systematic and dogmatic theology employing the "virtues of the analytic tradition."[5] Or as Oliver Crisp puts it, "analytic" here "involves the use of certain tools like logic to make sense of theological issues, where metaphysical concerns are central."[6] The primary critique, previously lodged by philosophers like Merold Westphal, is that Analytic Theology is more "onto-theology" (i.e., focused on an understanding of the metaphysical nature of God, the Trinity, etc.) than theology traditionally understood. Many analytic theologians have shown an appreciation for the anxiety that "analytic" actually means being both ahistorical and narrowly ontotheological when working in the analytic mode. But their confidence in the method compels them to proceed with an awareness of these dangers. Indeed, Crisp's book *Retrieving Doctrine*, which meant to demonstrate the analytical theological method, was neither ahistorical and only ontotheological where it was required.

Additionally, Analytic Theology claims to follow arguments to their logical conclusions, no matter where they lead, which might create an uncomfortable variability for theologians. This uncertainty regarding the orthodoxy of Analytic Theology's products is shored up in part by William Abraham's proposal that calls for an epistemology of theology: "a new sub-discipline in the borderlands between philosophy and theology. . . ."[7] This would be a "systematic, self-critical, historically informed" discipline that could counter the reservations of Analytic Theology's most capable skeptics. We will propose that Abraham's suggestion for an epistemology of theology focuses at the exact point where the Scriptures are most concerned with knowing. However, we will need to consider below what kind of epistemology is most commensurate to that project. For now, we must consider a broad critique of the Analytic Theology proposal and its relationship to the Scriptures.

Unfortunately, few scholars in *Analytic Theology* seem to genuinely consider the notion that the Scriptures might impose the criteria that guide

---

4. Rea's astute introduction exemplifies this clarity while demonstrating Rea's insight regarding some apprehension to Analytic Theology. "Introduction," 44.

5. Abraham, "Systematic Theology," 55.

6. Crisp, "On Analytic Theology," 37.

7. Abraham, "Systematic Theology," 67.

the process of answering questions that the Scriptures themselves inspire. There seems to be an unnecessary presumption that the Talmudic rabbis, Medieval Scholasticism, or Reformed systematicians ought to provide the frameworks for moving forward philosophically. Statements such as Randall Rauser's, that theological *bull*[8] ought to be held in check by "the rigorous demands of closely reasoned analysis," begs questions about the Scripture's role in that process of "checks and balances," not to mention other authorities within various traditions.[9] This concern is more pointed when considering Crisp's claim that an "analytic theologian might end up holding doctrine that is unorthodox, or even heretical."[10] Of course, Analytic Theology must "privilege some ways of conceiving of God over others," as all theologies must do.[11] And Rea tips his hat to the problem of privileging as being "highly contentious." But there is no substantive discussion about the role of Scripture, hermeneutical strictures, or even more, the criteria by which that "privileging" takes place.[12] This is not a minor shortcoming of the Analytic Theology proposal.[13]

---

8. "Bull" as in "bullshit" á la Frankfurt's essay "On Bullshit."
9. Rauser, "Theology as a Bull Session," 83.
10. Crisp, "On Analytic Theology," 46.
11. Rea, "Introduction," 25.
12. Ibid.

13. We are not making the case that being "analytic" does not terminably bind one to rejecting phenomenology. It should be noted that most of my critique about knowledge having some kind of inextricably phenomenological roots can be found in the *Analytic Theology* volume itself. In a Cartesian fashion (re: *The Meditations*), Rea and Crisp let the final chapters (chs. 12–14) be written by its most capable and cautionary scholars. Stump's (ch. 12) well-known work on theodicy within the analytic tradition is now calling for a deep consideration of narrative as the philosopher's way forward in the field. "The Problem of Evil." Westphal (ch. 13) reviews some of his longstanding phenomenologically-oriented critiques of analytic philosophy, but now more particularized for their move toward theology. He cites Merleau-Ponty as a point of center mass for philosophers, "True philosophy consists in re-learning to look at the world." "Hermeneutics and Holiness," 266.

There are, of course, many others who are "analytic" but do not fit the representational views of those expressed within *Analytic Theology*. Nussbaum has been exploring the analytic/phenomenological boundaries for a while now. E.g., Nussbaum, *Love's Knowledge*. Also, there are reputable *mysterions* in analytic philosophy, those who cannot see the gap between domesticated propositional knowledge and the breadth of physical reality as fundamentally insoluble. E.g., McGinn, *Problems in Philosophy*.

ANALYTIC THEOLOGY AND PHENOMENOLOGY

If the above critique captures anything in this wide net called Analytic Theology, then that style of philosophy appears to be at odds with what is typically termed phenomenology. We must now briefly consider what phenomenology is, why it is methodologically different from analytic theology. The reason for this foray is not to merely counter ballast analytic theology's precision with a messier, embodied, and more human face of philosophy. Rather, when we look at the work of biblical scholarship that explores the philosophical content of Scripture, we find that it is notably not analytic in process or product. In fact, biblical scholars have generally tended toward philosophers of phenomenology to express what they are finding in Scripture. That tendency toward phenomenology in biblical studies requires explanation.

What do we mean by phenomenology?[14] Dermot Moran pithily summarizes the discipline this way: "[T]he programme of phenomenology sought to reinvigorate philosophy by returning it to the life of the living human subject," to shift "the scope of philosophy to be about everything, to capture life as it is lived."[15] Granting Heidegger's point that phenomenology is not just one thing, we can still make some general comments that capture the thrust of it. Husserl, Heidegger, Sartre, Merleau-Ponty, Levinas, et al. have contributed uniquely to the project of phenomenology, but the continuity between these thinkers is what we are concerned to reflect here. We offer a modest list of distinguishing marks, a rough heuristic, that might indicate that we are thinking less in analytic and more in phenomenological modes:

1. continual return of our attention to the subject,

2. notions of inhabitation or indwelling as ultimate constraints and categories in philosophy,

3. heightening of embodiment,

4. rejection of the representational model of knowledge in favor of direct engagement with reality,

---

14. Heidegger rejects phenomenology as a singular method. He claims: "There is no such thing as one phenomenology, and if there could be such a thing it would never become anything like a philosophical technique." Heidegger, *The Basic Problems of Phenomenology*, 328.

15. Moran, *Introduction to Phenomenology*, 5.

5. and the insistence on *the other* (alterity) having some epistemic/moral authority on *the I*. In other words, I am not an autonomous rational agent, rather, I am always bound to my relationship with others.

An error that we can easily fall into here would be to paint these two camps, Analytic Theology and phenomenology, with such a broad brush that we are not able to capture either position in our exploration. However, these generalizations are meant to draw our attention back to modes and tendencies in the "biblical thinking about thinking."[16] We are not claiming that writers of the Tanakh were twentieth-century Frenchmen or cigarette smoking nihilists or even Gadamerians. They were not.[17] But with these generalities in hand, we can begin to survey biblical scholarship for marks of analytic and phenomenological tendencies regarding ancient Semitic thinking.

In this chapter, we contend that the call for rigor and clarity of *Analytic Theology* ought be heeded by all scholars. However, propositionally-reduced versions of Analytic Theology are actually a target of the Scripture's critique against an impoverished epistemology. Indeed, the Scriptures tend to shy away from propositional affirmations in favor of phenomenal experience as constitutive of knowledge. Precision and clarity become pressing concerns for YHWH and his prophet, but are rectified through phenomenal episodes, not propositionally derivable content.

Neither has there been an impetus from the narrative logic of the biblical texts to look for metaphysically centered solutions to the problems raised within them. Here, we maintain that these episodes of personal experience are the philosophical force of the Scripture's epistemological program. This phenomenal mode of knowing then presses the question upon analytic modes of theology: What can philosophical theologians hope to know and can they derive it without understanding the epistemological thrust of biblical narrative?

First, I will survey some of the literature of biblical studies that has identified these epistemological motifs more broadly in the Tanakh, and specifically in the Pentateuch. We will find these disparate studies tend toward phenomenological motifs of knowledge. Second, we will sample a story in the Pentateuch where knowing is present, relevant, and persistent: Deuteronomy 4.

16. Carasik, *Theologies of the Mind*, 1.
17. Although Westphal tells that by 1999 in the West, "We are all Gadamerians now." Westphal, "Taking Plantinga Seriously," 175.

Implications for theological epistemology will be addressed in the next chapter, but these act as prolegomena for philosophers and theologians who aspire to reflect the sacred texts in their work. Inasmuch as the criteria of Analytic Theology have yet to be refined,[18] a formative concern that has not been posed by its chief proponents is the philosophical stance of the Scriptures themselves. We will argue that if the Pentateuch has a detectable position on how philosophical investigation should proceed, then that directive cannot be shelved, *even for the sake of analytical clarity and precision.*

EPISTEMOLOGY IN BIBLICAL SCHOLARSHIP

Before moving into our final analysis of a biblical text, we should acknowledge that there has been a recent upsurge in interest regarding epistemology in biblical scholarship, both Christian and Jewish. Below, we will survey some of the key works that look at the texts and discern what kind of epistemological constructs are operative in them. The point is both to give a brief overview of the work in this emerging subfield, but also to demonstrate that the overlap in the independent observations of biblical scholarship does not center on an analytic version of epistemology.

Recent Biblical Scholarship on Epistemology

Philosophical theologies, which tend to be bent toward analytic philosophy, face a main difficulty: their claims directing us toward propositional forms of knowledge and ontologically-oriented investigations do not find much support in the biblical scholarship. Here, we must turn to that recent scholarship which is sensitive to reading the Tanakh for what is epistemologically native, or *emic*, to the text even though we necessarily read with our own epistemological constructs foreign, or *etic*, to those texts. The discernible trend amongst these findings is the prominence of embodiment, perception, authority, history, personal knowledge, intimate knowledge, ritual, and ethics. These constructs are often associated with Continental philosophy and specifically phenomenology. But these findings do not, in and of themselves, create an argument against Analytic Theology. For those

---

18. See my review of *Analytic Theology* in *Themelios*.

Biblical Knowing

specific concerns about propositionally-reductionistic epistemologies, we will have to look at the Pentateuch for ourselves.

We begin by considering two works that have a somewhat aloof relationship to the authority of the Scriptures.[19] By this, we mean that they are descriptions of epistemological structures and processes *of* Scripture, but not necessarily *in* the Scriptures. Meir Malul's 2002 seductively titled *Knowledge, Control, and Sex* surveys both the cultural-anthropological roots of knowledge and the textual data in the Tanakh.[20] Although it has received mixed reviews,[21] possibly due to it's broad interdisciplinary nature, Malul finds the following themes operative in biblical epistemology: embodiment, authority, power, sociological strata, and intimacy (i.e., sex).

Shlomo Biderman's *Scripture and Knowledge* addresses concerns of the epistemic role of Scripture itself within various religious traditions.[22] The role and not the content of a particular Scripture factors most significantly in his analysis. He generically describes Scripture's epistemological function as:

1. the entanglement of propositional and non-propositional knowledge,[23]

2. the view of knowledge as co-inhabitation of a *nomos*,[24] and

3. the authoritative role that Scripture must play over it's practitioners in order to be epistemically efficacious.[25]

While Biderman's work is not biblical scholarship *per se*, his conclusions overlap with what we will discover in the biblical scholarship:

1. propositions cannot form the core of epistemological perspective,

---

19. I regret that I did not have access to Yael Avrahami's work *The Senses of Scripture: Sensory Perception in the Hebrew Bible* (New York: Bloomsbury T. & T. Clark, 2011), which was delayed in going to press. I have spoken extensively with Dr. Avrahami and believe that there is broad agreement with her work and the ideas proposed here. I look forward to interacting with her ideas in future work.

20. Malul, *Knowledge, Control and Sex*.

21. "By the end of the book, I was disappointed that Malul's work had not yielded a greater cache of insights into Biblical epistemology. . . . In short, the value of this book lies in the processes, described so carefully by Malul." Zevit, Review: *Knowledge, Control and Sex*.

22. Biderman, *Scripture and Knowledge*.

23. Ibid., 95–96.

24. Ibid., 84.

25. Ibid., 103.

Analytic Theology and Biblical Scholarship

2. social and embodied beings form knowledge (i.e., co-inhabitiation of another *nomos*), and

3. the social role of authority figures most prominently in Scripture's epistemic utility.

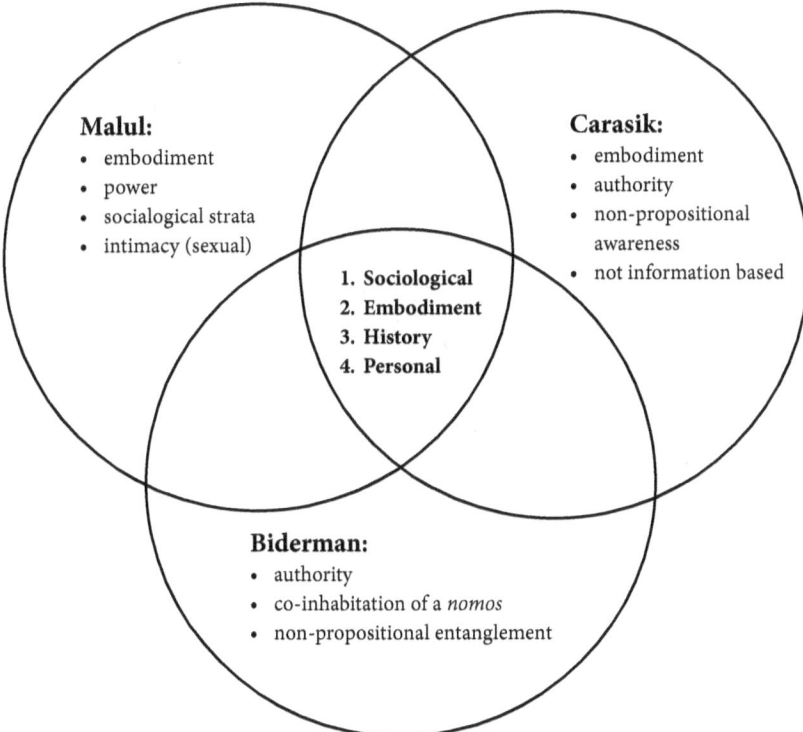

These two broadly epistemological works are not sufficient to draw conclusions about the content of the Tanakh itself. For this, we will turn to a spate of recent work, the last of which are retooled Ph.D. theses. First, Michael Carasik's work *Theologies of the Mind in Biblical Israel* is a monograph on "biblical thinking about thinking."[26] Although he frames the whole discussion in terms of "mentality," something akin to epistemology in his sights.[27]

Carasik's discoveries follow the language of sense perception throughout the Tanakh. His analysis is sometimes deficient in it use of the

---

26. Carasik, *Theologies*, 1.

27. Carasik reveals that what he means by mentality is actually something like knowing, thinking, and remembering. Ibid.,11.

Pentateuch, but his basic findings carry through. Primarily, he finds that authority in our knowing is derived from the divine realm. So he concludes that the Tanakh has "a positive evaluation of thought whose origin is in the divine realm and a negative evaluation of thoughts which originate in the human mind without impetus from the divine."[28] Social structure and authority mitigates proper knowledge. As for the individual knower, he discovers the embodied agent at the center of the Tanakh's "two complementary views of the mind: how the outside world influences the mind, and how the mind influences the outside world."[29] He even goes on the offensive against Enlightenment thinking regarding the widely cited use of memory in Deuteronomy. There, he sides with John Eaton claiming that the term "remember" (זקר) does not refer to "a mere matter of memorizing information. 'Nowhere does the sage speak of his educational aim as being to inculcate a body of knowledge.'"[30] Putting the Israelite knower back in her body, Carasik follows Eising's *Theological Dictionary of the Old Testament* entry for "remember" (זקר) and prefers it to be understood as "awareness" more than "recalling a memory."[31]

Following Carasik's text in 2007, Paternoster compiled essays from biblical scholars and philosophically-oriented theologians titled *The Bible and Epistemology: Biblical Soundings on the Knowledge of God*. The penultimate essay from *The Bible and Epistemology* is Murray Rae's "'Incline Your Ear So That You May Live': Principles of Biblical Epistemology." Rae summarizes the consensus among the biblical scholars and derives some theological conclusions from this collection of essays. He discerns at least three strands that persists throughout the observations of the biblical scholars: 1) knowing is relational, 2) knowing involved participation, and 3) knowing requires indwelling.[32]

We conclude this survey of biblical scholarship with three recent PhD theses. The first of these dissertations is Douglas Yoder's unpublished dissertation, *Tanakh Epistemology: A Philosophical Reading of an Ancient Semitic Text*; it is a wide-ranging exploration of a "native epistemology" in the Tanakh.[33] At over 200,000 words in length, it would be difficult to review it

28. Ibid., 2.
29. Ibid., 228–29.
30. Ibid., 56. Quoting from Eaton, "Memory and Encounter," 181.
31. See entry for זקר (Eising) in *The Theological Dictionary of the Old Testament*.
32. Rae, "Incline Your Ear."
33. Yoder, "Tanakh Epistemology."

justly here. In brief, Yoder contends that the Tanakh contains a persistent critique of rationalism in an epistemology that is native to the text. Arguing largely from Qohelet and Daniel, but also from the Pentateuch, he finds that Tanakh epistemology is 1) rational (i.e., that it can be justified), 2) relational, and 3) richly phenomenological.

Second of the PhD theses, Ryan O'Dowd's text, *The Wisdom of Torah: Epistemology in Deuteronomy and the Wisdom Literature*, is an excellent contribution to the subclass of texts on this matter.[34] O'Dowd finds epistemological continuity in his five aspects of knowledge as portrayed in Deuteronomy and the wisdom literature (both canonical and intertestamental). O'Dowd describes Israel's epistemology as:

1. Ontological: rooted in the creation narrative,[35]

2. Idealogical: situated in community and history (i.e., cannot get beyond or around our ideology, contra the presumption of science),

3. Liminal: it depends on "sociological boundaries, traditions, and 'rights of passage,'"[36]

4. Hermeneutical: not rationalist disengagement, but "in the bi-polar relationship humans live before God and his world. . . . Deuteronomy relies on this same bi-polar, experiential aspect of human life in this world. . . ."[37]

5. Ethical: "That Israel's cosmic, mythical worldview was grounded in the good and evil use of the human *yeṣer* demonstrates that ethics and knowing were always inseparable for Israel."[38]

---

34. O'Dowd, *The Wisdom of Torah*.

35. Ontological here means that it is sober reality: "The world as it really is." Ibid., 166.

36. Ibid., 168.

37. Ibid., 171.

38. Ibid., 173.

Biblical Knowing

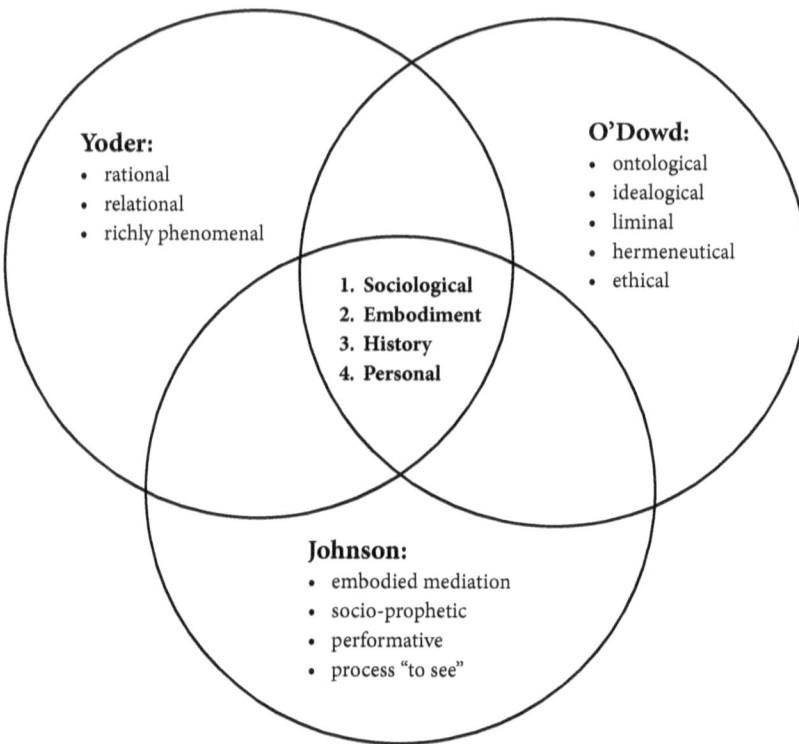

Third, my own doctoral thesis, *Error and Epistemological Process in the Pentateuch and Mark's Gospel,* has been thoroughly aired over the course of the prior chapters.[39] We only need to highlight one significant methodological difference from the above works. In this doctoral thesis, the story is followed as it is known in the canon, not prioritizing semantic field studies (i.e., What could "knowledge" [ידע] mean across these texts?) or word frequencies (i.e., Where does "knowledge" [ידע] occur the most?). My general findings were:

1. Knowledge is mediated through embodiment, not as a limitation, but because humanity is an intentionally created-to-know creature.
2. This embodied *creatureliness* demands that good knowledge (i.e., the kind that avoids error) occurs within a socio-prophetic structure. Specifically, knowing requires listening to and obeying the authenticated prophetic voices because they speak for God.

---

39. Johnson, "Error and Epistemological Process."

3. That socio-prophetic structure also demands one to perform what is prescribed by the prophet (i.e., the obedience dimension of number 3 above).

4. Only after the above have been performed, can the Israelite of the Pentateuch see what YHWH is showing them, and that "seeing" is termed "knowing."

Individually, these are interesting studies, but together, they beg a question in their overlapping observations: In what way can we understand the Tanakh to be speaking about knowledge in terms of the Analytic Theology described above when biblical scholarship indicates a preference for phenomenal descriptions of biblical epistemology? The recurring themes of embodiment, authority structures, personal knowledge, diachronic and historical orientation, ethics, and alterity appear to fit more with our provisional summary of phenomenology than anything we described in Analytic Theology.[40]

An objection that quickly comes to mind is that these biblical scholars might merely represent a group of Continentally-oriented scholarship and so their research into the philosophy of Scripture represents the philosophical tools in their toolbox more than something native to the texts themselves. Stated otherwise, these biblical scholars might have already been steeped in phenomenology before they came to these texts and therefore, their observations represent the mode in which they were already thinking about the texts. This objection is easiest to maintain in the absence of a thorough-going study of epistemology through the Scriptures. Hence, a response to this most serious objection must be found in the texts of the Scriptures themselves and an exploration of how the narrative logic deals with instances of knowledge, which we hope to have minimally demonstrated in this present work.[41]

---

40. We do find some of the above studies attempting to appropriate analytic language at times, but it is clear that the analytic language and quite possibly the constructs beneath the language are entirely *etic* to the Pentateuchal texts.

41. For an in-depth analysis of the epistemological process of the Pentateuch as a whole and within these particular instances, see: Johnson, "Error and Epistemological Process," 35–132.

Deuteronomy 4: Phenomenological Knowledge

There are several critiques of analytic method launched from within analytic philosophy itself concerning its narrow approach to a broad reality accompanied by idealistic views of the knower. These critiques are worth reviewing in brief. Alvin Goldman glibly descries his own field: "[E]pistemic agents are often examined who have unlimited logical competence and no significant limits on their investigational resources."[42] It is not only the agent that raises methodological concerns, but also the circumstances surrounding the most common illustrations employed. Jonathan Kvanvig critiques the analytic tradition exactly because of its myopic "focus on a single belief of a single person at a single time and also to the fact that the object of a belief is presumed to be a discrete proposition."[43] Our focus below will be on this noted contrast between knowing the breadth of reality against the desire to synchronically domesticate our knowledge in reductionist schemes.

Neither the knowing agents nor the circumstances are ideal when we look into the stories of the Scripture, to be sure. Further, knowing is portrayed as a diachronic process, rather than synchronic. It is a process which appears to be embodied and submitted to in order to comprehend what is being taught. Below, we will examine one last instance of human knowing and focus our attention on the process that ends in an instance of discernible knowledge for the reader of Scripture. Then we will assess whether or not a phenomenological or analytical approach helps us to best understand what the Scriptures might intend to convey. As a reminder, "analytic" is construed here as methodological clarity, precision and rigor and "involves the use of certain tools like logic to make sense of theological issues, where metaphysical concerns are central."[44] A phenomenological approach to theology would then lean toward construing theology in terms of embodiment, social roles, diachronic process, and therefore less propositionally, ontologically, and metaphysically oriented. However, it seems that both the traditionally impenetrable writing of phenomenology would benefit from the analytic method as much as the latter would be wise to do more than

---

42. Goldman, *Pathways to Knowledge*, 139.

43. This pithy quote from Zagzebski is a summary of Kvanvig's position. Zagzebski, *Virtues of the Mind*, 44; Kvanvig, *The Intellectual Virtues*, 181–82.

44. Crisp and Rae, eds., *Analytic Theology*, 37.

Analytic Theology and Biblical Scholarship

merely acknowledge that knowledge has a fundamentally phenomenological orientation in Scripture.

Canonically read, the rhetoric of the teaching in Deuteronomy 4 returns to the objects of the creation event in order to give instruction for Israel's future. Admonishing against idolatry, Deuteronomy lists a cavalcade of animals and celestial bodies that were forbidden to be recreated "in the likeness" as idols. The list of created things in Deuteronomy 4 comes across as stunningly coincidental to Genesis 1. Of specific interest, the creatures/objects on the list that were forbidden to be remade in their created "likeness" (תמונה) resemble most directly the creation account:[45]

Object Name	Genesis 1	Deuteronomy 4
Male/Female	זכר ונקבה 27	זכר או ניקבה 16
Beast	הבהמה 24–25	הבהמה 17
Winged birds	עוף כנף 21	כנף אשר תעוף 17
Creeping thing	ורמש 24	רמש 18
Fish/Sea	בדגת הים 26	דגה אשר במים 18
Stars	הכוכבים 16	הכוכבים 19

The list in Deuteronomy so closely resembles the creation list of Genesis 1 that it appears to form a prescription, describing these created objects as, "things that YHWH your God has allotted to all the peoples under the whole heaven" (Deut 4:19).[46] The implication is that these creatures/objects were created by God and therefore, they should not be confused with the creator. Moreover, the reason they should not is because these created things are not the same as the God who rescued them from Egypt (Deut 4:20).[47]

After Moses expounds the penalties for making idols in the likeness of created things he directly appeals to the theophany when YHWH spoke from the fire in Exodus (Deut 4:33), which only compares to the creation

---

45. The terms used to describe the created things throughout both texts are "kind" (למינה) in Gen 1 and "likeness" (תמונה) here in Deut 4. Whether or not these terms would have been lexically-connected in an ancient reader's mind, the notion of "similitude" is intended with items listed in both Gen 1 and Deut 4.

46. Christensen titles this section of his commentary: *Israel Is to Worship the Creator—Not Created Images (4:11–24): Deuteronomy 1:1—21:9*, 82–90; Cf. MacDonald, *Deuteronomy*, 192–98; Weinfeld, *Deuteronomy 1–11*, 194–214; Olson, *Deuteronomy and the Death of Moses*, 33–37; Fishbane, *Biblical Interpretation*, 321.

47. It is only here in Deut 4 where we see a special and direct appeal to creation.

Biblical Knowing

event itself (Deut 4:32). This comparison to the creation event is the only direct appeal of its kind in Deuteronomy. The narrator offers this conclusion, "To you it was shown *that you might know* (לדעת) that YHWH is God; there is no other besides him" (Deut 4:35), and then repeats, "*Know* (וידעת) therefore today . . . that YHWH is God in heaven above and on the earth beneath; there is no other" (Deut 4:39). Knowledge comes through relationship, experience, and as we have previously argued, prophetic interpretation. Moses' interpretive voice conjoins Israel's embodied, testimonial, and historical knowledge with her future knowledge of a fruitful land and covenant foretold throughout Deuteronomy.

In Deuteronomy 4, we have a call to listen (Deut 4:1), to remember (Deut 4:9), to forbid idols that image creation (Deut 4:15–24), and we have an appeal to knowledge based on what Israel has seen (Deut 4:35). Because of this theme that flourishes throughout Deuteronomy, O'Dowd concludes, "Israel's epistemology is grounded in the ontological and ethical nexus of the creation myth,"[48] and: "Significantly, 4:32–39 appeals to both senses where Israel's seeing signs and hearing testimony of God's works testify to his uniqueness. In verses 32–34, Israel is led to conclude that no such acts as the Horeb revelation or the Egypt deliverance have occurred since creation."[49]

Referring back to this one historical incident at Mount Sinai, Deuteronomy shapes Israel's knowledge. YHWH speaking from the fire at Horeb ties Israel back to the creation event itself. In arguing a case against the idolizing of the image of YHWH in terms of the creation event, Moses chides them, "Did any people ever *hear the voice* of a god speaking out of the midst of the fire, as you have heard, and still live" (Deut 4:33)?[50] The text states that the intended effect of them hearing YHWH's voice is so that they would know that YHWH is uniquely God (4:39) and that Moses is his prophet (Deut 5:23–27).[51]

In short, Deuteronomy 4 presents us with a turn from indicative history to imperative instruction: "And now O Israel, listen to the statutes . . ." (Deut 4:1). It then follows an appeal to what Israel's "eyes have seen"

48. O'Dowd, *The Wisdom of Torah*, 31.

49. Ibid., 41.

50. This specific utilization of שמע קול appears only in chapters 4 and 5 within Deuteronomy a total of six times. Cf. instances of *hear* and *voice* where it is not in the sense of obedience, rather an experience: Deut 4:33, 36; 5:23, 24, 25, 26.

51. This is not an argument for monotheism, rather it also serves as the phenomenological basis for proscribing the image of god/s made into idols (4:15).

with the comment that those who have "clung to YHWH your God are all alive today" (Deut 4:3–4).[52] After some portending of blessings and curses, we return to the epistemological crux of this unit. Particularly, "To you it was shown, *that you might know* that YHWH is God; there is no other besides him" (Deut 4:35). Setting aside the issue of monotheism, we may ask, "What was shown to Israel and how does the showing function in her epistemological process?"

Going back to the rhetorical beginning of this section (Deut 4:32), we see that the creation of heaven and earth is again invoked as the comparative example of what they have seen (e.g., they have heard the voice of God, seen the fire, and seen the signs and wonders). How do these perceivable demonstrations make any sense to the Israelites? We have contended that these *seeings* are only coherent to the Israelites if there is a voice to whom Israel listens *and* that prophetic voice can interpret what Israel is seeing. Mere seeing, as in witnessing, is not equivalent to knowing or believing as has been demonstrated in Genesis and Exodus.[53] Even the fact that Moses is *re*-interpreting this event, re-visiting it in Deuteronomy and re-explaining its significance, argues against the notion of brute seeing.[54]

The call for Israelites to remember what they saw requires a prior submission to listen to the voice of Moses "in order to see" those "great deeds of terror." The prior submission to Moses as prophet is captured in the continual "listen to his voice" statements. In other words, here in Deuteronomy 4 as in Exodus 14, *listening to Moses enables Israel to see the significance of the pillar of fire and the voice they heard for themselves.*

Exodus gives us clear impetus to argue that merely seeing the Mosaic signs, which Pharaoh witnessed as well, is insufficient as a basis for

---

52. MacDonald, *Deuteronomy*, 194.

53. O'Dowd, *The Wisdom of Torah*, 93–94.

54. Geller posits that universal wisdom in the ancient world is captured metaphorically by *seeing*. It prioritizes *seeing* as the confirmation of what one has heard by way of "seeing it for themselves" (48–51). Deuteronomy 4 reverses this logic, ironically using wisdom language, to say that because Israel has seen (in wisdom rhetoric), they must now listen to these commands, teach them to their children, etc. Geller does incorporate the concept of teacher/pupil from the wisdom tradition to show that it is being rhetorically employed in the sense of "listening to a teacher." But that is as far as he takes the analysis. He understands that listening now has the priority, and we want to build upon his proposal with some amendment. Geller, *Sacred Enigmas*, 50. Schellenberg also highlights "seeing" as preeminent in Qohelet and Job over hearing, which she takes to mean that immediate experience overrides traditional wisdom. Schellenberg, *Erkenntnis als Problem*, 181–85.

understanding what Israel saw. Even in their remembrance, Israel's youth must listen to Moses in order to understand what their parents saw. Listening to Moses, now enscripturated in the text of Deuteronomy, enables Israel to see in the future as they grow distant to those acts their parents once saw and understood through Moses in their national past.

When Deuteronomy says, "Know therefore today that YHWH is God," it is presuming upon that which Israel has seen, and significantly, how what they saw had been authoritatively interpreted to them by "listening to the voice of" their prophet Moses. *Therefore, listening to the voice of Moses takes epistemological priority over seeing.* Because they are listening to the voice of Moses and saw the fire and heard God's voice, we can expect them to know that YHWH is their God.[55]

In his conclusions regarding Deuteronomy's epistemology, O'Dowd begins with Deuteronomy's "Ontology and the Created Order." He says, "To be epistemologically engaged in ontology is to say that knowledge is acquired and justified on the basis of a preconceived understanding of reality (its origin, purpose, structure, etc.), and not with a move to 'disengaged' objectivity."[56] What we are arguing for here is O'Dowd's "preconceived understanding of reality" (i.e., the creation story) and how an Israelite would acquire it. In order for Israel to see what YHWH is showing her, she must listen to the "polyphonic voices" of the creation stories and Moses' instruction to her.[57]

Synthesis from the Pentateuch

This brief illustration from Deuteronomy is meant to establish, once again, an objective epistemological contention with which any theology, analytic or otherwise, must be confronted. Not only is knowledge present in a core narrative of Scripture (i.e., Deut 4), but also highly relevant, right at the

---

55. Seeing the fire and hearing the voice could act as a hendiadys, generically meaning "to witness an event." But we have argued that seeing must be interpreted by a prophetic voice and therefore listening has priority in the epistemological process. This is why we had to distinguish "hearing the voice of YHWH" (4:33) as merely witnessing an event from "listening to the voice of YHWH" (4:30) as the epistemological submission toward a prophetic authority. Accordingly, because they listened, they saw what was being shown and knew YHWH their God is unlike any other.

56. O'Dowd, *The Wisdom of Torah*, 163.

57. Ibid., 171.

Analytic Theology and Biblical Scholarship

center of the story. Synthesizing Deuteronomy 4 with the entirety of this study, we find:

1. There is a socio-prophetic role in knowing where authorities are established and the intended knowers either submit to or reject those authorities;
2. Knowing is a diachronic process, not a punctiliar moment in the narrative's logic, although is often comes to heightened points of illumination (e.g., Gen 2:23; Exod 14:31; Deut 4:35, Mark 8:29–33);
3. Knowledge requires the embodiment of instructions given by the authenticated authorities;
4. The biblical picture of proper knowing is relayed to us through phenomenological depiction, subjects in processes and relationships which lead them to know an objectively real world.

CONCLUSIONS

The weight of biblical scholarship along with our prior examination of the biblical texts suggests that the Scriptures fall more in the realm of a phenomenological description of epistemology than analytic modes of description. There is a clear priority given to heeding an authenticated voice, to seeing things afresh through the lenses of an interpreter, and to embodying a process in order to know. When propositional statements are averred, they do not perform the typical role of propositions in the analytic tradition, namely we cannot assess their accuracy to reality in predicate and logical relationships. Rather, proposition-like sentences act as indicators to the reader that the agents are in the diachronic process of knowing.

None of this negates the Analytic Theology project, but it should certainly cause one to pause and consider whether or not the epistemological process employed in Analytic Theology is commensurable with that about which the Scriptures appear to be concerned. Returning to our sketch of phenomenology, we said that indicators of phenomenological modes would feature:

1. continual return of our attention to the subject,
2. notions of inhabitation or indwelling as ultimate constraints and categories in philosophy,
3. heightening of embodiment,

4. rejection of the representational model of knowledge in favor of direct engagement with reality,
5. and the insistence on *the other* having some epistemic/moral authority on *the I*.

Even in our brief review of a key passage in the Pentateuch, we have shown that there is much more attention paid to the subject in the epistemological process than knowledge as an object. Embodiment of prophetic guidance has become a prerequisite for the journey toward proper knowledge. Sentences representing knowledge appear throughout Scripture, sometimes even giving the impression that they are factitive propositions. But upon closer examination, there are no definitive signals of propositional thinking in these texts. The ability of the other to intrude, even demand our submission, is fundamental to avoiding error. In fact, the central question raised by the Pentateuch's epistemological process appears to be: To what authoritative voice should we listen? As well, absent are the metaphysical concerns that figure so prominently in the prescriptions of Analytic Theology.

To be clear, we are not arguing here that the Analytic Theology project is wrong-headed or even bound for failure. However, we are broaching a significant question for theologians and philosophers who aspire to work in ways commensurable to the sacred texts from which they draw their doctrine. If good knowing per the Pentateuch begins with the question, "To whom should we ultimately listen," then it seems apropos to turn that same question on the analytic theologian. To reword our initial question posed at the fore of this chapter: Should the Scriptures be the epistemological guide for our theological prolegomena?

Again, the same question has been posed from within Analytic Theology by people such as Eleonore Stump. She claims that analytic philosophy's narrowness does not go far enough to describe a possible shortcoming of the analytic method if practiced merely by rote. Since Stump is both an insider of analytic philosophy and an expert, we will allow her the last word. In her recent work, *Wandering in Darkness*, she concludes about analytic method:

> Theories of knowledge that ignore or fail to account for whole varieties of knowledge are correspondingly incomplete; . . . it will be incomplete at best in its descriptions of reality; those parts of reality made accessible to us in experience, especially the experience

of persons and the knowledge of persons it generates, will be slighted.[58]

---

58. Stump, *Wandering in Darkness*, 59–60.

9

Implications for Theologians and the Church

FOR THE PURPOSE OF this text, it is impossible to describe all of the implications of the epistemological process as proposed here. But, in an effort to show the practical matters that have to do with the lives of theologians, philosophers, teachers, pastors, and more, we will briefly consider some reflections and paint pictures of what knowing looks like as a real life process. Further, we will describe some reverberations from thinking about the church's normal activities as epistemological processes, seeking to enliven our wisdom together in the church.

IMPLICATIONS FOR THEOLOGIANS

For those familiar with the work of T. F. Torrance, it will be obvious that we are not arguing for anything drastically different from Torrance's theological utilization of Polanyi's scientific epistemology.[1] Torrance sought to show that "[t]he task and problems of a scientific theology are not very different from"[2] a properly understood scientific epistemology. Torrance seeks to expound the affinity that theology and science share in their epistemological processes. This present work is only unique in that we have sought

---

1. Regarding some of Torrance's prolific writing on theology and science, see: *Theological Science*; *Belief*; *Reality and Evangelical Theology*; *God and Rationality*; *Christian Theology and Scientific Culture*; *Transformation and Convergence*; *Theology and Science*.

2. Torrance, *Theology and Scientific Culture*, 161.

to demonstrate that the biblical texts themselves share affinity with what Torrance and others have argued for regarding Polanyi's epistemology.[3]

If the view that we have argued for in this text befits an intentional pattern of epistemological process in the Scriptures, then what are the necessary implications for theologians and the church? We will suggest three critical ramifications that correspond to the centralizing aspects of epistemological process as we have discovered them: 1) determining the authenticated voices, 2) participating in prophetic direction, and 3) guiding others to see. We will then offer practical implications for how this could affect our views of preaching, teaching, discipling, and counseling in the local church and life contexts.

Genuflection: Determining Our Prophetic Voices

Knowing requires submission to prophetic voices, those who guide us. Whether we are young children learning our colors or adults trying to grasp quantum mechanics, we must acknowledge our guiding authorities in order to gain the skill of knowing that we seek. Trevor Hart draws this same conclusion where he says of theological epistemology:

> The pertinent question, the decision which we have to make, is not *whether* we will submit to such voices, but rather *which* voices we will submit to, and at what points and under what conditions shall we feel able or obliged to challenge what they are saying to us.[4]

There is no neutral position—autonomous humanity making choices—and so we must be aware of the prophetic voices operative over us and those that we want to be operative in our epistemological process.[5]

If authoritative voices inherently govern our theological formation, then recognizing who stands in that position of authority becomes a chief concern. Even more, recognizing who ought to stand in the position of guide is of ultimate consequence. For Christian theology, the relationship between theologian and Scripture must be meted out upon this boundary.

---

3. Of course, this is not a claim we can defend in full here. But we are also not alone in seeing these affinities. E.g., Gunton, "The Truth of Christology"; "Knowledge and Culture"; Hart, *Faith Thinking*. Although Polkinghorne regularly appeals to Polanyi, he only does so regarding the more individualistic and responsible rationalizing aspects of *Personal Knowledge*. Polkinghorne, *Theology in the Context of Science*, 73–75.

4. Hart, *Faith Thinking*, 177.

5. Torrance, "The Social Coefficient of Knowledge."

Biblical Knowing

For many of us, the Scriptures are the prophetic voice, quite literally the assemblage of the prophets' voices. The Scriptures have the ultimate position as prophet over the theologian, the voice that trumps all other voices. This does not mean that we can simply assert that the Scriptures guide us plainly in all circumstances. None have escaped the postmodern critique that has shown that all reading of the text is interpretation, bound up in our cultures, traditions, communities, and personalities. Hence, we must acknowledge the epistemological frameworks that we bring to our reading of the Scriptures.

The term genuflection means to reflect a disposition of deference or understanding of servility. The theologian's genuflection toward the Scriptures and other theologically influential voices must be sorted out in order to assess her epistemological goals. The Protestant Christian canon makes claims like those we found in Exodus: These texts can prophetically guide one to know both about God and *to know God himself* as a person—just as Moses guided the Israelites to know YHWH as their God and guided Egypt to know *about* Israel's god. If we choose to put Scripture in position as our prophetic guide, then Scripture determines who and what we can know.

Likewise, the theological voices to which we listen determine what kind of god we see in the sacred texts. Marcionite lenses guide us to different epistemological ends than would Luther's theological voice. But even if we grant the priority of Scripture as our prophetic voice, how does one adjudicate between the theological lenses with which we look *into* Scripture?[6] Even more, we have argued that if the content of the Christian canon has any authoritative sway, *then the Scriptures also look into us as we look into them.*

For Roman Catholicism, the historic prophetic voice of the unbroken Magisterium is *the* authoritative guide of the church's epistemological process, despite lingering concerns of the Magisterium's prophetic authentication. Claiming the Magisterium as our prophetic voice makes for a rather tidy epistemological process, but it does not actually help one to adjudicate between prophetic voices. Rather, it calls for basic genuflection to the voice of the Magisterium.

In the same vein, the Protestant Reformation's cry "back to the sources" (*ad fontes*) was meant to place Scripture back in position as the ultimate prophetic voice. That Protestant return to Scripture was not a bare call for individualistic readings of the texts, but rather a call to hear

---

6. We have argued here that the Scriptures "look into us" as well.

Implications for Theologians and the Church

different prophetic voices, perhaps in contrast to the singular voice of the Roman Catholic Magisterium. That is to say, theologians cannot casually assert that only Scripture or only The Magisterium act as their authority in the epistemological process as traditions, community, personal history, and more can play a subtle but significant role as a guiding voice to our reading of the texts.

While many things can guide the theologian in her reading, the pattern evinced in Scripture demands that theologians ought to justify their prophetic voice in terms of authentication. Genuflection towards a prophetically influential voice without justifying the authenticity of that voice creates first-order errors, knowledge *about* God and creation that is out of sorts with God's epistemological goals. A full description of acceptable authentication is a matter for another book, but at minimum, it is a repetitive process where trust is furnished, guidance is enacted, and reasons for future trust can be justified based on prior trust (e.g., the multiple authenticating acts of YHWH through Moses before the Israelites, Jesus' continual miracle ministry, etc.).

The question of prophetic voice is really a question of epistemological goal: What is it that we seek to know by means of this epistemological process? If one seeks to come to particular beliefs logically arranged, then one can data-mine the Scriptures in order to sort out those beliefs. This datamining approach offers both the pretense of submission to the Scriptures as prophetic guidance and rational agency in arriving at logical truths.

The problem with this approach is that it posits a different epistemological goal than what is espoused in Scripture: to know God and his kingdom (Exod 6:7; Mark 4:11; 9:1). Knowing God is clearly differentiated from *knowing about* God, because knowing God is depicted as having personal encounters with God himself.[7] For theology, if the goal is to know God himself and be able to see his kingdom, then *personal encounter with God appears to be a prerequisite for the practice of theology*. Genuflection toward the Scriptures then reflects the texts' authenticity and authority to construct an understanding of reality that shapes the theologian's understanding. Texts alone are incapable of rendering knowledge of a person. However, the text can act as an objective referent to the community's encounter with the God as His subject.

---

7. Compare Exodus' accounts of Israel's personal encounters with YHWH as her god versus Egypt's encounters with YHWH as Israel's god. As well, compare the disciples who knew Jesus (Mark 8–9) with Pilate who *knew about* Jesus (Mark 15:1–5).

Biblical Knowing

In short: if the theological enterprise sets the God referenced in Scripture as the epistemological goal of its quest, then the texts of Scripture, community confidence, and personal encounter with God must act as the primary prophetic voices that guide theologians in the process of knowing. In similitude with scientific knowing, theologians have recourse to convergence of observation just as the sciences have confirmation. God, who is the object of theological study, can be known and differentiated among competing theologies and gods (e.g., 1 Kgs 18). Better and worse understandings of this God can only be justified by theologians who both submit to the prophetic voice of Scripture and the personally encountered God of that Scripture in community. Theological enquiry that resides solely in the interpretation of the Scripture, community tradition, or in personal encounter with God has no way to discern authentication as it proceeds.

Participation: Enacting the Prophetic Direction

From the pattern observed in Scripture, participation under the guidance of Scripture and the Holy Spirit is also fundamental to theological knowledge. We cannot see that which is revealed to us by Scripture unless we enact what it requires. Knowing necessitates participation. Theological understanding will either come up vacant or go awry if theologians do not perform the process fixed in Scripture.

This could mean a host of manifestations depending on the inquirer, but it requires something from everyone who pursues Christian theological understanding. It means that theologically dissecting the Tanakh, the New Testament, or church doctrine will only yield fruitful understanding to the extent that ones lives the injunctions of those authorities. Analysis of "Loving your neighbor as yourself" (Lev 19:18) will yield some kind of knowledge about YHWH and his intentions only if someone actually practices the injunction.

As an illustration, one can learn something about the rules, the effort, and the skills required to play tennis, simply by observing a match. However, the mere observer and the tennis professional are seeing two different games when they sit next to each other at Wimbledon. There is an existential understanding of what-it-is-like-to-play-tennis that is absent in the mere observer's view.[8] Because of that absence, we cannot say that both the observer and tennis player saw the same thing when they watched the

---

8. See Hanson's analysis of "seeing" versus "seeing that." "Observation," 146.

Implications for Theologians and the Church

match, just as a doctor and layperson do not see the same thing when they look at the same X-ray. Knowing requires participation, and theological knowledge requires enacting the life of a servant of YHWH or disciple of Jesus. Clinical distance neither improves knowledge through objectivity nor renders knowledge that can be known only in fiduciary relationship (*in contractum*).

The implications of this requirement are manifest. Biblical scholars can analyze varying aspects of the texts in their hands (*in mortem* per Nietzsche), but they might never arrive at possible meanings intended by the author when they seek only axiomatic knowledge, reducing them to truths about the world. In other words, there is no process that will render the meaning of these texts outside of submitting to them and participating in their injunctions. Analyses can reveal the splendor of the texts and possibly their referent, but enacting reveals knowledge of the person: YHWH, Jesus, or others.

Michael Fishbane questions whether or not the Hebrew Bible interpreter (i.e., the hermeneut) has a unique text before her in the sense of literature, substance (ontology), or both. If both, then the duties of the hermeneut change accordingly:

> Hebrew Scripture is an ontologically unique literature: not because of its aesthetic style or topics of concern which are judged weak in comparison with contemporary medieval romances and epics but precisely because such externalities are merely the first of several garment-like layers concealing deeper and less-refracted aspects of divine truth whose core, the root of all roots, is God himself. ... The true hermeneut who is a seeker after God and not simply a purveyor of aesthetic tropes or normative rules will be drawn to this garmented bride (as the Torah is called in another text in this corpus) and will strip away the garments of Torah until he and the beloved one (God as discovered in the depths of Scripture) are one.[9]

Developing an epistemology of New Testament theology, Rosalind Selby concludes that the participatory element is crucial in order to accurately understand the texts themselves:

---

9. Fishbane, *The Garments of Torah*, 35. Even Noth probes the idea that Israel "re-presented" the Scripture in their sacramental life implying that "we would be impoverished if this manifoldness [different ways of proclaiming God's acts] were not continuously probed." "The 'Re-presentation' of the Old Testament In Proclamation," 88.

Biblical Knowing

> If we make a Polanyi-like commitment, in faith, to an epistemology and interpretation which maintains the centrality of God—his priority as the subject who founds us, and the givenness of his self-revelation through a text—logically we must pursue an ethics of reading which is true to that centrality.[10] ... *This* is the ethics of reading appropriate to an iconic text [the NT] which is a window onto the kingdom; we attend from the text to the "object" which is always subject as he reaches out to speak to us. We can never grasp this "object" and pin it down, rather we can gaze, read, study, and be self-critical in obedient response.[11]

Similarly, Lesslie Newbigin summarizes his theological epistemology: "We need to learn to know God as he is. There is no way by which we come to know a person except by dwelling in his or her story and, in the measure that may be possible, becoming part of it."[12] This requirement then weighs most heavily on the Christian theologian for it requires her to appraise her knowledge in light of her participation as a disciple of Jesus.

More than merely an ethical requirement of the theologian, participation by means of indwelling the life required by the Scriptures is how she understands the rich meaning of theological discourse.[13] Merely seeking to describe what Scripture says does not guarantee scholarly integrity, but it can obscure knowledge that cannot be had apart from participation. As a novice scientist who refuses to look down the microscope and listen to her professor removes the possibility of knowing cellular tonicity, so too is theological reality obscured from those who do not enjoin their lives to the texts.

Guidance: Helping Others to See

We have been arguing for a privileged position of theology as the task that seeks to know God and the secrets of his kingdom.[14] We have elevated the

---

10. Selby, *The Comical Doctrine*, 246.

11. Ibid., 248.

12. Newbigin, *Proper Confidence*, 88. Gunton makes a similar claim in his summary of Christian epistemology: "Knowledge and Culture," 99.

13. Cf. Moberly's suggestion that biblical theology is an "act of prayer." "How May We Speak of God?"

14. Dorman argues for a form of *heilsgeschichte methode* whereby the acknowledgment of the historical role of the Holy Spirit is acknowledged both in the Scriptures, theologians throughout history, and the current theological enterprise. The Holy Spirit

Implications for Theologians and the Church

criteria for assessing theological knowledge precisely because theology, seeking to follow what Scripture describes, must submit to the prophetic voice of Scripture and to God while also acting as a prophetic voice for others. If we believe that some theology has broader explanatory power than others, then theological insight seeking breadth of explanation must be submitted to Scriptural authority and derived by lived-participation as a disciple of Jesus.

Because theological writing and teaching claims to have insight, it must be judged as to whether it reflects proper epistemological process as evinced from Scripture. Theological claims will always act as guidance to others, and so ought to be measured with the highest scrutiny. It is patent from the Scriptures that those who act as a prophetic voice in God's community are held to higher account owing to the fact that they can *guide* others as easily as *misguide*.[15]

Thus, the epistemological goal is not merely individual, but is social as well. We do not strive to know what is being shown to us just so that we can know as an individual. We come to know God and His kingdom so that we can better point others to that same God and kingdom. Because all communicated theological knowledge becomes prophetic for others, the task demands accountability. The theologian must genuflect to an authenticated authority and participate in the life of a community of disciples. As theological knowledge grows, who God is (person) and what he is doing (kingdom) becomes the prophetic voice to others inside and outside of that community. This is the prophetic society anticipated in the New Covenant of Jeremiah.

> And no longer shall each one teach his neighbor and each his brother, saying, "Know YHWH," for they shall all know me, from the least of them to the greatest, declares YHWH. For I will forgive their iniquity, and I will remember their sin no more. (Jer 31:34)

In short: Epistemological process is fundamentally social and therefore, theological knowledge requires fiducial binding to a peculiar society: the church. Due to the accountability of the prophetic voice in that peculiar society, theologians guide others to pursue this epistemological process in submission to the same prophetic voice to whom they themselves have submitted. If this view is correct, then no theologian can claim to be

---

is then seen as the prophetic guide to the theologian. "The Future of Biblical Theology"; "Holy Spirit, History, Hermeneutics and Theology."

15. See Exod 32; Num 12; Deut 13:1–5; 18:15–22; Mark 8:11–21, et al.

experimenting harmlessly with theological ideas apart from the task of the church.

IMPLICATIONS FOR THE CHURCH

It will come as no surprise that the implications for a biblical epistemology in the church might not be radically different from the way many churches already operate. The three principles explored above—genuflection, participation, and guidance—seem to be at the center of much church liturgy and activity. Though there are many ways to express these three principles in an ecclesial tradition, some are more genuflective than others.

There are other aspects of the church that are worth considering as epistemological efforts. Briefly. We will discuss how the biblical epistemological process would inform our view of teaching, counseling, and discipleship—all of which are epistemological acts.

Teaching

The epistemological question for the teacher or preacher is one of primacy: What must be established first in order to bring others to know?[16] From the priorities that we found in Scripture, the primacy of our authentication as teachers is paramount. Notice that we did not claim that the issue of authoritative knowledge was supreme, although a teacher ought to know the Scriptures and life both soberly and authoritatively in order to bring others to know. However, without authentication, there is no fiduciary bond between the teacher and the apprentice. Without mutual commitment to the epistemological process, there is no genuine effort that can make knowing happen. Authentication is caught best by the well-worn phrase, "earning the right to be heard." After all, no one wants to expend effort under the apprenticeship of someone who may or may not guide us to know correctly. Authoritative knowledge then takes a back seat to authentication in teaching and preaching.

---

16. When addressing teaching I am including preaching into the category. I know that many have made distinctions about their differences, but when a person guides a group to see something that they could not previously see, then the epistemological process is at work. Whether or why we would call it either "teaching" or "preaching" is a slightly different matter that we need not take up.

Implications for Theologians and the Church

The best teaching exhibits the epistemological process with both the authority who is teaching and the learner fully committed to each other and to the process.[17] Some authorities are better guides. Some are more committed to the process, but not the learner. But in order to develop the skill to know something well, we must have reasons to commit to the process. Hence, authentication is not merely a badge worn by teachers, but the evidence of their fiduciary commitment to teaching counts too. Further, authentication includes the learner's sense that she will actually come to know something, to develop a skill of *getting it*. Thus, learning requires a bit of hope.

The trio of trust (i.e., faith), hope, and love fit nicely here in the category of authentication. We are not importing Paul's discussion into ours, but noticing that without reasons to trust the authority (faith), an expectation that a discernible skill will result (hope), and the commitment of both parties to each other and the act (love), good knowing is staved or truncated. Teachers and preachers submit to a biblical epistemology when they attend to their authenticity. Good teachers understand the reasons as to why they can be trusted and mistrusted. Such teachers cultivate those reasons to earn trust much like God Himself does with His own people throughout the Tanakh and New Testament. Relational stability, awareness of our own historical environs, vulnerability to be wrong, compassion, and the ability to commit are just some factors that enliven our authenticity among those we hope to teach. Brute appeals to power or authority usually deflate any epistemological confidence with learners. If God has created humanity to know in community, and Jesus' life exhibits that mission *par excellence*, then the New Testament ethic anticipates and expects that we will cultivate habits of authenticity.

As a practical example, I have found that when I am new to a group of students or parishioners, it is often better to teach in a way that I am showing my work, so to speak. I attempt to teach expositionally so that my students can see for themselves the fidelity of my teaching to the Scriptures. In the church, this might mean that a new pastor would preach with more exegetical transparency and avoid topical or theological sermons for the first year or so.

---

17. Without being lewd, this aspect of epistemological process—the committed affection to each other *and* the process—makes some sense of the overlap in meaning between "know" and "sexual intimacy" in Scripture.

Biblical Knowing

Submitting to Reality

We have intentionally held at bay the discussion regarding non-personal authorities, mainly because Scripture very rarely employs them. We could make the case that wisdom literature and parables often employ non-personal reality as a teaching authority, but there are borderline cases. The plain cases would be the use of *flora* and *fauna*. The Proverbs use the ant (*fauna*) as an authority on wisdom and work (6:6). Jesus' use of seeds and trees (*flora*) mean to instruct us about the nature of the kingdom of God (Mark 4:30–32). But even in those cases, it is the voice of a person directing us to reflect on those concrete realities that bring us to know. What about Balaam's donkey, is that not an authority from *fauna* (Num 22)? Certainly the symmetry in the narration is meant to indicate that the donkey sees what Balaam does not and that Balaam needs to be more like the donkey.[18] However, the donkey is in no way an impersonal object that teaches Balaam. As well, Paul claims in Romans 1 that all of creation brings us to awareness of God (*sensus divinitatis*). However, the kind and quality of that knowledge does not seem to act as an active authoritative guide in the process of knowing God Himself. Rather, creation is in a supportive role to the Holy Spirit which brings us to know God, just as the donkey is in a supporting role between Balaam and the messenger of YHWH.

But considering the ways in which reality can guide us to know has merit for there are direct implications for our preaching and teaching. Namely, we want to ensure that epistemological processes—especially in the church—are bent on knowing God, but also knowing the real world. More specifically, the objective world to which we make constant contact, keeps us sober about what we might and can know. For if our preaching is bent on bringing others to knowledge of some other world, knowledge that cannot be corrected or guided by reality (i.e., a Platonic heaven or a Semitic Netherworld), then we relinquish our ability to let reality guide and shape our knowledge. And as we have shown in this work, God is intent on using creation and His specially recognizable acts in creation to bring Israel to specific knowledge.

Even more than supporting roles, there are also direct ways in which objective reality acts as our authoritative guide, if we submit to its way of guiding us. If we want to know the historical context of a rock, how could

---

18. For a literary analysis of Num 22, see Johnson, "Error and Epistemological Process," 99–103.

Implications for Theologians and the Church

the rock itself guide us? We could pretend to be an authority over the rock, threatening it with a hammer and demand that it tells us what kind of a rock it is (e.g., sedentary, ultramafic, ore, glass, etc.) and how long it has been in the place we found it. Obviously, this is an absurd example. After all, why would a rock know our English language classifications for minerals? And, it is also absurd because rocks do not speak, at least, not directly. There are ways to determine what kind of a rock it is, according to the classifications that we have constructed, and even ways to determine its age and conditions of its origins. But we must submit to the rock's way of speaking to us. We must understand that rocks cannot prove their age or lineage by means of driver's license.

And so we can come to know something about a rock, but not by asking absurd questions. Rather, we can begin a properly contextualized epistemological process only when we are willing to ask the question: How can this rock tell us about itself? Similarly, I've been told that wild horses work much the same way. When captured, they will only let us know them after we enter their world on their terms. They become the authority on how we will know them, revealing only their ability to be sweet after we have spent the right amount of time with them, learned to lower our voice, monitor our eye movements, and so on. It has been observed that children and other-aged humans work in a very similar fashion, being the authority on how they will reveal themselves to others. When we are too aggressive, or ask absurd questions, then people will often close down, defend, hibernate from us, and no longer guide us to know the more vulnerable version of themselves.

Learning how to properly submit to creation in order to know it is also instructive for our treatment of Scripture. First, learning how creation reveals itself to us in an epistemological process helps us to ground our preaching and teaching in reality. The real world is not accidental to God's kingdom that has already come and is coming. And so knowing reality and groping toward our Maker by what has been made should not be accidental to our preaching. Second, we learn how to know God in Scripture by practicing on creation, by learning how to ask the right questions, and by learning to excise the absurd questions.

How does creation gain authentication with us? In all these instances—the objective reality of a rock in the world, a live animal thrashing, or even a foster child entering a new family—the reality of these people and things being in the world authenticates them. We are stepping well outside of the biblical account of knowing as a developed theme, but we are well within the presumptions of Scripture. The brute reality of events and objects, not the interpretation of these things, self-authenticates objects and events. An example would be helpful. YHWH as the pillar of fire, the objective reality of a baby in Mary's womb, Jesus' public miracles, the resurrection, the Holy Spirit poured out on the Gentiles, and more are all meant to function as revelation (i.e., revealing something about God and His covenants) precisely because they were objectively real events. These non-personal realities—events proffered to happen in the real world despite how anyone would interpret them—confronted those characters of Scripture and had to be epistemologically dealt with or denied.[19] They were authoritative inasmuch as they are authenticated as objectively real, recognizable (i.e., not secret), and demanding that the participants of those narratives no longer view themselves as the authority, no longer able to demand answers to absurd questions.

In the same vein, non-personal reality is submitted to by the scientist. Their questions are posited and modified in the scientific method precisely because the reality being studied is an authority on the study. The reality of molecular structures or animal behavior modifies the scientist's questions, rejects absurdities, and is authentic to the scientist because it is presumed to be real.

If this is even partially correct, the implications spill directly into teaching and preaching. Any authority who attempts to guide others in the epistemological process risks de-authentication when they extend knowing into the unreal, that which is not known by experience or cannot be known. Or, at the very least, the teacher must let reality sober and temper their knowledge. Seeking to explain the essences of the heavens or realities of which they have not personally understood can de-credit the speaker. What they espouse must respect the real world, and in some fundamental way, submit to its authority. It cannot be Platonic in the sense that it cannot posit the heavens as the true reality and the material world as the source of our deception. Our theology cannot be what Nietzsche called "world-fleeing."[20] Authentic teaching jibes with reality because it respects both the

---

19. A baby or resurrection are non-personal only in that they are a real situation that obliges the character's response, despite the fact that they involve persons.

20. Although he probably acquired the idea that Christianity is essentially a world-fleeing mentality from his good friend Franz Overbeck, the idea remains the same: "It was the sick and decaying who despised body and earth and invented the heavenly realm and the redemptive drops of blood. . . . Ungrateful, these people deemed themselves

Implications for Theologians and the Church

creation by YHWH and the image of God in humanity that can see beyond a broken reality, marred by sinners sinning in sinfulness.

Identifying Absurd Questions

Even our theological questions themselves must be circumscribed by reality and the prophetic interpretation of reality found in Scripture. There are some theological questions, even big questions, that run the risk of being epistemologically absurd. The Scriptures and reality itself preclude us from pursuing them. Even the question, "What *is* God?" may not turn out to be an epistemologically helpful question, depending on what is meant by it. Since, if God is like the rock, mustang, or child discussed above, then the manner and content which He has chosen to reveal Himself to humanity are both instructive and possibly binding.

For instance, we all agree that certain medical experiments, while they might provide very useful basic research, would be inappropriate to pursue. If we can agree that it is absurd to film how long it takes human infants to die without any human touch (a real research question at one point in history!), then we already believe that there is an ethical aspect to all research questions. Thus, all epistemological pursuits are fundamentally ethical in that some things that can be known should not be known. The matter of what questions are then unethical or absurd must be reconciled by some understanding of Scripture's ethical teaching. In other words, it seems that Scripture has already fixed an ethic generally in humanity and specifically in the church that circumscribes our epistemological pursuits. Our plain understanding that research requiring cruel human death, even though it may lead to a profound insight into human anthropology, would actually lead us away from understanding what it is to be a human in covenant with God. That line of research takes us away from the very thing we are trying to understand under the auspices of gaining more knowledge. As Nietzsche expressed it:

> They think they are honoring a thing if they de-historicize it, see it sub specie aeterni—if they make a mummy out of it. Everything that philosophers have handled, for thousands of years now, has been a conceptual mummy; nothing real escaped their hands alive.[21]

---

transported from their bodies and this earth." Nietzsche, *Thus Spoke Zarathustra*, 144–45.

21. Nietzsche, *Twilight of the Idols*, 464–565.

Biblical Knowing

Thus, preaching and teaching must be very careful to understand what kinds of pursuits are at stake. Further, good teaching and preaching develop the skill to identify bad questions, ones that inherently deceive us into thinking that we are knowing more and more through less and less covenantal constraints.

Earning the Right to Be Heard

Further, those preaching and teaching must work to clarify and reify their authentication. Ordination and university degrees do not imbue accreditation by fiat or magic. Ordination and theological training are merely entry ways which have, hopefully, already shaped the teacher along the way. Accreditation comes by fidelity to a call, which I would contend must be accredited through the church. Even more, fidelity to reality, loving the broken world, the learner, and the process enough to faithfully participate renews our accreditation. We must earn the right to be heard because we have been transformed in our discernment of the kingdom of God in its particulars. The impetus to teach and preach under the sway of our transformed view must be tested for its mettle and trueness to reality by accrediting agencies (e.g., denominational bodies, agencies, churches, etc.). Moreover, authenticity must be meted out with a willingness to let accreditation be established and re-established every so often.[22]

Finally, the authority of pastors and teachers requires authentication. By implication, authentication of the teacher is most clearly evinced by the teacher who is enacting the Scripture outside of the time of teaching. By living the prescriptions of Scripture, the pastor and teacher gain the skill of knowing the kingdom and its God. More precisely, they gain authentication to teach others when they hone their skilled knowledge outside the sermon or class, regularly evaluating their own ability to discern how the kingdom of God operates and in new instances. Skills are honed and then lost and good knowing requires checks and balances to ensure that the skill is still accreditable. Teachers who do not submit themselves to the most basic requirements of discipleship, cannot be accredited.

For instance, a teacher of Scripture who shows no interest in addressing the spiritual and physical poverty in their community appears to be

---

22. This is why I hesitate at the title "preacher," as it is a foreign term in post-Christian societies such as the United Kingdom and runs the risk of presuming authentication with the title itself.

at odds with the most rudimentary epistemological process outlined by Moses in the Pentateuch and then later reified by Jesus and others in the Gospels. It is genuinely difficult for the teacher to claim to be a skilled knower of Scripture if they do not tangibly perform what is prescribed at the most basic level. But what we must notice is that while their authority to speak is questionable, their authenticity to the church is what should make us skeptical about listening to their voice.

Discipleship and Counseling

The primary difference between the epistemological process in preaching and counseling will be the public versus private nature of the processes along with the monological versus dialogical nature. Although good preaching and teaching is dialogical to some extent, it has most often been modeled as monologue. Nevertheless, how is counseling a private dialogue framed toward knowing? What is meant to be known and how?

Many young pastors are shocked when people meet with us and begin to reveal extremely desperate situations, which often require intense counseling. We are in no way prepared for this from seminary training alone. The skill of counseling is the ability to see patterns emerge from the chaotic mess of self-reported particularities, to see what is significant and why. That visionary wisdom of the counsellor notices one pattern among many. But beyond noticing a pattern, skilled wisdom enables her to work out a process through which counselees will come to know themselves and the reality within which they struggle soberly. There can be many other facets of life mitigating the epistemological process of counseling: church discipline, family systems, self-identity, abuse, addiction, etc. But the consummate ability required of the counselor is *discernment*. The counseling process, like teaching, requires trust, hope, and love in order for both parties to know well.

If humans are created for deep covenantal relationship with God and others (including creation itself!), shattered family systems and individual relationships require a significant amount of savvy in order to understand what is central versus peripheral, and what takes primacy in the process of coming to know. Indeed, all counsellors will tell about the failure of counselees to commit to the fiduciary relationship for reasons of trust, hope, or failure to love. But the counsellor's role in the epistemological process is as an authority.

Biblical Knowing

Counseling, discipleship, and even the application portion of preaching all share this as common: humans need someone outside of themselves to guide them. Indeed, this was epistemically normal before the Fall (Gen 3). The man was "not good" when it was just YHWH Elohim and him in the Garden. The man needed both someone else (God) and reality itself (the animals) to lead him to see who his proper mate would be. With broken humanity after the Fall, we desperately need others so that we can come to know who we are soberly. Of the many things that we may want to say here, let us restrict ourselves to this thought: epistemological process in Scripture envisions a community of people who counsel, disciple, and coach one another because they cannot know themselves, each other, or God well without such external help. The particular role of counseling then becomes specialized, above and beyond that normative way of knowing well by means of regular counsel.[23]

Conclusion

While the above treatment is in no way full enough, it hopefully provokes further thought on how the church can benefit from seeing its own initiatives and activities as epistemological processes. Framing our counseling or preaching as acts of knowing forces us to think about how to structure the act of knowing and what types of ends are possible. Even more, this view allows us to understand some ways in which the process goes awry.

---

23. The wisdom literature has much to say about this (e.g., Prov 15:22; Ps 1) and unfortunately, wisdom literature is annexed as a means holy and sagacious insight, and thus, annexed out from our understanding of our normative knowing.

Bibliography

Abraham, William. "Systematic Theology as Analytic Theology." In *Analytic Theology*, edited by Oliver D. Crisp and Michael C. Rea, 54–69. New York: Oxford University Press, 2009.
Alston, William P. *Perceiving God: The Epistemology of Religious Experience*. Ithaca, NY: Cornell University Press, 1991.
Anderson, Gary A. *The Genesis of Perfection*. Louisville, KY: Westminster John Knox, 2003.
———. *Sin: A History*. New Haven, CT: Yale University Press, 2009.
Anderson, Gary A., and Michael E. Stone, editors. *A Synopsis of the Books of Adam and Eve*. 2nd ed. Early Judaism and Its Literature no. 17. Atlanta: Scholars, 1999.
Anderson, Hugh. "The Old Testament in Mark's Gospel." In *The Use of the Old Testament in the New and Other Essays: Studies in Honor of William Franklin Stinespring*, edited by James M. Efird, 280–306. Durham, NC: Duke University Press, 1972.
Anscombe, G. E. M. "On Brute Facts." *Analysis* 18.3 (1958) 69–72.
———. "What Is It to Believe Someone?" In *Rationality and Religious Belief*. University of Notre Dame Studies in the Philosophy of Religion, no. 1, edited by C. F. Delaney, 141–51. London: University of Notre Dame Press, 1979.
Anscombe, G. E. M., and Sidney Morgenbesser. "The Two Kinds of Error in Action." *Journal of Philosophy* 60.14, Symposium: Human Action (1963) 393–401.
Aristotle. *Posterior Analytics*. In *The Complete Works of Aristotle*. The Revised Oxford Translation, edited by Jonathan Barnes, 160–231. Princeton, NJ: Princeton University Press, 1984.
Axtell, Guy, editor. *Knowledge, Belief and Character: Readings in Virtue Epistemology*. Lanham, MD: Rowman & Littlefield, 2000.
———. "Recent Work on Virtue Epistemology." *American Philosophical Quarterly* 34.1 (1997) 1–26.
Baer, S., and Franz Delitzsch. *The Book of Genesis: The Hebrew Text After S. Baer and Delitzsch*. London: Williams and Norgate, 1890.
Bain News Service. "X-Ray of Roosevelt [shows bullet]." George Grantham Bain Collection (Library of Congress). Online: http://www.loc.gov/pictures/item/ggb2004010871/ (accessed September 12, 2012).
Barr, James. *The Concept of Biblical Theology: An Old Testament Perspective*. London: SCM, 1999.
———. *The Garden of Eden and the Hope of Immortality*. London: SCM, 1992.
Barth, Karl. *Church Dogmatics I/1*. Translated by Geoffrey Bromily et al. Edinburgh: T. & T. Clark, 1961.

Bibliography

———. *Church Dogmatics II/2*. Translated by Geoffrey Bromily et al. Edinburgh: T. & T. Clark, 1961.
———. *Church Dogmatics III/1*. Translated by Geoffrey Bromily et al. Edinburgh: T. & T. Clark, 1961.
———. *Church Dogmatics III/2*. Translated by Geoffrey Bromily et al. Edinburgh: T. & T. Clark, 1961.
———. *Church Dogmatics IV/1*. Translated by Geoffrey Bromily et al. Edinburgh: T. & T. Clark, 1961.
———. *Church Dogmatics IV/2*. Translated by Geoffrey Bromily et al. Edinburgh: T. & T. Clark, 1961.
Bartholomew, Craig. *Where Mortals Dwell: A Christian View of Place for Today*. Grand Rapids: Baker Academic, 2011.
Bartholomew, Craig, and Mike W. Goheen. "Story and Biblical Theology." In *Out of Egypt: Biblical Theology and Biblical Interpretation*. The Scripture and Hermeneutics Series, edited by Craig Bartholomew et al., 144–71. Carlisle, UK: Paternoster, 2004.
Bartholomew, Craig, and Ryan O'Dowd. *Old Testament Wisdom Literature: A Theological Introduction*. Downers Grove, IL: InterVarsity, 2011.
Bartholomew, Craig, et al., editors. *Out of Egypt: Biblical Theology and Biblical Interpretation*. The Scripture and Hermeneutics Series, vol. 5. Carlisle, UK: Paternoster, 2004.
Beale, G. K. *We Become What We Worship: A Biblical Theology of Idolatry*. Nottingham, UK: Apollos, 2008.
Beavis, Mary Ann. *Mark's Audience: The Literary and Social Setting of Mark 4.11–12*. Journal for the Study of the New Testament Supplement Series 33. Sheffield, UK: JSOT, 1989.
Bennema, Cornelius. "Christ, the Spirit and the Knowledge of God: A Study in Johnannine Epistemology." In *The Bible and Epistemology: Biblical Soundings on the Knowledge of God*, edited by Mary Healy and Robin Parry, 107–33. Milton Keynes, UK: Paternoster, 2007.
Berg, Werner. "Der Sündenfall Abrahams und Saras nach Gen 16:1–6." *Biblische Notizen* 19 (1982) 7–14.
Berkof, Louis. *Systematic Theology*. Edinburgh: Banner of Truth, 2000.
Biddle, Mark E. *Missing the Mark: Sin And Its Consequences in Biblical Theology*. Nashville, TN: Abingdon, 2005.
Biderman, Shlomo. *Scripture and Knowledge: An Essay on Religious Epistemology*. Leiden: Brill, 1995.
Blakley, J. Ted. "Incomprehension or Resistance?: The Markan Disciples and the Narrative Logic of Mark 4:1—8:30." Ph.D. diss., University of St Andrews, 2008.
Bornemann, Robert. "Toward a Biblical Theology." In *The Practice and Promise of Biblical Theology*, edited by John Reumann, 117–28. Minneapolis: Fortress, 1991.
Buber, Martin. *I and Thou*. Translated by Walter Kaufmann. Edinburgh: T. & T. Clark, 1970.
Buoninsegna, Duccio di. "The Transfiguration." ca. 1308–11, National Gallery, London. Online: http://commons.wikimedia.org/wiki/File:Duccio_di_Buoninsegna_-_Transfiguration_-_WGA06780.jpg (accessed September 12, 2012).
Braulik, Georg. *The Theology of Deuteronomy: Collected Essays of Georg Braulik*. Translated by Ulrika Lindblad. Richland Hills, TX: BIBAL, 1994.
Briggs, Richard. "Review Article: On Christian Theological Interpretation of Scripture Built upon the Foundation of the Apostles and the Prophets: The Contribution of

Bibliography

R. W. L. Moberly's *Prophecy and Discernment*." *Journal of Theological Interpretation* 4.2 (2010) 309–18.

Brocken Inaglory. "Two silhouette profiles or a white vase?," ca.2009, Wikimedia, http://en.wikipedia.org/wiki/File:Two_silhouette_profile_or_a_white_vase.jpg (accessed February 22, 2013).

Brueggemann, Walter. *The Creative Word: Canon as a Model for Biblical Education.* Philadelphia: Fortress, 1982.

———. *Genesis.* Interpretation. Atlanta: John Knox, 1982.

Calvin, Jean. *Commentaries on the First Book of Moses, Called Genesis.* Edinburgh: Calvin Translation Society, 1847.

———. *Commentaries on the Four Last Books of Moses, Arranged in the Form of a Harmony.* Translated by Charles William Bingham. Grand Rapids: Eerdmans, 1950.

———. *Commentary on a Harmony of the Evangelists, Matthew, Mark and Luke.* Vols. 1–3. Translated by William Pringle. Edinburgh: Calvin Translation Society, 1845–46.

———. *Institutes of the Christian Religion.* 1536 edition. Edited by John T. McNeill. Translated by Ford Lewis Battles. Louisville, KY: Westminster John Knox, 1960.

Carasik, Michael. *Theologies of the Mind in Biblical Israel.* Studies in Biblical Literature 85. Oxford: Lang, 2005.

Cassuto, Umberto. *A Commentary on the Book of Genesis.* Jerusalem: Magnes, 1961.

Christensen, Duane L. *Deuteronomy 1:1—21:9.* 2nd ed. Word Biblical Commentary 6A. Nashville, TN: Thomas Nelson, 2001.

———. *Deuteronomy 21:10—34:12.* Word Biblical Commentary 6B. Nashville, TN: Thomas Nelson, 2002.

Clark, W. Malcolm. "A Legal Background to the Yahwist's Use of 'Good and Evil' in Genesis 2–3." *Journal of Biblical Literature* 88 (1969) 266–78.

Coady, C. A. J. *Testimony—A Philosophical Study.* Oxford: Oxford University Press, 1994.

Collins, Adela Yarbro. *Mark.* Hermeneia. Minneapolis: Fortress, 2007.

Crisp, Oliver D. "On Analytic Theology." In *Analytic Theology*, edited by Oliver D. Crisp and Michael C. Rea, 33–53. New York: Oxford University Press, 2009.

———. *Retrieving Doctrine: Essays in Reformed Theology.* Milton Keynes, UK: Paternoster, 2011.

Crisp, Oliver D., and Michael C. Rea, editors. *Analytic Theology: New Essays in the Philosophy of Theology.* New York: Oxford University Press, 2009.

Davies, G. Henton. *Exodus: Introduction and Commentary.* Torch Bible Commentaries. London: SCM, 1967.

Delano, Jack. "Chicago, Illinois. Provident Hospital. Dr. B. W. Anthony discussing an x-ray negative with two interns." Library of Congress Prints and Photographs Division, http://www.loc.gov/pictures/item/owi2001002808/PP/ (accessed September 12, 2012).

Dewey, Joanna. "Mark as Interwoven Tapestry: Forecasts and Echoes for a Listening Audience." *Catholic Biblical Quarterly* 53 (1991) 221–36.

Documents of the II Vatican Council. "Dei Verbum." IV, 16. Online: http://www.vatican.va/archive/hist_councils/ii_vatican_council/documents/vat-ii_const_19651118_dei-verbum_en.html (accessed: 9 June 2010).

Dorman, Ted M. "The Future of Biblical Theology." In *Biblical Theology: Retrospect and Prospect*, edited by Scott J. Hafemann, 250–66. Leicester, UK: Apollos, 2002.

———. "Holy Spirit, History, Hermeneutics and Theology: Toward and Evangelical/Catholic Consensus." *Journal of Evangelical Theological Society* 41.3 (1998) 427–38.

Bibliography

Dretske, Fred I. "Précis of *Knowledge and the Flow of Information.*" In *Naturalizing Epistemology*, 2nd ed., edited by Hilary Kornblith, 217–38. Cambridge: MIT, 1997.

Eaton, John. "Memory and Encounter: An Educational Ideal." In *Of Prophets' Visions and the Wisdom of Sages*, edited by Heather A. McKay and David J. A. Clines, 179–91. JSOTSup 162. Sheffield, UK: JSOT, 1993.

Eichrodt, Walther. "Is Typological Exegesis an Appropriate Method?" In *Essays on Old Testament Hermeneutics*, edited by Claus Westermann, 224–45. London: SCM, 1963.

———. *Theology of the Old Testament*, vols. 1 & 2. Louisville, KY: Westminster John Knox, 1967.

Feldman, Richard. *Epistemology*. Foundations of Philosophy Series. Upper Saddle River, NJ: Prentice Hall, 2003.

Fenton, J. C. "Paul and Mark." In *Studies in the Gospels: Essays in Memory of R. H. Lightfoot*, edited by D. E. Nineham, 89–112. Oxford: Blackwell, 1955.

Fish, Stanley. *Is There a Text in This Class? The Authority of Interpretive Communities*. Cambridge: Harvard University Press, 1980.

Fishbane, Michael A. *Biblical Interpretation in Ancient Israel*. Oxford: Clarendon, 1985.

———. *Biblical Myth and Rabbinic Mythmaking*. Oxford: Oxford University Press, 2003.

———. *The Garments of Torah: Essays in Biblical Hermeneutics*. Indiana Studies in Biblical Literature. Bloomington, IN: Indiana University Press, 1992.

Foley, Richard. "Egoism in Epistemology." In *Socializing Epistemology: The Social Dimensions of Knowledge*, edited by Frederick F. Schmitt, 53–74. Lanham, MD: Rowman & Littlefield, 1994.

———. *Intellectual Trust in Oneself and Others*. Cambridge: Cambridge University Press, 2001.

Foster, John. *Church of the T'ang Dynasty*. London: SPCK, 1939.

Fox, Michael V. "The Epistemology of the Book of Proverbs." *Journal of Biblical Literature* 126.4 (2007) 669–84.

———. "Ideas of Wisdom in Proverbs 1–9." *Journal of Biblical Literature* 116.4 (1997) 613–33.

Frankfurt, Harry G. "On Bullshit". *The Raritan Reveiw* 6.2 (1986) 81–100.

Frege, Gottlob. *Grundgesetze der Arithmetik*. In *Translations from the Philosophical Writings of Gottlob Frege*, edited by Peter Geach and Max Black, 137–265. Oxford: Blackwell, 1960.

Fretheim, Terence E. *Exodus*. Interpretation. Louisville, KY: John Knox, 1991.

Geller, Stephen. *Sacred Enigmas: Literary Religion in the Hebrew Bible*. New York: Routledge, 1996.

Gerhardsson, Birger. "The Parable of the Sower and its Interpretation." *New Testament Studies* 14 (1968) 165–93.

Gettier, Edmund L. "Is Justified True Belief Knowledge?" *Analysis* 23.6 (1963) 121–23.

Gibson, Jeffrey B. "The Rebuke of the Disciples in Mark 8:14–21." *Journal for the Study of the New Testament* 27 (1986) 31–47.

Gödel, Kurt. "On Formally Undecided Propositions of *Principia Mathematica* and Related Systems." In *From Frege to Gödel*, edited by Jean Van Heijenoort, 592–617. Cambridge: Harvard University Press, 1977.

Goldman, Alvin I. *Pathways to Knowledge: Private and Public*. Oxford: Oxford University Press, 2002.

———. "What Is Justified Belief?" In *Naturalizing Epistemology*, 2nd ed., edited by Hilary Kornblith, 105–30. Cambridge: MIT, 1997.

Goodman, Nelson. "Reply to an Adverse Ally." *The Journal of Philosophy* 54.17 (1957) 531–35.
Goppelt, Leonhard. *Typos: The Typological Interpretation of the Old Testament in the New.* Translated by Donald H. Madvig. Grand Rapids: Eerdmans, 1982.
Gordon, R. P. "Where Have All the Prophets Gone? The 'Disappearing' Israelite Prophet against the Background of Ancient Near Eastern Prophecy." *Bulletin for Biblical Research* 5 (1995) 67–86.
Greco, J. "Virtues and Rules in Epistemology." In *Virtue Epistemology: Essays on Epistemic Virtue and Responsibility*, edited by L. Zagzebski and A. Fairweather, 117–41. Oxford: Oxford University Press, 2001.
Grene, Marjorie Glicksman. *The Knower and the Known*. London: Faber & Faber, 1966.
Grisanti, Michael A. "Was Israel Unable to Respond to God? A Study of Deuteronomy 29:2–4." *Bibliotheca Sacra* 163 (2006) 176–96.
Gunton, Colin. "Knowledge and Culture: Towards an Epistemology of the Concrete." In *The Gospel and Contemporary Culture*, edited by Hugh Montefiore, 84–102. London: Mowbray, 1992.
———. "The Truth of Christology." In *Belief in Science and in Christian Life: The Relevance of Michael Polanyi's Thought for Christian Faith and Life*, edited by T. F. Torrance, 91–107. Edinburgh: Handsel, 1980.
Hanson, Norwood. "Observation." In *Theories and Observation in Science*, edited by Richard E. Grandy, 129–46. Englewood Cliffs, NJ: Prentice-Hall, 1973.
Hardin Russell. *Trust and Trustworthiness*. The Russell Sage Foundation Series, vol. IV. New York: Russell Sage Foundation, 2002.
Hart, Trevor. *Faith Thinking: The Dynamics of Christian Theology*. Reprint. Eugene, OR: Wipf & Stock, 2005.
Hays, Richard. *Echoes of Scripture in the Letters of Paul*. New Haven, CT: Yale University Press, 1989.
Healy, Mary, and Robin Parry, editors. *The Bible and Epistemology: Biblical Soundings on the Knowledge of God*. Milton Keynes, UK: Paternoster, 2007.
Helm, Paul. "John Calvin, the *Sensus Divinitatis*, and the Noetic Effects of Sin." *International Journal for Philosophy of Religion* 43 (1998) 87–107.
———. Review of *Warranted Christian Belief*. *Mind* New Series 110.440 (2001) 1110–15.
Heidegger, Martin. *The Basic Problems of Phenomenology*. Studies in Phenomenology and Existential Philosophy. Rev. ed. Translated by Albert Hofstadter. Bloomington, IN: Indiana University Press, 1988.
Hempel, Carl G. "Studies in the Logic of Confirmation (I.)." *Mind*, New Series 54.213 (1945) 1–26.
Hicks, Peter. *Evangelicals & Truth: A Creative Proposal for a Post-modern Age*. Leicester, UK: Apollos, 1998.
Hill, David. *New Testament Prophecy*. Marshalls Theological Library. London: Marshall, Morgan & Scott, 1979.
Hollander, John. *The Figure of Echo: A Mode of Allusion in Milton and After*. Berkeley: University of California Press, 1981.
Houtman, Cornelis. *Exodus*. Historical Commentary on the Old Testament vol. 1. Translated by Johan Rebel. Leuven: Peeters, 2002.
Huemer, Michael. "Direct Realism and the Brain-in-a-Vat Argument." In *Epistemology*, edited by Michael Huemer, 575–89. New York: Routledge, 2002.

Bibliography

Hume, David. *A Treatise of Human Nature*. Edited by David Fate Norton and Mary J. Norton. New York: Oxford University Press, 2000.

Iverson, Kelly R. *Gentiles in the Gospel of Mark: "Even the Dogs Under the Table Eat the Children's Crumbs."* Library of New Testament Studies vol. 339. London: T. & T. Clark, 2007.

Jacobs, Struan. "Michael Polanyi and Thomas Kuhn: Priority and Credit." *Tradition and Discovery: The Polanyi Society* 33.2 (2006-7) 26-36.

Jastrow, Joseph. "The mind's eye", ca. 1899." Online: http://socrates.berkeley.edu/~kihlstrm/images/Jastrow/JastrowDuckPopSci.jpg (accessed September 12, 2012).

Johnson, Andrew M. "Error and Epistemological Process in the Pentateuch and Mark's Gospel: A Biblical Theology of Knowing from Foundational Texts." Ph.D. diss., University of St Andrews, 2011.

———. Review of *Analytic Theology: New Essays in the Philosophy of Theology*. *Themelios*, 35.3 (2011) 504-5.

Johnson, Mark. "Some Constraints on Embodied Analogical Understanding." In *Analogical Reasoning: Perspectives of Artificial Intelligence, Cognitive Science, and Philosophy*, Synthese Library vol. 197, edited by D. H. Helman, 25-40. New York: Springer, 1988.

Kant, Immanuel. *Fundamental Principles of the Metaphysics of Morals*. Translated by Thomas Kingsmill Abbott. New York: Cosimo, 2008.

Kee, Howard Clark. "The Transfiguration in Mark: Epiphany or Apocalyptic Vision?" In *Understanding the Sacred Text: Essays in Honor of Morton S. Enslin on the Hebrew Bible and Christian Beginnings*, edited by J. Reumann. 135-52. Valley Forge, PA: Judson, 1972.

Kelber, Werner H. *The Kingdom in Mark: A New Place and a New Time*. Minneapolis: Fortress, 1974.

Kermode, Frank. *The Genesis of Secrecy*. The Charles Eliot Norton Lectures, 1977-78. Cambridge: Harvard University Press, 1979.

Kierkegaard, Søren. *Philosophical Fragments/Johannes Climacus : Kierkegaard's Writings*. Edited and translated by Howard V. Hong and Edna H. Hong. Princeton, NJ: Princeton University Press, 1985.

Kim, Jaegwon. "What is 'Naturalized Epistemology'?" In *Naturalizing Epistemology*, 2nd ed., edited by Hilary Kornblith, 33-56. Cambridge: MIT, 1997.

Kitcher, Philip. "The Naturalists Return." *Philosophical Review* 101 (1992) 53-114.

Kline, Meredith G. *By Oath Consigned: A Reinterpretation of the Covenant Signs of Circumcision and Baptism*. Grand Rapids: Eerdmans, 1975.

Kornblith, Hilary. "What is Naturalized Epistemology?" In *Naturalizing Epistemology*, 2nd ed., edited by Hilary Kornblith, 1-14. Cambridge: MIT, 1997.

Kuhn, Thomas S. *The Structure of Scientific Revolutions*. 3rd ed. Chicago: University Of Chicago Press, 1996.

Kusch, Martin. *Knowledge by Agreement: The Programme of Communitarian Epistemology*. Oxford: Clarendon, 2002.

Kvanvig, Jonathan L. *The Intellectual Virtues and the Life of the Mind: On the Place of the Virtues in Epistemology*. Studies in Epistemology and Cognitive Theory. Savage, MD: Rowman & Littlefield, 1992.

Lackey, Jennifer. *Learning from Words: Testimony as a Source of Knowledge*. Oxford: Oxford University Press, 2008.

Lakoff, George, and Mark Johnson. *Metaphors We Live By*. Chicago: University of Chicago Press, 1980.
Lamont, John. "A Conception of Faith in the Greek Fathers." In *Analytic Theology*, edited by Oliver D. Crisp and Michael C. Rea, 87–116. New York: Oxford University Press, 2009.
Legge, James. *The Nestorian Monument of His-an Fu in Shen-his, China, Relating to the Diffusion of Christianity in China*. London: Trubner, 1888.
MacDonald, Nathan. *Deuteronomy and the Meaning of "Monotheism."* Forschungen zum Alten Testament 2 Reihe. Tübingen: Mohr Siebeck, 2003.
———. "Food and Diet in the Priestly Material of the Pentateuch." In *Theology on the Menu: Asceticism, Meat and Christian Diet*, edited by David Grumett and Rachel Muers, 17–30. London: Routledge, 2010.
———. *Not Bread Alone—The Uses of Food in the Old Testament*. Oxford: Oxford University Press, 2008.
———. "Recasting the Golden Calf: The Imaginative Potential of the Old Testament's Portrayal of Idolatry." In *Idolatry: False Worship in the Bible, Early Judaism and Christianity*, edited by Stephen C. Barton, 22–39. London: T. & T. Clark, 2007.
McConville, J. G. *Deuteronomy*. Apollos Old Testament Commentary, vol. 5. Leicester, UK: Apollos, 2002.
McGinn, Colin. *Problems in Philosophy: The Limits of Inquiry*. Oxford: Blackwell, 1993.
Malul, Meir. *Knowledge, Control and Sex; Studies in Biblical Thought, Culture and Worldview*. Tel Aviv: Archaeological Center, 2002.
Marcus, Joel. *Mark 1-8*. The Anchor Yale Bible. New Haven, CT: Yale University Press, 2009.
———. *Mark 8-16*. The Anchor Yale Bible. New Haven, CT: Yale University Press, 2009.
———. "Mark 4:10–12 and Marcan Epistemology." *Journal of Biblical Literature* 103.4 (1984) 557–74.
Matera, Frank J. "The Incomprehension of the Disciples and Peter's Confession (Mark 6:14—8:30)." *Biblica* 70.2 (1989) 153–72.
Meek, Esther Lightcap. "Contact with Reality: An Examination of Realism in the Work of Michael Polanyi." Ph.D. diss., Temple University, 1985.
———. *Longing to Know: The Philosophy of Knowledge for Ordinary People*. Grand Rapids: Brazos, 2003.
———. "'Recalled to Life': Contact with Reality." *Tradition and Discovery: The Polanyi Society* 26.3 (1999–2000) 72–83.
Merleau-Ponty, Maurice, *The Primacy of Perception*. Translated by James M. Edie. Evanston, IL: Northwestern University Press, 1964.
Mettinger, Tryvve N. D. *The Eden Narrative: A Literary and Religio-historical Study of Genesis 2-3*. Winona Lake, IN: Eisenbrauns, 2007.
Miller, Patrick D. *Deuteronomy*. Interpretation. Louisville, KY: John Knox, 1990.
———. *The Way of the Lord*. Grand Rapids: Eerdmans, 2007.
Milgrom, Jacob. *Leviticus 1-16: A New Translation with Introduction and Commentary*. The Anchor Bible 3. New York: Doubleday, 1991.
Moberly, R. W. L. "Did the Serpent Get It Right?" *Journal of Theological Studies* 39.1 (1988) 1–27.
———. "How May We Speak of God?: A Reconsideration of the Nature of Biblical Theology." *Tyndale Bulletin* 53.2 (2002) 177–202.

Bibliography

———. *Prophecy and Discernment*. Cambridge Studies in Christian Doctrine. Cambridge: Cambridge University Press, 2006.

———. *The Theology of the Book of Genesis*. Old Testament Theology. Cambridge: Cambridge University Press, 2009.

Moffet, Samuel. *A History of Christianity in Asia: Volume I*. San Francisco: HarperSanFrancisco, 1992.

Moran, Dermot. *Introduction to Phenomenology*. New York: Routledge, 2000.

Moser, Paul K. *The Elusive God: Reorienting Religious Epistemology*. New York: Cambridge University Press, 2008.

Nagel, Thomas. "What Is It Like To Be A Bat?" In *The Mind's I: Fantasies and Reflections on Self and Soul*, 391–402. Toronto: Bantam, 1982.

"NASA's first major attempt to tell the story of the US Space Program graphically," (Unknown photographer) ca.1962, University of Washington Libraries Digital Collections. Online: http://content.lib.washington.edu/u?/seattle,2384 (accessed September 12, 2012).

Nelson, Richard D. *Deuteronomy: A Commentary*. The Old Testament Library. Louisville, KY: Westminster John Knox, 2002.

Nestle, Eberhard, and Kurt Aland, editors. *Novum Testamentum Graece*. 27th ed. Stuttgart: Deutsche Bibelstiftung, 1998.

Newbigin, Lesslie. *Proper Confidence: Faith, Doubt, and Certainty in Christian Discipleship*. Grand Rapids: Eerdmans, 1995.

Nietzsche, Friedrich Wilhelm. *Thus Spoke Zarathustra*. Edited & translated by Walter Kaufmann. New York: Penguin, 1976.

———. *Twilight of the Idols*. In *The Portable Nietzsche*, 464–564. New York: Penguin, 1982.

———. *Writings from the Late Notebooks*. Edited by Rüdiger Bittner. Translated by Kate Sturge. Cambridge Texts in the History of Philosophy. Cambridge: Cambridge University Press, 2003.

Noth, Martin. *Exodus: A Commentary*. Old Testament Library. London: SCM, 1962.

———. *Numbers: A Commentary*. The Old Testament Library. London: SCM, 1968.

———. "The 'Re-presentation' of the Old Testament in Proclamation." In *Essays on Old Testament Interpretation*, 76–88. London: SCM, 1963.

Nussbaum, Martha C. *Love's Knowledge: Essays on Philosophy and Literature*. Oxford: Oxford University Press, 1990.

———. "Mill between Aristotle and Bentham." *Daedalus* 133.2 (2004) 60–68.

O'Dowd, Ryan P. "Memory on the Boundary: Epistemology in Deuteronomy." In *The Bible and Epistemology*, edited by Mary Healey and Robin Parry, 3–22. Carlisle, UK: Paternoster, 2007.

———. *The Wisdom of Torah: Epistemology in Deuteronomy and the Wisdom in Literature*. Forschungen zur Religion und Literatur des Alten und Neuen Testaments Band 225. Göttingen: Vandenhoeck & Ruprecht, 2009.

Olson, Dennis T. *Deuteronomy and the Death of Moses: A Theological Reading*. Overtures to Biblical Theology. Minneapolis: Fortress, 1994.

———. "Truth and the Torah." In *But Is It All True?: The Bible and the Question of Truth*, edited by Alan G. Padgett and Patrick R. Keifert, 16–33. Grand Rapids: Eerdmans, 2006.

Overholt, Thomas W. "Prophecy: The Problem of Cross-cultural Comparison." *Semeia* 21 (1981) 55–78.

Patrick, Dale. *The Rhetoric of Revelation in the Hebrew Bible*. Overtures to Biblical Theology. Minneapolis: Fortress, 1999.

Peels, Rik. "The Effects of Sin upon Human Moral Cognition." *Journal of Reformed Theology* 4 (2010) 42–69.

Plantinga, Alvin. *Warranted Christian Belief*. Oxford: Oxford University Press, 2000.

Plantinga Jr., Cornelius. *Not the Way It's Supposed to Be: A Breviary of Sin*. Grand Rapids: Eerdmans, 1995.

Polanyi, Michael. *Personal Knowledge: Towards a Post-Critical Philosophy*. Chicago: University of Chicago Press, 1974.

———. *The Tacit Dimension*. Chicago: University of Chicago Press, 2009.

Polkinghorne, John. *Theology in the Context of Science*. London: SPCK, 2008.

Quine, W. V. O. "Epistemology Naturalized." In *Naturalizing Epistemology*, 2nd ed., edited by Hilary Kornblith, 15–32. Cambridge: MIT, 1997.

———. "Natural Kinds." In *Ontological Relativity and Other Essays*, 114–38. New York: Columbia University Press, 1969.

———. *Ontological Relativity and Other Essays*. New York: Columbia University Press, 1969.

Rae, Murray A. "'Incline Your Ear So That You May Live': Principles of Biblical Epistemology." In *The Bible and Epistemology*, edited by Mary Healey and Robin Parry, 161–80. Carlisle, UK: Paternoster, 2007.

———. *Kierkegaard's Vision of the Incarnation: By Faith Transformed*. Oxford: Oxford University Press, 1998.

Rahner, Karl. *The Church and the Sacraments*. New York: Hyperion, 1994.

———. *Theological Investigations*, vol. IV. Translated by Cornelius Ernst. Baltimore, MD: Helicon, 1961.

Ramanan, Venkata K. *Nagarjuna's Philosophy: As Presented in the Maha-Prajnaparamita-Sastra*. New Delhi: Motilal Banarsidass, 1986.

Rauser, Randal. "Theology as a Bull Session." In *Analytic Theology*, edited by Oliver D. Crisp and Michael C. Rea, 70–84. New York: Oxford University Press, 2009.

Rea, Michael C. "Introduction." In *Analytic Theology*, edited by Oliver D Crisp and Michael C. Rea, 1–32. New York: Oxford University Press, 2009.

Rendtorff, Rolf. *Canon and Theology: Overtures to an Old Testament Theology*. Overtures to Biblical Theology. Minneapolis: Augsburg Fortress, 1993.

Reno, R. R. "Theology's Continental Captivity." *First Things* 162 (2006) 26–33.

Reumann, John, editor. *The Practice and Promise of Biblical Theology*. Minneapolis: Fortress, 1991.

Ricoeur, Paul. *The Conflict of Interpretations*. Edited by Don Hide. Evanston, IL: Northwestern University Press, 1974.

———. "'Original Sin': A Study in Meaning." In *The Conflict of Interpretations*, edited by Don Hide, 269–86. Evanston, IL: Northwestern University Press, 1974.

———. *The Symbolism of Evil*. Translated by Emerson Buchanan. Religious Perspectives Series, vol. XVII. Boston: Beacon, 1967.

Rijn, Rembrandt Harmenszoon van. "The Baptism of the Ethiopian Chamberlain", ca. 1626. Online: http://www.rkd.nl/rkddb/(S(mjpgeoz4s0rtpn555z1duqfe))/detail.aspx# (accessed September 12, 2012).

Robinson, Robert B. "Narrative Theology and Biblical Theology." In *The Practice and Promise of Biblical Theology*, edited by John Reumann, 129–42. Minneapolis: Fortress, 1991.

Bibliography

Rowland, Wade. *Galileo's Mistake: A New Look at the Epic Confrontation between Galileo and the Church*. New York: Arcade, 2003.

Rudman, Dominic. "A Little Knowledge Is a Dangerous Thing: Crossing Forbidden Boundaries in Gen 3–4." In *Studies in the Book of Genesis*, 461–66. Leuven: Peeters, 2001.

Saeki, P. Y. *The Nestorian Monument in China*. London: SPCK, 1916.

Savran, George W. D. "Beastly Speech: Intertextuality, Balaam's Ass, and the Garden of Eden." *Journal for the Study of the Old Testament* 64 (1994) 33–55.

Schellenberg, Annette. *Erkenntnis als Problem: Qohelet und die alttestamentliche Diskussion um das menschliche Erkennen*. Orbis Biblicus et Orientalis no. 188. Göttingen: Vandenhoeck & Reprecht, 2002.

Scott, William Taussig, and Martin X. Moleski. *Michael Polanyi: Scientist and Philosopher*. New York: Oxford University Press, 2005.

Selby, Rosalind. *The Comical Doctrine: An Epistemology of New Testament Hermeneutics*. Paternoster Biblical Monographs. Milton Keynes, UK: Paternoster, 2006.

Sellars, Wilfrid. *Empiricism and the Philosophy of Mind*. Cambridge: Harvard University Press, 1997.

———. *Science, Perception and Reality*. London: Routledge & Kegan Paul, 1963.

Septuaginta. Edited by Alfred Rahlfs and Robert Hanhart. Stuttgart: Deutsche Biblegesellschaft, 2006.

Shea, William R., and Mariano Artigas. *Galileo in Rome: The Rise and Fall of a Troublesome Genius*. New York: Oxford University Press, 2003.

Sklar, Jay. *Sin, Impurity, Sacrifice, Atonement: The Priestly Conceptions*. Hebrew Bible monographs 2. Sheffield, UK: Sheffield Phoenix, 2005.

Sosa, Ernest. "The Raft and the Pyramid: Coherence versus Foundations in the Theory of Knowledge." *Midwest Studies in Philosophy* 5.1 (1980) 3–26.

Stanley, Jason, and Timothy Williamson. "Knowing How." *The Journal of Philosophy* 98.8 (2001) 411–44.

Stegman, Thomas D. S.J. "'The Spirit of Wisdom and Understanding': Epistemology in Luke-Acts." In *The Bible and Epistemology: Biblical Soundings on the Knowledge of God*, edited by Mary Healy and Robin Parry, 88–106. Milton Keynes, UK: Paternoster, 2007.

Stone, Kenneth. *Practicing Safer Texts: Food, Sex and Bible in Queer Perspective*. Queering Theology Series. London: T. & T. Clark, 2005.

Stordalen, T. *Echoes of Eden: Genesis 2–3 and Symbolism of the Eden Garden in Biblical Hebrew Literature*. Contributions to Biblical Exegesis and Theology 25. Leuven: Peeters, 2000.

Strecker, Georg. "The Law in the Sermon on the Mount, and the Sermon on the Mount as Law." In *The Practice and Promise of Biblical Theology*, edited by John Reumann, 35–49. Minneapolis: Fortress, 1991.

Stump, Eleonore. *Wandering in the Darkness: Narrative and the Problem of Suffering*. Oxford: Oxford University Press, 2010.

Tang, Li. *A Study of the History of Nestorian Christianity in China and Its Literature in Chinese: Together with a New English Translation of the Dunhuang Nestorian Documents*. New York: Lang, 2001.

Takakusu, J. "The Name of 'Messiah' Found in a Buddhist Book: The Nestorian Missionary Adam, Presbyter, Papas of China, Translating a Buddhist Sutra." *Varietes* or *T'oung pao* (December 1896) 581–91.

Bibliography

Taylor, Charles. "Overcoming Epistemology." In *Philosophical Arguments*, 1–19. Cambridge: Harvard University Press, 1995.
———. "Transcendental Arguments." In *Philosophical Arguments*, 20–33. Cambridge: Harvard University Press, 1995.
Tolbert, Mary Ann. *Sowing the Gospel: Mark's World in Literary-Historical Perspective*. Minneapolis: Fortress, 1989.
Torrance, Thomas F., editor. *Belief in Science and in Christian Life: The Relevance of Michael Polanyi's Thought for Christian Faith and Life*. Edinburgh: Handsel, 1980.
———. *God and Rationality*. London: Oxford University Press, 1971.
———. "One Aspect of the Biblical Conception of Faith." *Expository Times* 68.4 (1957) 111–14.
———. *Reality and Evangelical Theology: The Realism of Christian Revelation*. Downers Grove, IL: InterVarsity, 1999.
———. *Reality and Scientific Theology*. Theology and Science at the Frontiers of Knowledge no. 1. Edinburgh: Scottish Academic Press, 1985.
———. *Theological Science*. The Hewet Lectures for 1959. London: Oxford University Press, 1969.
———. *Theology and Scientific Culture*. The Theological Lectures at The Queen's University, Belfast for 1980. Belfast: Christian Journals, 1980.
———. *Transformation and Convergence in the Frame of Knowledge: Explorations in the Interrelations of Scientific and Theological Enterprise*. Belfast: Christian Journals, 1984.
Treier, Daniel J. *Virtue and the Voice of God: Toward Theology as Wisdom*. Grand Rapids: Eerdmans, 2006.
Van der Kooi, Cornelis. "The Assurance of Faith: A Theme in Reformed Dogmatics in Light of Alvin Plantinga's Epistemology." *Neue Zeitschrift für systematische Theologie und Religionsphilosophie* 40.1 (1998) 91–106.
VanGemeren, Willem A., editor. *New International Dictionary of Old Testament Theology and Exegesis*. 5 vols. Grand Rapids: Zondervan, 1997.
Vanhoozer, Kevin. *The Drama of Doctrine: A Canonical Linguistic Approach to Christian Theology*. Louisville, KY: Westminster John Knox, 2005.
———. "Lost in Interpretation? Truth, Scripture and Hermeneutics." *Journal of the Evangelical Theological Society* 48.1 (2005) 89–114.
———. *Is There a Meaning in This Text?: The Bible, the Reader, and the Morality of Literary Knowledge*. Grand Rapids: Zondervan, 1998.
Vasholz, Robert I. *The Old Testament Canon in the Old Testament Church: The Internal Rationale for Old Testament Canonicity*. Ancient Near Eastern Texts and Studies, vol. 7. Lampeter, UK: Mellen, 1990.
Von Rad, Gerhard. *Deuteronomy: A Commentary*. London: SCM, 1966.
———. *Genesis—A Commentary*. Rev. ed. Louisville, KY: Westminster John Knox, 1972.
———. *The Message of the Prophet*. Translated by D. M. G. Stalker. London: SCM, 1968.
———. *Wisdom in Israel*. Translated by James D. Martin. Nashville: Abington, 1986.
Waltke, Bruce K., and Cathi J. Fredricks. *Genesis: A Commentary*. Grand Rapids: Zondervan, 2001.
Watson, Francis. *Text and Truth: Redefining Biblical Theology*. Grand Rapids: Eerdmans, 1997.
Watts, Rikki E. *Isaiah's New Exodus and Mark*. Wissenschaftliche Untersuchungen zum Neuen Testament, 2, Reihe, 88. Tübingen: Mohr Siebeck, 1997.

Bibliography

Weinfeld, Moshe. *Deuteronomy 1–11: A New Translation with Introduction and Commentary*. The Anchor Bible 5. New York: Doubleday, 1991.
Wenham, Gordon. *Genesis 1–15*. Word Biblical Commentary vol. 1. Nashville: Thomas Nelson, 1987.
Westermann, Claus. *Genesis: An Introduction*. Minneapolis: Fortress, 1992.
Westphal, Merold. "Hermeneutics and Holiness." In *Analytic Theology*, edited by Oliver D Crisp and Michael C. Rea, 265–79. New York: Oxford University Press, 2009.
———. "Overcoming Onto-theology." In *Overcoming Onto-theology: Toward a Postmodern Christian Faith*, 1–28. New York: Fordham University Press, 2001.
———. "Taking Plantinga Seriously: Advice to Christian Philosophers." *Faith and Philosophy* 16.2 (1999) 173–81.
———. "Taking St. Paul Seriously: Sin as an Epistemological Category." In *Christian Philosophy*, 200–226. Notre Dame, IN: University of Notre Dame Press, 1990.
Wolters, Albert M. *Creation Regained: Biblical Basics for a Reformational Worldview*. Grand Rapids: Eerdmans, 1998.
Wolterstorff, Nicholas. *Reason within the Bounds of Religion*. 2nd ed. Grand Rapids: Eerdmans, 1976.
Wright, N. T. *Jesus and the Victory of God*. Christian Origins and the Question of God, vol. 2. London: SPCK, 1996.
Yagoda, Benjamin. *When You Catch an Adjective, Kill It*. New York: Broadway, 2007.
Yoder, Douglas. "Tanakh Epistemology: A Philosophical Reading of an Ancient Semitic Text." Ph.D. diss., Claremont Graduate University, 2007.
Zagzebski, Linda Trinkaus. *Virtues of the Mind: An Inquiry into the Nature of Virtue and the Ethical Foundations of Knowledge*. Cambridge: Cambridge University Press, 1996.
Zevit, Ziony. Review of *Knowledge, Control and Sex: Studies in Biblical Thought, Culture and Worldview* by Meir Malul. *Journal of the American Oriental Society* 123.3 (2003) 670–72.

Scripture Index

OLD TESTAMENT

Genesis

1–4	23
1–3	52, 54
1–2	24, 54
1	21, 23–25, 195
1:4	24, 25, 54
1:10	24, 54
1:12	24, 25, 54
1:16	195
1:17	24
1:18	24, 25, 54
1:21	24, 25, 54, 195
1:24	195
1:25	24, 54
1:26	53, 195
1:27	195
1:28	23, 25, 53
1:29	24
1:31	24, 25, 30, 54
1:33	25, 47
2–3	10, 11, 14, 24, 36, 39, 43, 47–49, 52–56, 64, 65, 96, 176, 178, 221, 225, 228
2–4	53
2	10, 22–25, 27–29, 31–37, 39–43, 51, 52, 61, 62
2:15–25	27, 43
2:15–17	40
2:16–17	56
2:18–22	27
2:18–20	25
2:24–25	26
2:9	37, 54
2:15	24, 56
2:16	24
2:17	27, 53, 79
2:19	24, 54
2:20	33
2:21	24, 56
2:22	24, 56
2:23	24, 30, 36, 56, 90, 116, 199
2:24	37, 79
2:25	62
3	10, 22–24, 26, 29, 31, 36, 40, 42–45, 47–55, 57–59, 61–63, 73, 77–79, 109, 218
3:1–6	17, 27
3:14–14	61
3:3	53
3:4	58
3:5	53
3:6	24, 54, 55, 59, 62, 63, 79
3:7	62, 116
3:12	57
3:13	58, 79, 92
3:17	41, 43, 48, 49, 55, 60, 76, 79, 116, 179
3:19	24, 56
3:22	56, 59
3:23	24, 56
3:24	79
4:1	38, 47
4:17	38, 47
4:25	38, 47
16	55, 94

Scripture Index

Genesis (*cont.*)

16:3–4	55
16:2	55
21:12	55
22	112
22:14	112
26:8	78–80
27	55
27:8	55
27:13	55
27:43	55
39:10	55

Exodus

1–14	68, 69
1	68
1:8–22	68
1:8	68, 69
2:4	73
3–34	84
3:1—4:17	130
3:21–22	79
3:7	68
4–12	85
4	74, 75, 82, 150
4:27–31	75
4:27–28	130
4:29–31	75, 89, 130
4:21	99
4:31	142, 150
5:2	68, 69
6:4–5	73
6:3	68
6:7	68, 128, 205
7–12	130
7:3	73, 99
7:5	68
7:13	99
7:17	68, 128
8:10	68
8:22	68
9:7	99
9:14	68
9:16	10, 69
9:29	68
9:30	68
9:34	10, 69, 99
10:2	68, 128
10:7	93
11:7	68
14	67, 70, 197
14:13–14	130, 142
14:30–31	70, 71, 130
14:4	68
14:13	70, 71, 93
14:18	68
14:31	67, 78, 90, 93, 142, 199
15:22–27	76
15:1	111
15:26	76, 77
16	76, 77
16:9–29	77
16:22–26	76
16:4	76
16:5	77
16:12	76, 77
16:15	77
16:16	77
16:20	77
16:29	77
20–31	78
20:23	79
23:33	93
25	79
31:3	137
32	78, 79, 209
32:1	78
32:4	78
32:6	79
32:8	79
32:20	78
32:21	60, 61, 78, 80
32:23	78
32:24	78
32:27	79
34:12	93
36:1	137

Exodus (*cont.*)

36:31	137
40:34	85

Leviticus

1–16	90
5:14–19	8
19:18	111, 206
19:34	111
26:5	114

Numbers

12	81, 134, 209
12:1–2	82
12:6–8	82
12:2	81, 82
12:3	82
12:5	82
12:8	82
12:12	82
16	81, 133, 134
16:1–40	83
16:3	133
16:7	133
16:28	83
16:30	83
22–24	81
22	31, 212
27:12–23	90

Deuteronomy

1–11	195
1:39	62, 93
1:43	62
4	186, 194–99
4:3–4	197
4:15–24	196
4:16–19	195
4:36–37	108
4:1	196
4:9	196
4:15	196
4:19	195
4:20	195
4:30	198
4:32	196, 197
4:33	195, 196, 198
4:35	90, 196, 197, 199
4:36	196
4:39	196
5:23–27	196
5:23	196
5:24	196
5:25	196
5:26	196
7:16	93
7:18	75
12:10	114
13	46, 59, 83, 84, 90
13:1–5	209
13:1–4	84
13:5	85
18	46, 59, 83, 86, 87, 90, 108, 109
18:9–14	86
18:15–22	59, 86, 128, 209
18:15	46, 86, 109
18:18	86, 109
18:21	86
29–30	73
29	83, 87, 89, 99, 100, 103, 104, 120
29:2–4	83, 96, 100
29:3–4	76, 83
29:4	3, 74, 103
29:19	1
30:1–6	104
30:15–20	91, 96
30:6	89
31:1–8	90
34:9	91, 95

Joshua

2	91
3	92

Scripture Index

Joshua (*cont.*)

3:4	92
3:10	92
4	91
4:1–7	91
4:24	92
5:6	91, 95
6:22–25	91
7:10–26	92
22:7–8	91
22:2	91
22:5	91
23:11–13	93
23:13	93

Judges

2	95
2:10–11	93
2:11–13	93
2:14–15	93
2:17–18	93
2:1	92
2:2	92
2:10	92, 93
2:19	93
6	94
9:7	80

1 Samuel

1:20	94
3:4–21	94
3:19–20	94
3:20	94
6:6	99
8:7	94
8:9	94
8:19	94, 95
8:22	94
15:19	95
15:20	95
15:22	95
15:24	10, 95
30:16	80

1 Kings

3:14	1
12:28	78
13	60
18	133, 134, 142, 206
20	95
20:23–25	95
21:17–19	111
22:35–38	111

2 Kings

18	95
18:12	95

Psalm

1	218
26:3	1
82:5	1

Proverbs

1–9	135, 138
1:1–5	137
1:5	138
1:8	138
1:33	138
2:1–2	138
2:13	1
3:1	138
3:13	137
4:10–16	137
4:1	138
4:10	138
5:7	138
7–8	137
7:24	138
8:6	138
8:32	138
8:33	138
8:34	138
9:9–10	137
10–31	138
10:8	125

Proverbs (cont.)

12:31–32	138
12:15	138
13:2–3	139
13:1	137–39
15:22	218
19:20	138
19:27	138
21:28	138
22:17	138
23:19	138
23:22	138
25:12	138
28:9	138

Ecclesiastes

12:10	140

Isaiah

6	103, 105, 106
6:9–10	3, 76, 89, 100, 103, 104, 106
6:9	99

Jeremiah

31:34	128, 209

Ezekiel

33:32	39

Hosea

8	70
13:13	138

Joel

1	70

Amos

7:14	39

Haggai

1	70

Malachi

3:1	115
4:6	115

~

NEW TESTAMENT

Matthew

5:21–26	165
5:21–22	8
5:23:24	8
19:16–22	166
26:26	63

Mark

1–8	225
1–3	102
2:1–12	133
3:13–19	102
3:5	73, 99
3:14	102
4–9	105, 106, 166
4:1—9:17	108
4:1—8:30	220
4	102–4, 106, 108, 150
4:1–20	82
4:1–10	100
4:11–12	100
4:10–12	103
4:13–34	100
4:13–20	105
4:22–23	166
4:30–34	6
4:30–32	212
4:10	98
4:11	99, 101, 102, 205
4:12	100, 102, 103
4:22	105

Scripture Index

Mark (*cont.*)

4:23	105, 106
4:24	105
4:33	108
4:41	106
5:27	108
6	108
6:1–6	106
6:7–12	106
6:30–44	106, 112
6:51–52	120
6:2	108
6:4	107
6:7	102
6:11	106, 108
6:12	102
6:13	102
6:14	108
6:16	108
6:20	108
6:29	108
6:37	120
6:52	73, 99
6:55	108
7:14–23	107
7:24–30	112
7:5	1
7:14	106, 108
7:25	108
8–16	109
8–9	134, 205
8	98, 102, 134
8:1–10	106
8:11–21	209
8:17–21	142
8:17–18	99, 120
8:22–26	100, 101
8:27–30	46
8:29–33	199
8:30–33	161
8:31–38	150
8:31–33	109
8:17	73, 99
8:18	102, 106, 108
8:29	46, 109, 150, 161
9	108
9:2–13	46
9:1	106, 205
9:7	46, 108, 120
10	166
10:17–22	166
10:35–45	101
10:46–52	101
10:36	101
11:27–30	107
13:5	107
13:22	107
15:1–5	205

Luke

1:1–4	111
1:2–3	114
1:16–17	115
1:1	113
1:3	113, 114
1:4	113, 114, 115
1:54	115
1:55	115
1:73	115
13:25–27	8
17:11–19	112
18	166
18:18–23	166
24	113
24:16	115
24:27	115, 116
24:31	116
24:32	116
24:34	118
24:42	117
24:45	117

John

4	112
6:2	108
6:4	107

John (cont.)

6:11	108
6:14	108
6:16	108
6:20	108
6:29	108
7:14–23	107
7:14	108
8:12	1
8:18	108
11:27–33	107
12	118
12:35	1
12:40	73
13:5	107
13:22	107
13:27	79
21:30–31	111
20	6, 118
20:29–31	118
20:30–31	110, 112, 120
20:20	119
20:24	119
20:25	119
20:27	119

Acts

1:6–11	6
1:6–7	117
2	109
2:22	142
2:36	114
2:43	142
4:30	142
5:12	142
6:8	142
7:36	142
8:30–31	67
8:35	67
9:26	5
9:30	5
10	6
14:3	142
15	6
15:12	142

Romans

1	212
5	57

1 Corinthians

5:12	3
10:7	80
13:12	2

2 Corinthians

5:7	1

Ephesians

1:3	144
1:8	144
1:9	144
1:17	144
1:18	144
2:1–10	145
2:1	1, 145, 146
2:10	1, 146
3:3	144
3:4	144
3:10	144
3:19	144
4:1	145
4:13	144
4:17	1
4:18	144
5:8–10	147
5:8	1, 145
5:15	144, 145
5:17	144, 146

Philippians

3:1	114

1 Thessalonians

2:13	40

Scripture Index

1 Timothy
2   57

Hebrews
6:19   114
13:22–25   143

Name and Subject Index

Abraham, William, 183
analytic philosophy, 123, 151–52, 163, 167, 179, 182, 184, 200
Analytic Theology, 181–87, 193–94, 199–200
Anderson, Gary, 51, 57
Anderson, Hugh, 107
Anscombe, G. E. M., 156, 175, 177
Anthony, B.W., 35
Aristotle, 4, 25, 172, 219, 226
Artigas, Mariano, 18
asphaleia, 113–15
Axtell, Guy, 171

Barr, James, 49, 59
Barth, Karl, 25–27, 37, 41, 49, 53
Bartholomew, Craig, 30, 144, 156
Beale, G. K., 104
Beavis, Mary Ann, 103
Bennema, Cornelius, 118
Berg, Werner, 55
Biddle, Mark, 57
Biderman, Shlomo, 188–89
Blakely, J. Ted, 6
Braulik, Georg, 88
Briggs, Richard, 74
brute seeing, 3, 66–67, 70, 77, 197

Calvin, John, 26, 32, 37, 80, 109, 150, 174, 176–77
Carasik, Michael, 15, 38, 181, 186, 189–90
Cassuto, Umberto, 25, 27
Christensen, Duane, 84, 195
Clark, Malcolm, 49–50

Coady, C. A. J., 177
Collins, Adela Yarbro, 102
confession, 79, 81, 100–101, 150, 166
Continental philosophy, 151, 187
creatureliness, 30–31, 192
Crisp, Oliver, 167, 183–84, 194

Davies, G. Henton, 78–79
Delano, Jack, 35
Deuteronomic, (constucts), 83, 91, 98, 102, 104, 107, 120
Dewey, Joanna, 110
differentia, 4, 11, 25–26, 29, 43, 47, 62, 156, 164, 205–6
discovery, 23–32, 47, 122–24, 131–32, 151
Dorman, Ted, 221
Dostoyevsky, Fyodor, 162
Dretske, Fred, 169

eating, 28, 36, 38, 44, 54, 56, 60, 63–64, 71, 79, 117
Eaton, John, 190
Eichrodt, Walther, 40, 106
embodiment, 29–36, 47, 62, 90, 111, 116–17, 125, 128, 140–41, 146–47, 156–61, 164, 185–200
epistemology, theories of
  Naturalized Epistemology, 169–71, 179
  Reformed Epistemology, 167, 173–80

Name and Subject Index

epistemology, theories of (*cont.*)
    Scientific Epistemology, 12, 17, 23, 97, 122–25, 141, 171, 179, 180, 202
    Traditional Analysis of Knowledge, 167, 169, 179
    Virtue Epistemology, 171–73, 179
eureka, 31–32, 116, 118
Eve, 29, 51, 57, 79 178

facts, brute, 156
Feldman, Richard, 167
Fish, Stanley, 132
Fishbane, Michael, 195, 207
Foley, Richard, 40, 177
Fox, Michael, 124, 135, 141
Frankfurt, Harry, 184
Frege, Gottlob, 129, 155, 161
Fretheim, Terence, 77

Gadamer, Hans-Georg, 31, 132, 186
Galileo, 17–19
Geller, Stephen, 17, 197
genuflection, 203–5, 210
genus, 4, 25–26, 47, 156
Gerhardsson, Birger, 105
Gettier, Edmund, 168–69, 175
Gibson, Jeffrey, 6
Gödel, Kurt, 170
golden calf, 61, 78–80
Goldman, Alvin , 13, 40, 123, 152, 169, 174, 177, 194
Goodman, Nelson, 170
Goppelt, Leonhard, 107
Gordon, R. P., 39
Greco, J., 171
Grene, Marjorie, 38, 171
Grisanti, Michael, 104
Gunton, Colin, 203, 208

Hanson, Norwood, 127, 206
Hardin, Russell, 177
Hart, Trevor, 203

Hays, Richard, 104
Heidegger, Martin, 185
Hempel, Carl, 157, 170
Hicks, Peter, 153, 155
Hill, David, 107
Hollander, John, 104
Hume, David, 156, 169–70
Husserl, Edmund, 185

Isaianic (constucts), 101–5, 107
Iverson, Kelly, 6, 100–101

Jacobs, Struan, 131–32
Johnson, Andrew, 7, 74, 81, 98, 107, 192–93, 212
Johnson, Mark, 34, 47, 140

Kant, Immanuel, 30, 111, 125, 172
Kee, Howard Clark, 106
Kelber, Werner, 46, 102
Kepler, Johannes, 17–19, 127
Kermode, Frank, 102–3
Kierkegaard, Søren, 7–11, 28, 177–78
Kim, Jaegwon, 169
Kitcher, Phillip, 169
knowledge
    of good and evil, 24, 27, 29, 38, 40, 48–53, 59, 63, 73, 93, 116, 191
    plot, 68–71
    propositional knowledge, 23, 153, 155, 159, 167, 184
    sacramental , 36–40, 43–44, 48, 52, 55–57, 62–63, 78–80
    sexual knowledge, 23, 30, 38, 47, 49, 189, 211
"know"(ידע [*yada*]), 12, 15, 27
Kuhn, Thomas, 9–10, 123–24, 131–32
Kusch, Martin, 175, 177
Kvanvig, Jonathan, 13–14, 123, 171–72, 174–75, 194

Name and Subject Index

Lackey, Jennifer, 177
Lakoff, George, 34, 47, 140
Legge, James, 111
Levinas, Emmanuel, 185

MacDonald, Nathan, 38, 51, 80, 195, 197
Malul, Meir, 30, 188-89
Marcus, Joel, 103, 109
marriage, 28, 36, 38-39, 44, 96
Matera, Frank, 100
maxim, maximic language, 9, 26, 122-25, 134-41, 143-49
McConville, Gordon, 84
McGinn, Colin, 184
Meek, Esther, 31, 33, 35-36, 40, 115, 123, 125, 133, 160
Merleau-Ponty, Maurice, 30, 184
metanoia, 9-10
Mettinger, Tryvve, 76
Milgrom, Jacob, 90
Miller, Patrick, 86
miracles, 3, 99, 102, 141-42, 214
Moberly, Walter, 17, 40, 42-43, 49-51, 58-59, 74, 208
Moffet, Samuel, 111
Moleski, Martin, 124
Moran, Dermot, 185

Nagel, Thomas, 33
Nelson, Richard, 88
Newbigin, Lesslie, 208
Nietzsche, Friedrich, 154, 180, 207, 214-15
noetic effect, 4, 8
Noth, Martin, 78, 80, 207
Nussbaum, Martha, 172, 184

O'Dowd, Ryan, 84, 135, 144, 191-92, 196-98
Olson, Dennis, 31, 109, 195
Overholt, Thomas, 39

parable, 99-100, 103, 105, 150, 212
Patrick, Dale, 42
phenomenology, 30, 151, 184-87, 193-94, 199
Plantinga, Alvin, 13, 173-79
Platonism, 19, 162, 170
Polanyi, Michael, 17, 19, 23, 26, 31, 33-35, 38-39, 41-42, 97, 122-37, 139-40, 147, 151, 155, 158, 171, 179-80, 202-3, 208
Polkinghorne, John, 203
prophetic authentication, 17, 74, 82, 84, 86, 90, 149
propositions, 8, 13-14, 23, 26, 30, 39, 59, 123-25, 129, 140, 150-88, 194, 199-200

Quine, W. V. O., 160, 169-71, 179

Rad, Gerhard von, 27, 49-50, 106, 134, 137-40
Rae, Murray, 8-10, 28, 190
Rauser, Randall, 184
Rea, Michael, 152, 182-84
Rendtorff, Rolf, 106
Reno, R. R., 170
rhetoric,, 3, 14, 26, 36, 42, 48, 52-57, 79, 83-84, 110-15, 118, 120, 143, 146, 166, 195, 197
Ricoeur, Paul, 11, 29, 58
Rowland, Wade, 18
Rudman, Dominc, 53, 56

sacrament, 36-40, 43-44, 56-57, 63, 78-79
Sartre, Jean-Paul, 185
Savran, George, 31
Schellenberg, Annette, 31, 49, 52, 197
Scott, William, 124
Selby, Rosalind, 207-8
Sellars, Wilfred, 169

Name and Subject Index

serpent, 17, 31, 42–43, 48–54, 56–63, 70, 79, 109, 130, 150, 178
Shea, William, 18
Sklar, Jay, 90
Sosa, Ernest, 171
special authentication, 17, 82, 85–87
Stanley, Jason, 155, 179
Stegman, Thomas, 113, 115
Stone, Kenneth, 38
Stordalen, T., 31, 52
Strecker, Georg, 165–66
Stump, Eleonore, 123, 152, 167, 179, 184, 200–201

Taylor, Charles, 30–31, 73, 160
Tolbert, Mary Ann, 102
Torrance, T. F., 153, 158–59, 202–3
Transfiguration, 45–46, 101–2, 106, 108, 120
Treier, Daniel, 52
trust, 1–5, 40–41, 54–61, 74–75, 80–81, 87–89, 115, 118–20, 123–30, 146, 157, 176–78, 205, 211, 217, 222–23
truth, 8–11, 42, 59, 114, 132, 139, 153, 159–61, 164–65, 166–78, 205, 207

Van der Kooi, Cornelis, 175–76, 179
Vasholz, Robert, 85
Venkata, Ramanan, 165

Waltke, Bruce, 27
Watts, Rikki, 103
Wenham, Gordon, 55
Westermann, Claus, 49–50
Westphal, Merold, 30, 152, 166, 176, 183–84, 186
Williamson, Timothy, 155, 179
wisdom, 54, 56, 80, 97–98, 122–48, 172, 191, 196–97, 212, 217–18
Wolters, Albert, 61
Wolterstorff, Nicholas, 30, 173–74
Wright, N. T., 107

Yagoda, Benjamin, 7
Yoder, Douglas, 190–92

Zagzebski, Linda, 14, 123, 171–74, 194
Zevit, Ziony, 188

www.ingramcontent.com/pod-product-compliance
Lightning Source LLC
Chambersburg PA
CBHW031726230426
43669CB00007B/253